WATER~~~~
of Western
Europe

TOTAL LENGTHS OF INLAND
WATERWAYS CURRENTLY NAVIGABLE

England & Wales	3374 miles/	5430 km
Scotland	167 miles/	268 km
Ireland	446 miles/	717 km
France	4700 miles/	7560 km
West Germany	2920 miles/	4700 km
Belgium	969 miles/	1560 km
Holland	4600 miles/	7400 km
Sweden	865 miles/	1392 km

*Waterways of the more complicated networks are
indicated in simplified form. For detailed planning, refer
to individual country maps.*

0 KM	100	200	300	400	
0 MILES		100		200	300

THE GUINNESS GUIDE TO

WATERWAYS
of Western
Europe

One of the last of the French horsedrawn working boats, seen on the Canal latéral à la Loire at Guétin in 1968. Known as a berrichon, these wooden craft were designed to fit the now disused locks of the Canal du Berry. This example was loaded with about 100 tons of cement and progress was a tedious affair, the normal run in a day's operation being no more than about 16 km/ 10 miles.

THE GUINNESS GUIDE TO

WATERWAYS of Western Europe

Hugh McKnight

GUINNESS SUPERLATIVES LIMITED
2 Cecil Court, London Road, Enfield, Middlesex

Photography and maps : © Hugh McKnight

Editor: Beatrice Frei

Copyright © Hugh McKnight and Guinness Superlatives Ltd 1978
Published in Great Britain by
Guinness Superlatives Ltd
2 Cecil Court
London Road, Enfield, Middlesex
Set in Times 11/12
Printed and bound in Great Britain by
Morrison & Gibb Limited, Edinburgh and London
Typesetters: Computacomp (UK) Limited, Fort William and London
ISBN 0 900424 48 6

Contents

Author's Note and Acknowledgements

Every effort has been made to ensure the accuracy of the information contained in this book. However, neither author nor publisher can be held responsible for any errors that may have been included. It is recommended that proper navigational charts are used when cruising the more hazardous routes.

This book is almost totally the result of first-hand knowledge and observation: consequently it was not found necessary to consult many official bodies or authorities. Willing help was, however, offered by the Swedish Tourist Office, London and the Northern Ireland Tourist Board, Belfast. Derek Dann, Managing Director of Emerald Star Line, Dublin and Michael Streat of Blue Line Cruisers (France) Ltd have both provided facilities and information, for which I am most grateful. Special thanks are due to many friends who have shared my boating experiences over a number of years: especially June and John Humphries, the Rt. Hon. The Lord Harvington, John Liley and Robert Shopland, Editor of *Waterways World*. Throughout, my publishers have been more than agreeable to work with and in this connection I would particularly like to mention Beatrice Frei, my Editor. All photographs are by the author or from the Collection of Hugh McKnight Photography, except where credited otherwise.

Introduction

'Of all the creatures of commercial enterprise, a canal barge is by far the most delightful to consider. It may spread its sails, and then you see it sailing high above the tree-tops and the windmill, sailing on the aqueduct, sailing through the green corn-lands: the most picturesque of things amphibious.

The chimney smokes for dinner as you go along; the banks of the canal slowly unroll their scenery to contemplative eyes; the barge floats by great forests and through great cities with their public buildings and their lamps at night; and for the bargee, in his floating home, "travelling abed", it is merely as if he were listening to another man's story or turning the leaves of a picture book in which he had no concern. He may take his afternoon walk in some foreign country on the banks of the canal, and then come home to dinner at his own fireside. ...

I am sure I would rather be a bargee than occupy any position under Heaven that required attendance at an office.'

Robert Louis Stevenson certainly knew the delights of waterway travel and his comments of a century ago apply equally well today.

A boat on river or canal offers a rare opportunity for civilised travel. Unhurried, free from the worries and dangers of cruising at sea, able to visit the towns and villages of ordinary people, where few tourists are likely to break the spell: all this is made possible through the waterways network of Western Europe.

When I was four years old, my father acted on a characteristic impulse, returning from his office one evening with a small rowing boat lashed to the roof of the car. After several sorties into the muddy and tidal waters of the Thames below Teddington, he

In a world of mass production, there is a great satisfaction in the ownership of a traditional onetime working boat. The author's horse-drawn ice breaker was built in timber with rolled iron sheathing by the Birmingham Canal Navigations Company in October 1895. After a useful life of some 60 years, she became derelict and was subsequently fitted with a boatman's cabin and engine room. The power unit is a Swedish-built hot bulb semi-diesel Seffle, imported in 1961 but of a design little changed since about 1910. Much admired wherever she travels, Parry II may be a part of English canal history but is nevertheless a comfortable and adaptable pleasure craft.

added an ancient outboard motor to our little vessel. For several summers, weekends were devoted to river picnics. Never travelling through more than a handful of locks, it was left to me to seek more ambitious waterway horizons. On joining the Inland Waterways Association at the age of 14, I did so more in the belief that here was a campaign worth supporting, rather than with any detailed knowledge of Britain's waterways system. Practical exploration followed slowly, first in the London area and gradually spreading throughout England and Wales. In the summer of 1961 I completed a circular cruise from the Thames to Llangollen in a 12 ft/3·7 m camping dinghy and spent several weeks living with working narrow boat families on the Grand Union Canal. I also lent a hand to early restoration schemes on the Basingstoke Canal and the Southern Stratford. Soon, most of my friends were people who shared this interest and I determined to earn a living as a self-employed writer and photographer specialising in waterways – a field offering great scope and little competition.

My first visit abroad, in 1957, had provided brief glimpses of French waterway traffic on the Rhône and Saône at Lyon, but it was not until a decade later, when I was thoroughly familiar with Britain's rivers and canals, that I considered investigating waterways throughout the rest of Europe. For two enjoyable weeks in late September, I joined a group of canal enthusiast friends for a memorable discovery of navigations in Burgundy. Here, we found a thriving commercial network, virtually ignored by pleasure craft. It was like a journey back through time to British waterways as they were before the Second World War.

Since then, I have returned to Europe as often as possible, mostly in hired craft and several times as a guest aboard a large sea-going motor yacht. A chance encounter with Norris McWhirter, of *The Guinness Book of Records*, while boating on the Canal du Midi, resulted in a friendship which was directly responsible for this present volume.

Only a wealthy fulltime waterways traveller can expect to have explored every canal branch and backwater of Europe, a task that would take many years. Therefore, while setting out to broadly describe all areas of Western Europe, I have focused my attention on regions that I know best. This is a collection of personal highlights, selected as being subjects and places most likely to interest the reader.

This book is a celebration of waterways: the commercial and pleasure boats, buildings, bridges, aqueducts, people and scenery that combine to make a unique and little-known world. It is my hope that yachtsmen and canal boaters alike will derive pleasure and practical help from these pages.

Hugh McKnight, The Clock House, Shepperton-on-Thames, 1978.

A History of Inland Waterways

While portions of natural rivers had been used for transport since pre-historic times, it was not until the 14th century that a type of lock was devised for overcoming changes in level in Holland, and thus the possibility of creating cross-country artificial navigations was presented. But canal transport was slow in its development, so that it was not until the 17th century in France and Britain that anything other than very local schemes were undertaken.

England's remarkable canal and river network was largely engineered between about 1760 and 1830 when the advent of railways presented faster transport methods. In Britain, the creation of navigable waterways was left mainly to private enterprise, resulting in a variety of different craft sizes, many of which were of tiny capacity by modern standards. On the Continent of Europe, Governments generally had much greater involvement, with the result that waterways were more integrated. The canal building era was an exciting time, allowing for undreamed of industrial expansion and opening up large areas for agricultural and urbanised improvement.

Fortunes were made by promoters and freight carriers; passenger transport achieved previously unknown sophistication and a fascinating record of the age is preserved not only in the waterways themselves but also through copious documents and contemporary illustrations.

A selection of this rich store of material is presented on the next few pages with the aim of showing something of the flavour of the time. Canal prosperity was all too short lived in Britain, although commercial transport by water continued to make a useful economic contribution, in spite of an almost total lack of modernisation and investment. Elsewhere in Europe, commercial carriage is still actively encouraged, while pleasure boating, now the mainstay of most British navigations, is considerably less widespread.

A selection of English canal tokens, issued by waterway companies for use by those concerned with their construction. The central example, showing navvies' tools, was produced by the Basingstoke Canal Co.

The Theory of Navigable Canals, a hand coloured engraving published in the Encyclopaedia Londinensis *of 1800. Water powered inclined planes were designed as an alternative to locks, although they never achieved wide popularity in Britain. The Canal Age produced many remarkable schemes at a time when navigation building was seen to be an instant method of making large profits.*

Above: *life on an English canal narrow boat in the 1880s. Conditions for boaters were harsh and there was much public concern to improve them.* Below: *an early 19th-century engraving showing Limehouse Dock, at the junction of the Regent's Canal and the Thames.*

Above: *produce being unloaded from a horse barge at Tottenham Mills on the Lee Navigation, north of London, early 19th century. Handling of goods relied heavily on manual labour, a situation which lasted on many British canals until their final commercial disuse.*

Below: *a canal narrow boat arriving at a riverside village. This charming Victorian painting by R Gallon probably depicts the Upper Thames, where canal craft were common until the early decades of the 20th century.*

Right: *commercial and pleasure traffic on Germany's River Neckar at Heidelberg in the middle of the 19th century.*

Below: *the wonder of its age, France's Canal du Midi was the subject of a board game, designed for an Archbishop of Narbonne. Locks and other special features are illustrated and doubtless the rules imposed penalties for landing on particular hazards. Courtesy, Archives de la Haute-Garonne.*

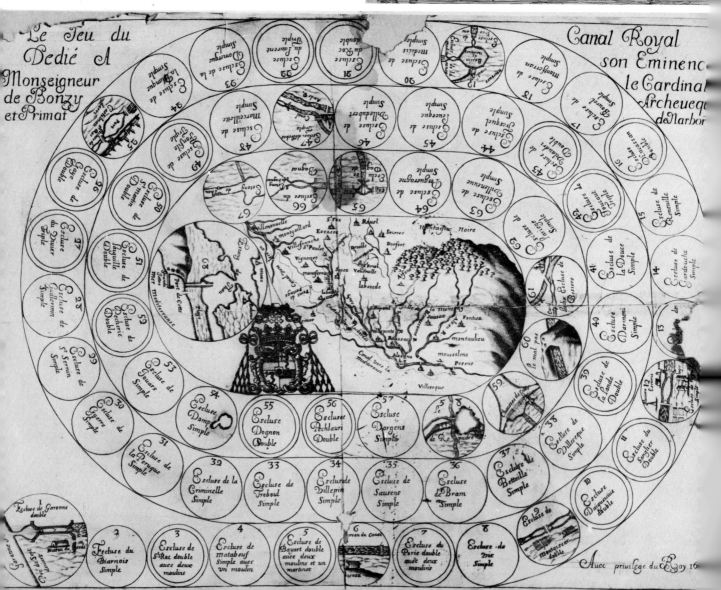

Commercial Traffic

Inland waterways were developed largely for the carriage of freight, and in spite of any recently encouraged rôle in the fields of tourism or pleasure boating, it is the cargo carrying vessels, their crews and way of life that provide a navigation with much of its character.

Among smaller types of canal barge, few substantial changes have been made in design for upwards of half a century, while in rare instances vessels are virtually as they were two hundred years ago. But the pattern of traffic is now rapidly altering as we progress towards the end of the 20th century. Smaller waterways and their boats are subjected to harsh economic pressures and looking to the future, inland water transport is only fully viable where really large loads can be carried over substantial distances. Thus, on Continental routes, the most commercially virile navigations are those capable of accommodating craft of 1350 tons or more. The improvement schemes widely in progress or carried out in recent decades should ensure that these areas will enjoy increasing volumes of traffic in the years ahead.

Only ten years ago, the author discovered horse-drawn barges on the canals of France, the last of their line and now a mere memory. In the case of recently flourishing navigations built for 350-tonners, traffic is frequently on the decline. Fortunately, it is these canals (such as the Nivernais) which are best suited to leisurely holiday boating, so they should enjoy an assured future.

Road transport, higher wages and a general demand for improved living standards have all but killed off the traditional narrow boat in England: yet until well into the 1960s the canals were unthinkable without the gay contribution they made to the scene. In this atmosphere of change, although this book is mainly concerned with the present, it was felt desirable to also include pictures from the recent past. It is hoped that this will not present a false impression of the waterways: rather that it offers an insight into a world that existed only a short time ago.

There is little romance in a pair of 1350-ton barges with diesel engines thundering as they career along a concrete-lined channel; at least not by comparison with the relaxed journeyings of a family-operated *péniche* or narrow boat with friendly smoking chimney. But such is the price of progress.

Under tow from its chain-driven electric tug, a barge slides up the shaded approach to the great tunnel at Pouilly-en-Auxois on the Canal du Bourgogne in Central France. The operation is long and noisy.

Below: *The birthplace of the modern English canal system: Worsley, on the Bridgewater Canal near Manchester. For two centuries from its opening to traffic in 1761, the waterway conveyed large amounts of goods: craft of today are for pleasure. This diesel powered* short boat *was photographed in the summer of 1965 as it made its way towards Manchester with a load of coal.*

Above: *tearing downriver towards the Mediterranean, one of the Rhône barges passes an ancient fortified village near Avignon. Modern navigation works have resulted in much easier conditions for traffic.*

Opposite: *the crew of a German barge attend to their mooring hawsers in readiness to enter a lock on the River Neckar. Working and living conditions for Continental boat people are generally excellent.*

A contrast in official attitudes to waterways freight: above, *one of the huge Princes Irene locks on Holland's Rhine-Amsterdam Canal, with guillotine gate raised to allow the numerous barges to leave the chamber. Above,* right: *coal traffic in 'Tom Pudding' compartment boats on Yorkshire's Aire & Calder Navigation in Goole. Craft* have changed little since the end of the last century.

Below: *coasters still trade to the unlikely port of Norwich, on the River Yare. Opposite: an elderly wooden motor barge on the Garonne Latéral Canal, near Bordeaux.*

Above: *one of the Rhine's most modern and powerful tugs surges into the strong current at Loreley. Thick fog or serious floods are the only conditions likely to halt the constant traffic.*

Below: *shipping Renault motor cars down the Seine between Billancourt and the company's main works at Flins. Photograph, Keystone Press Agency.*

The Canal Pioneers

Pleasure cruising on the inland waterways of Britain is now so firmly established as part of the holiday scene, that it is difficult to appreciate that – Thames and Broads apart – until after the Second World War the canal traveller was a considerable rarity. In their early days inland waterways enjoyed a brisk traffic in passengers as well as freight, but the explosion of railway building after about 1840 so changed travel patterns, that to elect to go by water was the prerogative of the curious eccentric.

Towards the latter part of the 19th century, both Thames and Broads became recognised holiday areas, with craft ranging from camping skiffs to steam launches and sailing wherries readily available. It seemed as if everyone wished to emulate Jerome K Jerome's *Three Men in a Boat* (1889), which in its more contemplative moments vividly recalls the idyllic character of summer on the river almost a century ago.

These were the days when skiffs '*equipped with the best fittings*' could be supplied to '*the nobility*

and gentry of the surrounding locality, inclusive of housing, dressing room and attendance' at a mere £15·75 for a six month season. On the Norfolk Broads, during the 1890s, there were bargains like 'The Water Lily, *4-ton Una-rig yacht. Good sleeping accommodation in Cabin for 6 persons. £3 per week. With Man, £4.*' Guides were available like G Christopher Davies' *Broads Handbook* (1891) which clearly catalogued a form of boating etiquette:

'*Do not, in the neighbourhood of other yachts or houses, indulge in songs and revelry after eleven pm., even at regatta times. Bathe only before eight o'clock in the morning, if in sight of other vessels or moored in a frequented part of the river. Ladies are not expected to turn out before eight, but after that*

While construction of the railway network resulted in savage competition for waterborne freight in Britain, the consequent improved access to the countryside encouraged popularity of pleasure boating, especially on the River Thames. Salter's of Oxford established a regular service of tripping steamers, working over the middle reaches of the navigation. This early 20th-century painting by R Murdoch Wright was one of a series showing the firm's fleet, and published in postcard form. Here, the vessel Cliveden *is seen in Cliveden Reach, upstream of Maidenhead.*

Salter's Oxford and Kingston Steamer passing CLIVEDEN

CLIVEDEN.

time they are entitled to be free from any annoyance. Young men who lounge in a nude state on boats when ladies are passing (and I have known Norwich youths to do this) may be saluted with dust shot, or the end of a quant.'

But to leave the established pleasure waterways and select coal barges and uncouth boatmen for your companions was the act of a real individualist. Many of the pioneers have left graphic accounts of their adventures. Sometimes these are important social histories, commenting on the conditions of the people who made their living along these largely ignored arteries of trade. One man whose life-work was a campaign to improve the lot of the canal families was George Smith of Coalville. At great personal and financial sacrifice, he probed, investigated, reported and agitated on behalf of the illiterate narrow boat people of the English canals. His campaigns in the Press did achieve changes in legislation designed to improve living conditions (although frequently these regulations were totally ignored as much as 60 years after his death).

The flavour of a George Smith investigation is admirably conveyed by the following extract from his *Canal Adventures by Moonlight* (1881). It is taken from Part II, *Six Days in a Monkey Boat.* He is attempting to find a narrow boat aboard which to travel northwards up the Grand Junction Canal to the Midlands:

'After getting part of a hasty street-stall breakfast upon Maida Hill tunnel, and the remainder with a friend, the toll clerk connected with the Regent's Canal, to my great joy and delight Mr T——, with his good natured face, made his appearance out of the tunnel at nine o'clock; the delay, he said, had arisen in consequence of the watchman not calling him at the proper time for the first turn. The boat was filled with rice, leather, paraffin, hemp-seed, and oil, as full as it could be crammed, and where my books and other sundry lots and paraphernalia were to be stored was a mystery I could not solve; however, with a little managing room was made ...

'With a crack of Charlie's whip off we moved towards Kensal Green, leaving the dead dogs, cats and other masses of animal corruption floating upon the Paddington sewage basin, behind us, the stench of which, and the filth of London, followed us for many miles beyond Bull's Bridge, which place, together with Cowley Lock and other places in the neighbourhood, stand, in regard to the filth of London, like Solomon's leeches, always asking for more; and it is fortunate for the Londoners that there are such places ...

'After passing through these odorating scenes of the London streets and gutters, we came upon

somewhat of a contrast in the shape of two big, coarse, burly, half-nude either boatwomen or tramps, who had been making use of the hot summer's sun to dry their linen – which had evidently been washed in the canal – on the hedges, while these nymphs were bathing. At any rate, when we passed their toilet was not quite arranged, while, to say the least, our presence did not put them to much inconvenience or discomfiture. This sort of disgraceful proceeding was going on in broad daylight, within the sound of the church-bells of the Capital of Christendom, and the passing and re-passing of canal boats upon which were herds of men, women, and children of both sexes and all ages.'

Other Victorian travellers sought peace and beauty on the waterways. And no account is more tempting than a description of a journey no longer possible. In 1868, there appeared a slim volume – now much sought after – from the pen of J B Dashwood, entitled *The Thames to the Solent by Canal and Sea.* Charmingly illustrated with engravings, this records the passage of an open sailing boat from Weybridge to Portsmouth, part of the route including the Wey & Arun Junction Canal, then within sight of its final closure to traffic. Water shortages resulted in Dashwood being made to take with him a boatman to ensure that locks were properly closed behind him, and conditions encountered made him comment that it was doubtful if the canal would remain open to navigation much longer. His description vividly recalls a summer day of long ago:

'The scenery, immediately on quitting Bramley, becomes lovely, and we were still blessed with the most splendid weather. The Canal winds its way under the shade of woods on each side, which come quite down to the water's edge, where the water-lilies, both white and yellow, were floating in profusion. The birds were singing most energetically, as if to make up for lost time during the past wet and cold spring and summer, and the little moorhens ducked under water, with wild screams on all sides, as we approached.'

Pioneers like Mr and Mrs Dashwood and their Pomeranian dog used a small open boat and relied on inns for their overnight accommodation. Other adventurers elected to carry all comforts with them, and in the absence of suitable pleasure craft with cabins would strike a bargain for the hire and temporary conversion of a freight boat, usually with man and horse. Thus did Reginald Blunt get afloat

Some Victorian waterways travellers. Top: *when a group of young ladies undertook a canoe voyage down the Warwickshire Avon in 1884, most of the locks were derelict and they were forced to shoot weirs and make portages.* Above, left: *one of the illustrations from J L Molloy's* Our Autumn Holiday on French Rivers *of 1874. The party's outrigger 'four' was specially built for the trip and shipped out from England.* Above, right: *one of the problems facing J B Dashwood in navigating his little sailing boat through the Wey & Arun Canal in 1868 was a series of towpath gates which the horse was expected to jump!* Left: *under tow by steam tug on the River Saône in 1887, an adventurous journey completed by Philip Hamerton aboard a roughly converted* berrichon.

on the canals of Southern England during the late 1880s; his description of a voyage from the Thames at Reading, via the Kennet & Avon Canal and the Wilts & Berks Canal (defunct since 1914) and so back to the Thames at Abingdon, was published in the *Pall Mall Magazine*. He set sail aboard the narrow boat *Ada*, with his brother, a captain and mate and a third man secured in Reading market place for 10p per day. During a three week trip, they worked through more than 130 locks and the expedition was agreed to be a complete success. The costs of the exercise are a cause of envy and wonderment:

'*Including everything – hire of boat, canoe, and horse; wages of crew; furnishing of cabin; food and forage; liquor, fuel, canal charges, gratuities, etc. – came to just £12 per week.*'

Also during the 1880s, the popular and prolific writer William Black had built a vessel designed to pass through narrow canal locks while being also capable (just) of negotiating the fast-flowing Severn Estuary between the Gloucester & Sharpness Canal and the Bristol Avon. Thus he was able to make a journey from the Thames via Warwick, Birmingham, Worcester, Bath and back to the Thames at Reading. The 443 pages of his *The Strange Adventures of a House-Boat* rank as the most long-winded and verbose outpourings in canal literature. The majority concerns personal happenings and philosophy of minimal interest to the modern reader. But where the excitement of canal navigation becomes intense, he is a good reporter. As in his account of taking his horse-drawn vessel through the Worcester & Birmingham Canal's 2726 yd/2492 m West Hill Tunnel:

'*Then appeared a black and grimy little steam launch; there was a production of papers; we were furnished with a lamp to be fixed at the bow; and thereupon the burly little steamer proceeded to head the long line. How that line was formed it is hard to say; but it was clear we were to be at the tail end of it; and, indeed, as barge after barge moved away, we had no more than time to throw a rope to the last of them and get attached. The huge black snake before us was disappearing into the bowels of the earth with a marvellous rapidity; one had to steer as straight as one could for the small and narrow arch at the base of that mighty mass of masonry; the semicircular opening seemed to close around us; and the next moment we were in darkness. This sudden plunge into the unknown was sufficiently startling; for now there was no welcome star of light far away ahead, while the red glow of our saloon told us nothing of our whereabouts or our proper course ...*'

The campaigns of George Smith and the travelogues of other writers had created a slight canal cult by the early 1890s. Nevertheless, each fresh expedition involved its participants with a world where there was little practical information readily to hand. As a partial remedy, F E Prothero and W A Clark of The Cruising Club, produced *A New Oarsman's Guide to the Rivers and Canals of Great Britain and Ireland* (1896). In this remarkably comprehensive work, numerous rivers are included that never find mention in current books on navigable waterways. And the remark in the Preface that: '*Few canals are worth a visit for their own sake or except as links in a through route. The principal exceptions are the Basingstoke, the ten miles of the Kennet & Avon from Bradford to Bath, the Brecon and the Welsh Section of the Shropshire Union*' seems to have been ignored in the main body of the text as it deserved.

At about this time, the greatest canal pioneer of all was busily cruising, compiling statistics and gathering information for his classic *Bradshaw's Canals and Navigable Rivers of England and Wales* (1904). He was Henry Rodolph de Salis, a director of the leading narrow boat traders, Fellows, Morton & Clayton Ltd. His title page describes the work as: '*A Handbook of Inland Navigation for Manufacturers, Merchants, Traders, and Others: compiled, after a Personal Survey of the whole of the waterways.*' If pleasure boatmen can be classed as 'Others', de Salis' efforts were not without point, for *Bradshaw's Canals*, reprinted several times, remains a leading reference work. Quite simply, it comprises tables of place names and distances, imbued with a poetry that is surely unique in the English language. Who cannot respond with interest to mention of the Spon Lane Locks Branch, Figure of Three Locks, Drypool Basin or Three Holes Bridge?

For his waterborne excursions, de Salis would use trading craft from the FMC fleet, but more often was to be seen aboard one of the series of three steam-driven narrow beam inspection launches which he had constructed, all with the name *Dragon Fly*. An indefatigable canal publicist, he logged more than 14 000 miles/22 530 km by inland waterway in England and Wales in the eleven years leading to publication of his book.

Easily the most appealing canal log of these pioneering days is C J Aubertin's *A Caravan Afloat* (c 1914), in which the writer set forth with his family in a horse-drawn craft not unlike Noah's Ark. This 33 ft/10 m device was built for around £40, not including interior fittings. In a charmingly whimsical style, Aubertin easily conveys the spirit and joy of canal boating:

'*The water gurgled pleasantly against the bows as the old horse did his steady three miles an hour. A pine wood cast a grateful shade across the canal, and the valley beneath us was one sweep of purple heather interspersed with stacks of brown peat. I lolled in the stern giving the rudder the occasional twist necessary to keep us out of the bank. Beside me was a map which made it plain that the nearest road was some two miles off – and that only a dotted line (not recommended to cyclists) which terminated in World's End. The Canal was eerie. There had evidently been difficulties of construction in crossing the peatlands. The waterway ran above the level of the surrounding country, and one side of it was composed of old barges, now mere rotting timbers, among which purple loose strife struggled for life with ranker water-side growths.*'

Other canal writers of the early 20th century include E Temple Thurston, whose *The Flower of Gloster* (1911) is a charmingly written account of boating on the Oxford, Stratford and Thames & Severn Canals.

During the late 1920s and 30s, a Capt J Carr-Ellison, father of the present Chairman of the Northumbrian Water Authority, completed many hair-raising canal journeys by a steam launch named *Thetis* and an early converted narrow boat called *Susan Sheila*. His unpublished records, kindly made available by his son, recall voyages through such vanished routes as the Grantham, Cromford, Derby and Montgomeryshire Canals. The narrow boat conversion (one of the first) was powered by a Coventry Victor diesel engine which spent its winters driving a van on the family estates. Each spring, at the start of the boating season, a mechanical transplant was arranged! And when thick weed, as on the Llangollen Canal, made powered progress too difficult, a forestry horse named Doll was pressed into service.

One classic account, which resulted to a large extent in the post War explosion of canal boating, was L T C Rolt's magic *Narrow Boat*, describing a summer cruise shortly before the world was changed by the 1939–45 War. In due course, Tom Rolt was involved with formation of the Inland Waterways Association in 1946, and suddenly pioneering had become a normal activity. Our amenity waterways have since experienced an undreamed of tourist boom.

To travel British waterways was a great adventure, but by comparison the rivers and canals of mainland Europe offered even more excitement. One not infrequent hazard facing British explorers was the risk of being arrested on suspicion of

Above: *Capt Carr-Ellison's steam launch* Thetis *in one of the Kennet & Avon Canal's 29 Devizes locks during the early 1930s.* Below: *H R de Salis ensconced in a deck chair aboard a narrow boat on the Grantham Canal, during one of his many canal cruises in the late 1890s.*

spying! This fate befell Robert Louis Stevenson, and is recorded in his *An Inland Voyage*, a tale of canoeing through Northern France in 1878.

A similar thing happened to Philip Hamerton, while travelling aboard a hired barge through Central France (*The Saône, A Summer Voyage*, 1887.) With memories of the Franco-Prussian War still vivid, all foreigners were deemed untrustworthy! On arriving at Pontailler aboard his converted *berrichon Boussemroum*, Hamerton and his companions were accused of making plans of a military nature, in spite of their protestations that they were merely sketching for pleasure! They argued that had they really been intent on espionage, they would '*never travel in such a visible and peculiar apparatus as the* Boussemroum *and its contents.*' This merely brought the reply that extreme openness and frankness might be made use of to conceal illegal designs! Regulations were produced which empowered the gendarmes '*to arrest persons making plans or sketches of roads, rivers, canals and public works such as bridges*'. Accordingly, the travellers were placed under armed guard aboard their vessel, while enquiries were made at a higher level. For 24 hours, there seemed every possibility of prison. However, their innocence established, the party was allowed to resume its cruise. Hamerton's narrative is full of Saône life of the day: the bargemen, steam tugs and farming communities. In many respects, this part of France has changed little during the intervening century.

Our Autumn Holiday on French Rivers (1874) by J L Molloy, achieves the very highest standards of Victorian book production with a richly embossed and gilded cover and numerous witty drawings. It chronicles the adventures of five English gentlemen who tackle the Seine, Loire and several connecting canals in an outrigger sculling boat. Soon after the beginning of their expedition they sank and almost drowned one of their number.

The hire of holiday craft on the Continent is even now nothing like as easy or widespread as in Britain. Nevertheless, in 1906 H F Tomalin, accompanied by an accomplished photographer, Arthur Marshall, set out for the Dutch province of Friesland, where they secured a *booier*, or sailing barge. The resulting record of Dutch waterways, *Three Vagabonds in Friesland*, shows a style of life that has totally disappeared. Almost everything from groceries to people then travelled by water. The inhabitants of rural areas wore traditional costume and the sky was filled with the dark shapes of picturesque barge sails.

Far more ambitious was the marathon journey of Donald Maxwell chronicled in *A Cruise Across Europe* (1907). This entailed navigating from Holland to the Black Sea, with a passage of the legendary (now defunct) Ludwig's Canal in Bavaria. Chosen vehicle was a small sailing barge named *Walrus*. As if to underline the rarity of such an enterprise, the travellers were arrested in Dordrecht, and their effects thoroughly examined. When it was concluded that these eccentrics were not spies, they were allowed to take a tow up the Rhine, thereafter using a chain-tug for the Main. In Bamberg, *Walrus* was delayed for a week while necessary permission was sought to pass through Ludwig's Canal to the Danube; in the whole 172 km/107 miles of this forgotten navigation fewer than ten other craft were encountered. Maxwell comments that the waterway was as if the Wey & Arun Canal had lost itself upon a spur of the Alps. Being engineless, they resorted to taking turns to bow haul their craft from the towpath, a tiring procedure indeed. Reaching the Danube, frequent and time consuming inspections were demanded by Customs officials, from Bulgaria on one bank and Romania on the other. Finally, prostrate on his bunk with a malaria attack, Maxwell arrived at the Black Sea, having completed the most strenuous inland voyage recorded this century!

An almost identical cruise was carried out twenty years later by the American Negley Farson, aboard a 26 ft/8 m yawl called *Flame*. (*Sailing Across Europe*, 1927.) By this time Ludwig's Canal was choked with weed. For four days the Farsons coped also with a group of travelling musicians who were determined to earn a passage to Vienna. Eventually the weed drove them away!

In recognition of a desire to cater for canal and river tourists, there have long been passenger steamers, running scheduled services over routes as different as the Rhine and Sweden's Göta Canal. Admirable travellers' tales have resulted, but they can in no way compare with the private inland mariner, tackling unknown waters of foreign lands. Sometimes not even knowing in advance whether his chosen navigation was still in commission until he arrived at the first lock!

After the last War, cruising through Europe has become less of a pioneering exercise, although it may still be tinged with adventure. One notable exponent who has taken his British motor yacht to virtually every corner of Western Europe is Roger Pilkington. In a succession of *Small Boat* books, Dr Pilkington has shown that twenty summers may happily be passed in this manner, with further waters yet to be conquered or newly opened navigations to be penetrated.

Choice of a Boat

In all probability, there is no such thing as a boat which is suitable for all waterways of Western Europe. Certain craft which are well adapted to non-tidal rivers and canals are positively dangerous on large lakes or the open sea. Equally, sea-going cruisers are frequently too large in respect of beam, draught and headroom for many of the smaller navigations. But, with the exception of particularly restricted waterways like the narrow beam (6 ft 10 in/2·08 m) canals of the English Midlands, the best compromise would perhaps be a 25 ft/7·62 m wide beam cruiser which can be trailed behind a family car: thus it can safely be transported by car ferry and is not too small or underpowered to tackle the majority of commercial navigations.

Inland boating inevitably entails frequent contact with locksides, jetties and even other craft. A major consideration, therefore, is a strong hull. Timber, iron, steel, glass reinforced plastic and ferro-cement are all available; properly protected steel is perhaps best of all. Steering positions vary from the stern (where there is much to be said for the immediate response of a tiller rather than wheel), to centre cockpit and even bow. Remembering that all round visibility is essential when entering restricted lock entrances and bridge holes, a stern tiller is the writer's personal choice.

Ignoring the type of boat you may already have available, there is little question that the *best* vessel is akin to those which work the waterways commercially. Locks and other equipment were designed with them in mind. Besides, there is much satisfaction to be derived from ownership of former working boats and if they have satisfactorily completed a life laden with freight, they should be able to cope adequately with the more sedate existence of carrying passengers. Thus, the converted narrow boat cannot be bettered for the English canal system, a fact emphasised by the majority of hire firms whose fleets are based on modern replicas. And on the mainland of Europe, one of the smaller barges, no longer competitive for trading purposes, is ideal.

Generally, it is a good rule to own a boat slightly larger than essential for your needs: the extra space will pay dividends. When considering the question of power units, a similar rule applies. Additional speed can sometimes be required and to operate at maximum revolutions during normal cruising is expensive on fuel, noisy and allows for no safety factor. With the exception of the smallest class of powered boat, an inboard diesel engine is always best, both for running costs, reliability and ease of locating help in the event of a breakdown.

Most important, the would-be boat owner is strongly advised to hire, borrow or otherwise become familiar with his chosen type of vessel before purchasing one of his own. In this way an ideal holiday home will become just that and not an expensive reminder of inexperience.

Canoe: *A manually propelled canoe – Canadian variety or Kayak – offers a freedom that some owners of more sophisticated vessels might envy. Equipment is of necessity reduced to the barest of camping essentials, and provided with a simple arrangement of two wheels mounted on an axle, portages round locks or obstructions are overcome with minimum delay. Traditionally of timber but more often canvas on a frame or glass reinforced plastic, the canoe opens up prospects of exploration of waterways that are totally barred to even the smallest of motorised craft. This example is seen in the Baltic archipelago off Sweden's east coast at Trosa.*

Inflatable dinghy: *Perhaps the most adaptable boat of all is the inflatable dinghy. Complete with outboard motor, oars, floorboards and elementary camping equipment, it can be carried in the boot of a small car. Extremely seaworthy and stable, such boats can be manhandled over obstacles and even navigated down weirs as demonstrated by the picture taken on Glasgow's River Kelvin during a marathon race. Do not confuse the quality product costing several hundred*

pounds with insubstantial beach toys available on garage forecourts. Inflatables have been much used by the author in exploring remote or semi-navigable waterways.

Camping boat: *Rather belonging to a past era, the dinghy, skiff or punt fitted with a canvas awning supported on hoops is a cheap but surprisingly comfortable method of getting afloat. The punt shown, once owned by waterway enthusiast Viscount St Davids, is fitted with an outboard motor well and its considerable length in proportion to the narrow beam produces a surprising turn of speed with virtually no wash. The writer's first 4000 miles/6440 km of canal and river travel throughout England and Wales were completed in a similar 12 ft/3·66 m motorised dinghy. Old established Thames boatyards are fertile hunting grounds for such boats, many of which are upwards of 70 years old.*

Trailed cruiser: *For the family that seeks weekend cruising on a local river with the opportunity of annual holidays further afield or abroad, this is the best solution. Hulls not exceeding 25 ft/7·6 m can be towed safely by a medium-powered car and the boat may even be used as a caravan while in transit, reducing costs by saving hotel bills! The most common construction is glass reinforced plastic, a maintenance free (or nearly so) material. The greater cost of an inboard diesel engine compared with a thirsty petrol outboard is outweighed by lower fuel bills and generally increased convenience.*

Wide beam inland cruiser: *The needs of holiday hirers on the English Broads and Thames have produced craft with the space and luxury of weekend cottages. The 39 ft/11·88 m* Caribbean *has, by installation of a diesel engine under the aft deck, achieved living areas all on one level; with forward steering, massive deck space and 'domestic' furniture, these boats sleep seven to eight in the sort of comfort that you would expect at home. Moulded throughout in GRP, they are sufficiently seaworthy for lake crossings in suitable conditions. The illustration shows one of the Blue Line Cruisers' fleet on the Canal du Midi in the South of France.*

Seagoing motor yacht: *Luxurious in every respect and capable of prolonged sea voyages at a speed of 10 knots, the twin engined diesel yacht is the ultimate in European waterway travel. There are few navigations not visited by Lord Harvington in his fine vessel* Melita, *shown here in a Rhône lock. She was built specifically to the most generous dimensions possible on Continental rivers and canals and occasionally takes on board local human ballast if the wheelhouse fails to clear an abnormally low bridge.*

Converted narrow boat: *The 'cult' craft of the English canals, rugged and spacious with a remarkable 70 ft/21·3 m length on a 7 ft/2·13 m beam. In converted form, the original cargo space beyond boatman's cabin and engine room, provides a living area where up to ten people can enjoy a high standard of comfort. Ferret, shown here, was built in 1926 with iron sides and elm planked bottom. She is by no means the oldest of her breed still in regular use.*

Traditional Dutch sailing barge: *Beautifully adapted to sailing the shallow lakes of Holland and yet fully seaworthy, this timber-built Dutch barge is an ideal craft for waterway use. Motorised, and designed on the lines of former working boats, it can reach all waterway systems of Western Europe and negotiate most locks (excepting the narrow beam canals of England).*

Modern 'narrow boat': *Whereas an unconverted narrow boat could be purchased in the early 1960s for a few hundred pounds, demand rapidly outstripped supply. Equipped with the most basic fittings, one would now cost several thousand. In consequence, a thriving business has grown up in the construction of new steel-hulled 'narrow boats', incorporating a mixture of traditional features and modern innovations. The 32 ft/9·8 m example shown is fitted with four berths, a pleasant open plan interior and an 8 hp Sabb diesel engine.*

Auxiliary sailing cruiser: *Cabin sloops and other types of smaller sailing cruiser are designed primarily for sea or lake use. But with mast lowered for passage through fixed bridges they have great potential for canal or river navigation. Adequate fendering must be devised to protect topsides from abrasion and where there is a fixed keel, due consideration must be given to the permitted draught of a waterway.*

Converted péniche: *Unquestionably the ideal choice for Continental use is the smaller type of former freight barge, with steel hull and superstructure. Many can be seen as mobile houseboats on the Seine in Paris or moored in Dutch towns (the most fruitful hunting ground for would-be purchasers). That illustrated is American-owned and was encountered on the Meuse in Belgium.*

27

Boat Handling and Practicalities

Inland Navigation

Thousands of families set out on their first ever holidays afloat every year in Britain with, at most, half an hour's instruction from the hire cruiser company. Accidents are few and those which do occur usually result from a lack of common sense which is not easily instilled in individuals where it is already totally lacking! Every practical manual of inland boating aims to convert simple ideas into complicated written instructions, a tendency which this book attempts to avoid. But a few remarks of general advice might perhaps be of help, even if only to build confidence with the complete novice.

Anyone embarking on boat ownership for the first time is unlikely to have absolutely no previous experience: the chances are that they will have been afloat with friends, hired a cruiser or at the very least studied the subject to the extent of having some notion of what is involved. (Without such previous grounding, you would in any event be most unwise to become a boat owner, for this would prove a costly exercise if it was not to your liking, or that of your family.)

If you drive a car, you will already have experience of being in control of a large and complicated machine. Here, the similarity with boats ends. On still-water canals, difficulties that do arise generally occur with ample time to take preventive action. The first point to notice is that nothing happens instantaneously: engage forward gear and the boat will take a little time to reach normal cruising speed. Likewise with steering, where movement of wheel or tiller produces a delayed response. Always anticipate events, leaving yourself plenty of time to correct a fault. Apart from displaying poor watermanship, it is stupid to approach a mooring or lock at high speed, relying on your reverse gear to produce an instant braking effect; act slowly and deliberately, making due allowance for wind and water currents.

On most waterways, the rule is to keep to the right. Local variations are signposted or otherwise made clear. In shallow navigations, deep draughted craft may wish to stay in the deepest part of the channel – generally the centre, or on the *outside* of bends. Thus, an approaching laden barge may signal for you to pass on the *wrong* side. Always acknowledge these signals, so that both helmsmen are certain what their intentions are.

Always keep within speed limits. These are strictly enforced on many European waterways, and your travel time between one lock and another may be noted by keepers in touch by telephone. It is not unknown for fines to be imposed. The point to watch is whether you are producing a wash; not only does this result in waste of fuel for little extra speed, but it causes damage to banks, draws silt into the channel and might endanger or ground other craft.

When mooring, even for a short time, avoid doing so on what is obviously private property, on sharp bends, in narrow sections, or wherever you could inconvenience other traffic. Often, lock keepers can advise on suitable locations.

Navigation in rivers and tidal estuaries demands greater seamanship. If travelling against a current, you have better control than going with it, so always turn your bows *into* the stream when mooring up. A suitable anchor attached to plenty of heavy chain (*at least* three times the average depth of the water) should be kept ready for immediate use in the event of an engine failure. Travelling at night (normally forbidden on hire craft) adds to the hazards, and obviously regulation navigation lights should be carried. On inland waters, this is a practice best avoided, unless you know the area extremely well.

Equipment

Hire craft are supplied with the gear necessary for the waters on which they are to be used. Private boats will need to be fitted out to cope with the special circumstances found on inland waterways. First, mooring ropes: strong lines of perhaps 50 ft/15 m should be attached to bow and stern. There are occasions when more rope is required, for example in exceptionally deep locks. When tying up at established mooring places, bollards or rings can generally be discovered on the banks. But failing these, you will have to supply your own, in the form of steel spikes at least 2 ft/60 cm long – anything shorter may well be tweaked from the ground by the wash of passing traffic. A heavy sledge hammer is needed to drive them in. Do not worry unduly if your knowledge of knots is very basic. Ability to tie a rope so that it cannot pull free accidentally, but can be released in an emergency, is all that is vital on inland waters. But do carry a sharp knife for cutting ropes if you need to get away suddenly. The author once woke up at 3 am to discover that torrential rain had raised the level of the canal well above the towpath, with the mooring bollards submerged out of sight!

As long as the boat is large enough to provide stowage on the roof, a stout gangplank will help passengers get ashore, especially if the water is too shallow to moor directly alongside the bank. A bicycle is invaluable for shopping expeditions (especially for a pre-breakfast ride to the nearest *boulangerie*) as well as for sending one crew member ahead down the towpath to alert the next lock keeper.

In England and Wales, lock windlasses (handles) should be carried for operating unmanned locks. Two different sized sockets fit the great majority of paddles, and windlasses designed for dual use are widely obtainable at canal boatyards. Having acquired a supply of windlasses, next purchase a heavy duty magnet (obtainable from many chandlers) for recovering them and other metal objects that have been dropped in the water. Everyone suffers from canal debris twisted around the propeller. A small plastic sack will impair performance, while a good haul of rubbish can cut the engine dead. Best of all is a watertight weed hatch, allowing access to the propeller from inside

The Coventry Canal's Hartshill dry dock was the only solution to removal of barbed wire from the propeller of this motorised ice breaker.

the boat; failing this, it is usually possible by lying on the stern to cut the offending matter with a long-handled knife, or sharp blade attached to a stick. Sooner or later you will be unfortunate enough to collect strands of barbed wire which can sometimes be removed with a powerful pair of bolt cutters. As a last resort, the boat may have to go into dry dock.

In addition to navigation lights, a strong white headlamp producing a broad beam is necessary for negotiating tunnels; a good hand torch makes a reasonable substitute.

Adequate water, gas and fuel storage removes the worry of constantly running out, especially in regions far from replenishments. Portable water and fuel carriers are advised for emergency use. Plenty of hose (fitted with tap connectors of the type in local use) is generally necessary on the English canals. Elsewhere, water supplies *normally* have hoses attached. Boat hooks or shafts of different lengths are most useful in recovering objects dropped overboard, for 'shafting' the boat off mud and − with care − pushing the boat away from obstructions. Be sure to fit a really powerful horn as an audible warning to other craft and to attract lock or bridge keepers. Avoid the use of car horns: they can be confusing.

A tool chest able to cope with all running repairs, together with a range of engine spares, is vital especially when far from home. Even the least mechanically-minded boater can normally get out of trouble with the aid of a local garage.

The sight of pristine white-hulled yachts hung

A detail of the remarkable Pontcysyllte Aqueduct, carrying the Welsh Section of the Shropshire Union Canal over the River Dee near Llangollen, North Wales. The structure of 19 arches stands at a maximum height of 121 ft/37 m above the fast-flowing river, the total span from bank to bank being 1007 ft/307 m. A cast iron trough of narrow beam also comprises a towpath. Designed by Thomas Telford with William Jessop, the aqueduct was opened to boats in 1805. It remains unique among world waterways.

overall with car tyres as protection when passing through locks is common on the French canals. Ideally, a steel or timber barge-type hull is painted black and needs no further fendering except on bow and stern. But more lightly constructed craft should be well supplied with fend-offs, either purpose-made in plastic and securely fastened, or adapted from small car tyres. These are not pretty, but they are effective if drilled top and bottom for tying and efficient draining.

Lock Working

Yachtsmen on passage from coast to coast regard canal locks with a degree of dread. Their inland boating enthusiast friends look on them as a pleasant enforced interlude, a chance to chat to the local people and possibly obtain fresh fruit and vegetables. Except for the larger, mechanised structures, locks are manually operated, often by the boat crew in England and Wales, almost always with the aid of keepers elsewhere. As a means of overcoming changes in level, the lock is an ingenious device and if treated with due caution, is easily negotiated. Experts have developed certain time-saving short cuts, many of which are calculated to upset the people responsible for their maintenance.

If working uphill, land a crew member to empty the chamber (if necessary) by opening the paddles at the lower end. Next open the bottom gates and take the boat in, securing it with lines fore and aft. Close lower gates and paddles and open the sluices at the upper end. If there is any choice, work ground-mounted paddles first, followed by those fitted on the gates. Admit water *slowly* to avoid creating a powerful cascade. Adjust the ropes as the boat rises in the chamber. When a level has been made, open the top gates, take the boat out under power and close gates and paddles behind you if this is the accepted procedure for those particular (unattended) locks. Where no payment is made, the lock keeper may be given a small tip, but this is perhaps best reserved for some particular service, such as

supplying water or information. Downhill locks demand operation according to a reverse procedure: the lack of water turbulence makes the undertaking rather easier.

Locks are sometimes encountered in multiples of up to as many as seven chambers and even 2-rise pairs demand more than normal advance consideration. Act slowly and deliberately, with each crew member attending to his allotted task. Avoid wasting water, especially by leaving paddles partly open when you depart.

The most common difficulties encountered with locks are mooring too close to the top gates when descending, with the result that the boat is stranded on the gate-sill; allowing the craft to be trapped by gate projections when rising; and losing control of a windlass when raising a paddle. This last eventuality can be very dangerous, for a rapidly rotating handle can cause serious injury, especially if flying off the spindle and striking someone. Always keep a firm hold of the handle while winding, secure the *pawl* (catch) when the paddle is fully raised, and, in

There are numerous opportunities for day cruises lasting several hours. Here, purpose built wide boat Avon *navigates an attractive length of the Kennet & Avon Canal near Hungerford, Berkshire.*

Some of the stages of working a manually operated lock on the Grand Union Canal at Stoke Bruerne, Northamptonshire. Top left: *chamber full, a downhill* *boat enters*. Top right: *crew members raise the lower gate paddles to empty the lock*. Centre left: *lock now empty, a converted narrow boat enters from below,*

while crew member waits to close the gate. Centre right: *gates shut, a top ground paddle has been drawn and the chamber starts to fill*. Bottom left: *opening a top ground* *paddle with the portable 'windlass'*. Bottom right: *top gates are open and the boat proceeds to the next lock, where the procedure is repeated!*

the case of removable windlasses, take it off the spindle.

Everything is much easier at manned mechanised locks. Follow the keeper's instructions (sometimes problematical if gabbled in a foreign language from a remote loud-speaker!) and moor where requested. Attend to your ropes as the water level changes and be prepared to leave smartly if commercial traffic is in the vicinity.

After your first dozen locks, you will think that you know all the tricks. Beware! Many locks have their own idiosyncrasies and the oldest of old dogs is always learning new tricks.

Emergencies

A dictum among boating people is that serious accidents always result from a combination of mistakes. A well-run boat is a safe boat. But, equally true, the sophisticated range of machinery, explosive fuel and gas and aqueous surroundings must be treated with respect. The catalogue of untoward happenings that follows have all been experienced by the writer at first hand: it could be helpful to know what to do when disaster does strike.

When town youths spit on you from bridges, the response is expression of disgust. But if under fire from air guns or well-aimed bricks, more positive action is demanded. Provided you can catch the culprits, dirty bilge water is an effective redress. If real damage has resulted, the police should be alerted, although in Great Britain this seldom seems to result in anything more severe than an official warning. The same class of person can usually be blamed for depositing refuse, blocking bridge holes or preventing lock gates opening wide enough for the boat to pass. In each case, the obstruction must be raked clear, using a *keb* – a useful device similar to a long-handled garden fork with the teeth bent at right angles to the shaft. Sometimes a narrow lock proves just too narrow to accept a boat: either the lock walls have caved in slightly, or the boat has 'spread'. The most effective solution is to produce a 'flush' of water by quickly raising and lowering the upper paddles. If that fails, resort to a block and tackle or seek advice from the waterway authority.

It is only too easy for someone to fall overboard. For this reason a steering position providing an all-round view of the boat is a great advantage. If someone is in the water, put the engine into neutral

Two privately owned cruisers work through one of the Håverud Locks on Sweden's enchanting Dalsland Canal.

gear immediately and preferably turn it off. Throw a life buoy to the victim and, if he is a poor swimmer or obviously in difficulties, jump in to offer help.

Fire on a boat is particularly nasty, and it cannot be too strongly emphasised that care must be taken with butane gas and petrol. Supply all parts of the vessel with *large* fire extinguishers and be sure that everyone knows where they are located.

Sinking, as the result of a collision or through striking debris on the canal bed, is a hazard most likely to be encountered by owners of older timber-built boats. If possible move the craft to shallow water and try to haul the damaged section clear. Stem the flow with anything suitable to hand such as a cushion, forced against the hole. Make a temporary repair with canvas, tar, clay or a quick-setting compound like Plastic Padding, until it is possible to obtain professional help.

Other problems, appalling though they may seem at the time, can usually be overcome through ingenuity. A breached weir or section of canal bank will drain a waterway in record time. The writer well remembers this happening on the Canal du Nivernais near the start of a two week circular cruise. But by pleading with the authorities to allow him to continue at minimum speed over the rapidly appearing mud, the safety of the next lock was eventually reached. Emergency stoppages are often insuperable: at the best a delay of several days must be endured until the trouble has been rectified.

The most worrying experience in this chapter of unfortunate happenings was recounted by a friend travelling down the River Rhône with a brand new cruiser. Securely moored for the evening in Arles. he enjoyed dinner ashore. On returning to the quay there was no sign of the boat: just an expanse of swirling water in the darkness! There followed a nail-biting night of police stations and telephone calls, before setting out at first light along the riverbank. By an extraordinary stroke of good fortune a boatman had seen the cruiser drifting through the dusk and had towed it to a place of safety. Later, it was learned that she been cast off by vandals. With the knowledge of hindsight, an anchor on the riverbed would have been a wise precaution.

Organisation of a Successful Cruise

When hiring a boat, you can be reasonably sure that she will be awaiting your arrival, fully equipped and even stocked with food if you have made out an order in advance. But some items must be taken from home. First, a comprehensive medicine chest is essential in order to cope with any minor family mishaps. This applies particularly to boating abroad. Suitable clothes, from swim-wear to warm pullovers and proper waterproofs should take care of most eventualities. Remember also comfortable non-slip shoes.

Entertainment in the form of books and games can be included, although there is always so much of interest happening on a waterway holiday that one is likely not to need either.

At least one member of the party should take a camera to record the journey. One splendid way of commemorating the holiday is to compile a 'scrap book', consisting of photographs, picture post cards, maps, pressed wild flowers and other souvenirs. If boating abroad, the scope can be enlarged to include wine bottle labels, entry tickets to museums or other attractions, and even the small change from your pocket at the end of the trip! Younger members of the family will enjoy being involved in this operation.

Some planning in advance of the holiday will pay dividends. If possible, obtain detailed route maps and a guide book to the area and work out a flexible schedule, day by day.

Expenses

If travelling by hire cruiser or your own boat, the costs may well include transport from home to where the craft is based. Where a considerable distance is involved, as in the case of a journey from

Fresh French bread from a travelling salesman flagged down on the Canal du Midi.

Two pages from a scrap book recording a family holiday on the Canal du Midi, Southern France.

England to join a boat on the Canal du Midi in the South of France, you have a choice of getting there by air, rail or car. Hire companies will usually make necessary ticket or car ferry bookings and, if driving, it is likely that an overnight hotel stop on the outward and return journeys should be arranged, preferably confirmed in advance. Once settled on to your boat, the main costs are food – a substantial item, especially in Sweden and Germany. If the budget can be stretched, do aim to eat ashore from time to time, for this adds considerably to the enjoyment of a foreign cruise.

Shopping abroad is great fun, and with self-service supermarkets established in virtually every village, language problems are readily overcome. It is far cheaper to adapt your eating habits to accord with local products, rather than buy familiar but expensive imported goods.

Documentation

Apart from passports, there is now normally no additional paperwork necessary for British people hiring cruisers abroad. If 'going foreign' in your own boat, obtain a Certificate of Registry for the craft or an International Certificate for Pleasure Navigation from the Royal Yachting Association, Victoria Way, Woking, Surrey. This will enable you to obtain the Green Card from the Customs on arrival at your foreign port of entry. Armed with this, you are entitled to travel for a period (usually

six months in any year) without paying import duty on the boat. The other necessity is a certificate of insurance covering the craft for third party liability.

When cruising in England and Wales, navigation permits must be obtained from the appropriate waterway authority. These are normally included in the cost of cruiser hire. In Germany, Ireland Sweden, Belgium and Holland, lock or bridge tolls will be charged on arrival. Except in a few isolated instances, use of the French waterways is free.

All the foregoing remarks apply to craft less than 15 tons displacement, where Germany is concerned. Larger vessels are subject to many additional regulations. In every case, it is most advisable to seek confirmation of arrangements with the appropriate national tourist offices in England, before commencing a holiday.

Insurance

When hiring, be sure to check that adequate third party and personal cover is offered by the operating company. The private boat owner should obtain third party cover (at least) as a protection for any damage that may result to other craft or waterway equipment. This is a legal requirement imposed by most navigation authorities. Additionally, comprehensive insurance cover is a wise precaution. A recent survey of the craft, proving it to be fully seaworthy, is normally required by the insurers, as is specific identification of the waters on which she will be used. Temporary cover for foreign navigation or tidal waters (if otherwise excluded) should be obtained in advance of making a journey beyond the quoted limits.

England & Wales

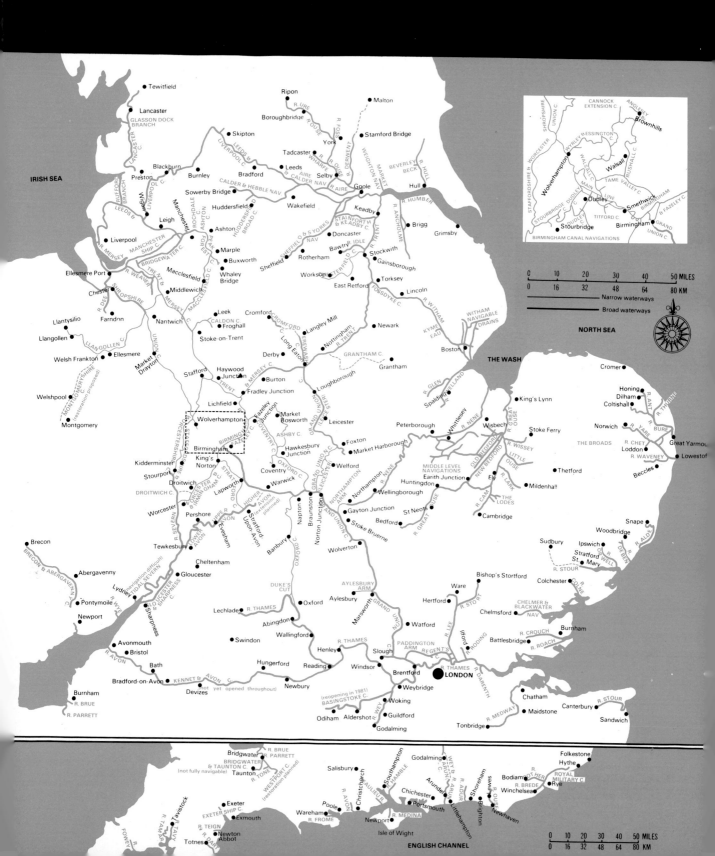

IRISH SEA

NORTH SEA

THE WASH

ENGLISH CHANNEL

Tewitfield
Lancaster
GLASSON DOCK BRANCH
Ripon
R. URE
Malton
Boroughbridge
R. OUSE
R. FOSS
Stamford Bridge
Skipton
Tadcaster
York
R. DERWENT
Blackburn
R. WYRE
Preston
Leeds
R. WHARFE
WEIGHTON NAV
LEEDS & LIVERPOOL C.
LANCASTER C.
RUFFORD BRANCH
Burnley
Bradford
Selby
MARKET WEIGHTON NAV
BEVERLEY BECK
R. HULL
Sowerby Bridge
AIRE & CALDER NAV
R. AIRE
Goole
Hull
CALDER & HEBBLE NAV
Huddersfield
Wakefield
Keadby
R. HUMBER
Liverpool
Leigh
Manchester
ROCHDALE C.
HUDDERSFIELD BROAD C.
ASHTON C.
STAINFORTH & KEADBY C.
Brigg
Grimsby
MANCHESTER SHIP C.
Ellesmere Port
R. MERSEY
PEAK FOREST C.
Marple
Buxworth
Doncaster
R. DON
SHEFFIELD & S YORKS NAV
R. ANCHOLME
Macclesfield
Whaley Bridge
Bawtry
R. IDLE
Stockwith
Gainsborough
Chester
R. DEE
R. WEAVER
Middlewich
MACCLESFIELD C.
Sheffield
Rotherham
Worksop
CHESTERFIELD C.
Torksey
SHROPSHIRE UNION C.
TRENT & MERSEY C.
Nantwich
Leek
CALDON C.
Froghall
East Retford
R. TRENT
Lincoln
FOSSDYKE C.
WITHAM NAVIGABLE DRAINS
Llantysilio
Llangollen
LLANGOLLEN C.
Welsh Frankton
Ellesmere
Market Drayton
Cromford
CROMFORD C.
Stoke-on-Trent
Langley Mill
EREWASH C.
Newark
R. WITHAM
KYME EAU
Boston
MONTGOMERYSHIRE C. (restoration proposed)
Welshpool
Stafford
Haywood Junction
Derby
Long Eaton
Nottingham
R. TRENT
R. GLEN
R. WELLAND
Montgomery
Lichfield
Fradley Junction
TRENT & MERSEY C.
Burton
GRANTHAM C.
Grantham
Loughborough
Spalding
Whittlesey
R. NENE
King's Lynn
Cromer
Honing
R. ANT
Dilham
R. THURNE
Coltishall
SHROPSHIRE UNION C.
STAFFS & WORCS C.
Wolverhampton
FAZELEY JUNCTION
Market Bosworth
ASHBY C.
R. SOAR
Leicester
GRAND UNION C.
Peterborough
Wisbech
R. GREAT OUSE
Stoke Ferry
R. WISSEY
Norwich
R. YARE
R. BURE
THE BROADS
R. CHET
Loddon
R. WAVENEY
Great Yarmouth
Lowestoft
Birmingham
King's Norton
WORCESTER & BIRMINGHAM C.
Hawkesbury Junction
COVENTRY C.
OXFORD C.
Foxton
Welford
Market Harborough
NORTHAMPTON ARM
Northampton
MIDDLE LEVEL NAVIGATIONS
OLD BEDFORD
NEW BEDFORD
Earith Junction
Ely
R. LARK
THE LODES
R. CAM
Thetford
Mildenhall
Beccles
Kidderminster
Stourport
Droitwich
DROITWICH C.
STRATFORD C.
Warwick
GRAND UNION C.
Coventry
Wellingborough
Huntingdon
R. NENE
St Neots
Gayton Junction
Cambridge
Snape
Woodbridge
R. DEBEN
Worcester
Pershore
R. SEVERN
HIGHER AVON (extension planned)
Stratford-Upon-Avon
LOWER AVON
Evesham
Napton
Braunston
OXFORD C.
Norton Junction
Stoke Bruerne
Bedford
R. GREAT OUSE
Ipswich
R. ORWELL
Stratford St. Mary
R. STOUR
Sudbury
Brecon
BRECON & ABERGAVENNY C.
Abergavenny
Lydney
TIDAL SEVERN
navigation difficult
Tewkesbury
Cheltenham
Gloucester
GLOUCESTER & SHARPNESS C.
Banbury
Wolverton
Bishop's Stortford
Ware
Hertford
R. STORT
Colchester
R. COLNE
CHELMER & BLACKWATER NAV
Chelmsford
Pontymoile
Newport
R. WYE
Sharpness
DUKE'S CUT
Lechlade
R. THAMES
Oxford
Aylesbury
AYLESBURY ARM
Marsworth
GRAND UNION C.
R. LEE
Watford
Ilford
R. RODING
Burnham
R. CROUCH
Battlesbridge
R. ROACH
Avonmouth
Bristol
R. AVON
Bath
Abingdon
Swindon
Wallingford
Henley
R. THAMES
Slough
PADDINGTON ARM
REGENT'S C.
R. LEE
R. RODING
Bradford-on-Avon
KENNET & AVON C.
(not yet opened throughout)
Hungerford
Reading
Windsor
Brentford
R. THAMES
R. DARENT
LONDON
Chatham
Canterbury
R. STOUR
Sandwich
Burnham
R. BRUE
Devizes
Newbury
(reopening in 1981)
BASINGSTOKE C.
Weybridge
Woking
Odiham
Aldershot
Guildford
Godalming
R. WEY
R. MEDWAY
Maidstone
Tonbridge
R. PARRETT
Bridgwater
R. BRUE
R. PARRETT
BRIDGWATER & TAUNTON C.
(not fully navigable)
Taunton
R. TONE
WESTPORT C.
(restoration planned)
Salisbury
R. AVON
Christchurch
Southampton
R. HAMBLE
Godalming
WEY & ARUN C.
Arundel
R. ARUN
Chichester
R. ROTHER
Shoreham
R. ADUR
R. BREDE
Bodiam
ROYAL MILITARY C.
Folkestone
Hythe
Exeter
EXETER SHIP C.
Exmouth
Wareham
Poole
R. FROME
Newport
R. MEDINA
Isle of Wight
Portsmouth
Littlehampton
Brighton
R. OUSE
Winchelsea
Rye
Newhaven
R. TEIGN
Newton Abbot
R. TAW
R. TAVY
Tavistock
R. DART
Totnes
FOWEY

```
0    10    20    30    40    50 MILES
0  16   32    48    64    80 KM
                          ──── Narrow waterways
                          ──── Broad waterways
```

BIRMINGHAM CANAL NAVIGATIONS

CANNOCK EXTENSION C.
SHROPSHIRE UNION C.
ANGLESEY C.
Brownhills
WYRLEY & ESSINGTON C.
WALSALL C.
RUSHALL C.
Walsall
Wolverhampton
STAFFORDSHIRE & WORCESTER C.
BIRMINGHAM MAIN LINE
TAME VALLEY C.
STOURBRIDGE C.
DUDLEY C.
Dudley
Smethwick
BIRMINGHAM & FAZELEY C.
TITFORD C.
Stourbridge
Birmingham
GRAND UNION C.

```
0    10    20    30    40    50 MILES
0  16   32    48    64    80 KM
```

Routes Across England

The great complexity of the canal and river network of England and Wales is such that a complete book is required to even try to do them justice. (*The Shell Book of Inland Waterways* runs almost to 500 pages, and even there, the author had little space to be expansive.) Therefore, it is proposed to offer something of the flavour of the various regions of the system; and then to concentrate on three individual navigations. Each happens to be a particular favourite of the writer: but if that is seen as insufficient reason for their selection, it might be added that the Leeds & Liverpool Canal is a fine example of a coast-to-coast wide beam waterway; Shakespeare's Avon is a thoroughly typical English river, made all the more special through having been made navigable from dereliction by voluntary effort; and of all narrow beam canals, the little Oxford has unique appeal.

Study of the map on page 37 reveals the great scope of the subject. It is possible to navigate from Tonbridge or Godalming in the south to Ripon or Skipton in the north; to enter the network from the East Coast via the Thames, Wash or Humber and emerge on the far side of England in the Severn or Mersey. These feats can be achieved with little effort, provided your chosen boat conforms to the rather exacting dimensions of the English canals. To penetrate virtually *everywhere* maximum sizes are 46 ft length × 7 ft beam × 2 ft draught × 5 ft 11 in height above water/14·02 m × 2·13 m × 0·61 m × 1·8 m. For serious exploration, the 7 ft/2·13 m beam is essential, as otherwise the mass of narrow canals would be inaccessible. But, apart from the Middle Level Navigations, between the Nene and Great Ouse, a length of 60 ft/18·29 m is permitted almost everywhere, and the figures for draught and headroom can generally be increased without problems. Wide beam boats over 7 ft/2·13 m have extensive cruising grounds based on the Thames, South West, North West, East Anglia and North East, but the only communication between north and south features narrow locks. But for the 17 of the Grand Union Canal's Leicester Section, at Watford and Foxton, this difficulty would be solved.

As restoration of derelict navigations progresses, new possibilities will materialise. With the eventual reopening of the whole Kennet & Avon Canal, wide beam craft will be able to cruise from the Thames at Reading to the Bristol Avon, but this is not expected until the mid-1980s at the earliest. Active consideration is being given to creation of a wide beam waterway along the Higher Avon, between the Grand Union Canal in Warwick and the river upstream of Stratford; when finished, this totally new line will offer a wide beam link from London to the Severn. One other long term prospect must also be mentioned: resuscitation of the disused 18·5 miles/29·8 km Wey & Arun Canal between Guildford and the South Coast via the Arun. Closed in 1871 but now being repaired at several points by the Wey & Arun Canal Trust, this idea has great appeal. But such an achievement is not likely for many years.

To an extent rarely to be found elsewhere in Europe, the English waterways have changed little since their construction which reached its height in the late 18th and early 19th centuries. Many present an illusion of travelling through Georgian England that would be difficult to discover by any other means. They are exceptionally rich in original architecture and industrial archaeology. Another unique quality is the very large number of circular cruising routes available within the scope of a one or two week holiday. The map suggests many alternatives, including the Thames–Oxford–Grand Union – 253 miles/407 km, two energetic weeks; the Avon–Severn Ring; the Cheshire Ring, Marple–Manchester–Middlewich–Macclesfield; and, for a long weekend, the fascinating London Circular Cruise, using the Thames, Grand Union and Regent's Canal.

The South

Britain's best known and most heavily used river is the Thames, splendidly maintained throughout its locked reaches from Teddington to beyond Lechlade in Gloucestershire. The Royal River features Hampton Court and Windsor Castle, Henley Regatta in early summer, the ancient University town of Oxford, numbers of stately homes, picture postcard villages, fine churches, many elegant bridges and a succession of fascinating waterside houses, emphasising that the Thames has long been a popular setting in which to live. All 44 locks are manned, those downstream of Oxford being mechanised. At the height of summer some reaches are exceptionally busy with long delays at locks in the most favoured areas. But for most of the year the river is peaceful, especially in its uppermost 30 miles/48 km. Hire cruisers, passenger craft, rowing boats and motorised day launches are available from numerous yards. A connection is made between the Upper Thames and the Wey Navigation at Weybridge. This charming 17th-century navigation extends to Godalming with the rural Basingstoke Canal joining it at West Byfleet; complete restoration is in progress on the Basingstoke, with a likely reopening date in 1981.

At Reading, the Kennet & Avon Canal heads westwards through delicious Berkshire and Wiltshire scenery to join the Avon in Georgian Bath. Substantial lengths are currently available for use and all but a short portion east of Newbury should be reopened by 1982 after many years of fund-raising, campaigning and rebuilding work by the Kennet & Avon Canal Trust in conjunction with the British Waterways Board. Two entries to the Oxford Canal exist above Oxford (see page 74). As a long term prospect, some work is in progress to recreate the disused Thames & Severn and Stroudwater Canals from Inglesham to the Gloucester & Sharpness Canal.

The Thames in London provides access to a number of wide beam navigations: most important is the Grand Union, reached from Brentford and offering a connection to the Midlands and beyond. Even in the Metropolitan suburbs there are surprisingly rural sections, and as it heads northwards through Hertfordshire to Northamptonshire and Warwickshire, the Grand Union is always interesting and often beautiful. Bull's Bridge, Southall, marks the start of the Paddington Arm, which, together with the Regent's Canal skirts the north side of London from west to east, and joins the Thames at Limehouse Basin, downstream of Tower Bridge. From this same point, the River Lee passes through industrial surroundings as far as Enfield where it begins to become quite pleasing en route to Hertford. Considerably more attractive is its tributary the River Stort, with a succession of old water mills between Rye House and Bishop's Stortford.

For craft able to negotiate the Thames Estuary, the River Medway can be reached. Its lower, tidal section below Maidstone is in complete contrast to the upper river through the hop fields and orchards of Kent. Until such time as the Wey & Arun Canal is reopened, a range of south coast waterways remains isolated from the network. Generally tidal, they are frequently shortened forms of longer navigations that once featured canalised extensions with locks in their higher reaches.

The Midlands

Birmingham is the centre of a spider's web of canals, with cruising routes radiating in every direction. More than 100 miles/161 km of waterways are available in the Birmingham Canal Navigations system alone (see inset map on page

St John's Lock, Lechlade, Gloucestershire, near the head of navigation on England's most popular river, the Thames.

A 2-rise narrow lock on the Gower Branch of the intricate Birmingham Canal Navigations, with a working boat.

37). Like the majority of Midlands canals, these are narrow beam and once carried huge annual tonnages of cargo to supply the needs of industry. In places they are very urban and rather neglected (although some local authority schemes have achieved dramatic improvements). The melancholy charm of the BCN is perhaps an acquired taste, although there is always much interest in industrial archaeological remains; in places real countryside will be encountered. Most travellers regard the area as offering convenient connections between one navigation and another, but it is not unknown for enthusiasts to undertake extensive journeys around the BCN for its own sake. Numerous circular trips are possible.

With the exception of the Grand Union Canal (wide beam from the Birmingham outskirts) all routes from the BCN have narrow locks and bridges. These include the Birmingham & Fazeley Canal (to the Coventry Canal at Fazeley Junction); the Worcester & Birmingham Canal (for the Northern Stratford Canal and River Severn); the Shropshire Union Canal, reached from the Staffordshire & Worcestershire Canal at Wolverhampton; and the Staffordshire & Worcestershire itself which may also be joined via the Stourbridge Canal. All these lines are full of character and regularly used by pleasure craft with frequent services available at boatyards and ample hire boats.

The East Midlands may be regarded as extending from the central part of the Grand Union near the show village of Stoke Bruerne and its Waterways Museum (see page 234). Beyond the 3056 yd/ 2794 m Blisworth Tunnel, the narrow beam Northampton Arm falls towards the River Nene, while further north, at Norton Junction, Long Buckby, the Grand Union's extensive Leicester Line links with the Trent. Its lower reaches are formed by the canalised River Soar, a little known but pleasant river, somewhat prone to flooding after heavy rain. Trent Junction is a four-way crossroads. To the north, the Erewash Canal progresses to a terminus at Langley Mill; eastwards, the Trent Navigation passes through the heart of Nottingham and eventually into the Humber; while to the west, the lengthy Trent & Mersey Canal runs through Burton and near Stafford to the Potteries and the North West.

The Severn Navigation, one of England's major rivers. A narrow beam canal cruiser heads upstream past Wainlode Hill on a reach 7 miles/11 km above Gloucester.

The South West

Two substantial rivers, the Severn and its tributary the Avon are the leading navigations. The broad Severn Estuary features one of the greatest tidal rises and falls in Britain and its swift current makes the journey between Avonmouth and Sharpness a hazardous one for canal boats. The funnelling effect of the river produces a tidal bore up the natural course of the waterway between Sharpness and Gloucester. One of Britain's most spectacular natural phenomena and perceptible about 260 times a year, the bore consists of a series of seven waves reaching a maximum height of 9 ft/2·7 m. The effect of an ebb tide is instantly reversed on arrival of the bore which can be ridden in a motor cruiser. This potentially dangerous exercise has been enjoyed by the author but is definitely only for the expert with local knowledge. Largest bores coincide with spring and autumn equinoctial tides. Since 1827, most traffic has been able to avoid this difficult passage by taking the Gloucester & Sharpness Ship Canal from the estuary to Gloucester Docks, the Sharpness Sea Lock being operable for two to three hours before high water. The Upper Severn is navigable to a little above Stourport and the 18th-century basins of the Staffordshire & Worcestershire Canal. In the early 19th century, barges could continue to Welshpool, 86 miles/138·4 km beyond the present limit. The Severn is a lordly river and periodic flooding has always inhibited development of its high banks which tend to restrict vision of the surrounding countryside. Junctions are made with the Lower Avon at Tewkesbury (see page 67); the Worcester & Birmingham Canal in Worcester; and the 8·5 mile/13·7 km Droitwich Canal at Hawford, which is currently being restored by the Droitwich Canals Trust to provide a convenient circular route using portions of the Severn and Worcester & Birmingham Canal.

The Bristol Avon continues the line of the Kennet & Avon Canal from Bath to Bristol and below the city docks via the Avon Gorge, where it is tidal, to the Severn Estuary. Upstream, on the north shore, only a short distance of the once extensive River Wye Navigation remains of use to craft larger than canoes, providing telling evidence of how our waterways network has wantonly been allowed to contract over the last century. In South Wales, the only substantial surviving length of waterway is the isolated Brecon & Abergavenny Canal, situated almost totally within the Brecon Beacons National Park. Although a mere 33·25 miles/53·5 km long, its scenery is quite outstanding and there is ample scope for a week's holiday aboard one of a number of local hire cruisers. Tripping craft and rowing boats are also available.

A number of short Devon waterways, while disconnected from the national network, are rich in recreational potential. Among them are the Bridgwater & Taunton Canal (whose locks are mostly disused) and the Exeter Ship Canal, opened in 1566 and thus the first navigation in Britain with pound locks.

East Anglia

The Broadland waterways in Norfolk and Suffolk are among the most popular boating navigations in the world. Through routes total about 127 miles/204·4 km and are formed by the courses of five rivers which widen into a series of very natural-seeming lakes that resulted from medieval peat workings. Heavily under pressure, with more than 12 000 registered craft enabling something like an annual quarter of a million people to take holidays afloat each year, the Broads contrive to maintain a unique beauty. The constituent elements include windmills and reed beds, a thriving fauna and flora and, in places away from the water, the Breckland or sandy heaths of Norfolk, once covered by dense forest. Boating facilities are extremely well developed, with the hire of cruisers handled by two leading agencies: Blakes of Wroxham and Hoseasons of Lowestoft. Parts of Broadland have been designated as nature reserves. In commercial traffic terms, these waters were the preserve of the sailing wherry, of which a sole example, *Albion*, remains. The courses of the Rivers Bure, Ant and Waveney once continued above their present limits of navigation, but locks have been derelict since the late 1920s and early 1930s and the only surviving lock in Broadland is between Oulton Broad and Lowestoft Harbour.

While no connection has ever existed between the Broads and the Fenland waterways, one could be created moderately easily by canalising the Upper Waveney for about 32 miles/51·5 km above Geldeston to meet the source of the Little Ouse or Brandon River which in turn runs into the Great Ouse. Popular among waterway enthusiasts, such a notion has to date met with little support from the relevant authorities. A very extensive network of Fenland rivers and canals, bordered on one side by the Nene and on the other by the Great Ouse, drains into the Wash. Between the two, the Middle Level Navigations, constructed and maintained partly for their drainage function, make possible transfer from one river to the other. Generally improved in recent years, the MLN is prone to weeding in mid-summer and is rather difficult to enter from the tidal Ouse below Denver Sluice. Passing through extremely flat and fertile tracts of potato and strawberry field, the Middle Level is remote and not without its own rather special interest.

No less than 20 miles/32·2 km of the most direct line between the Wash and the Upper Great Ouse consists of the totally straight and tidal New Bedford River. A much more interesting alternative is via the Ouse to Ely and the Old West River. Upstream of Earith Junction, the Ouse is a charming navigation, most of the locks being fitted with at least one set of guillotine gates. The topmost 10 miles/16 km to Bedford were derelict by 1939, but pressure from the Great Ouse Restoration Society brought about complete restoration with seven new locks. Bedford was finally reconnected to the network with the termination of the Anglian Water Authority's rebuilding programme in 1978. Several Ouse tributaries include the River Cam to Cambridge.

The Nene is joined to the Grand Union Canal at Northampton, where there is a flight of narrow locks. Its pretty and winding course to Peterborough is punctuated by a series of locks of 1930s vintage, equipped with heavy manually-operated guillotine gates. This fact tends to limit the numbers of craft visiting this lovely navigation. Among other rivers entering the Wash is the River Witham, passing through Boston to join the Foss Dyke Navigation (of Roman origin) at Lincoln; this in turn makes a junction with the tidal Trent at Torksey.

The North West

The area features a range of routes from the mighty Manchester Ship Canal to narrow beam canals.

Newby Hall on the banks of the River Ure in Yorkshire.

Trent & Mersey and Shropshire Union Main Lines both make their way towards the Mersey. Each boasts really fine branch lines in the form of the Caldon Canal (restored in the early 1970s) and the ever-popular Llangollen Canal, terminating some distance beyond the great Pontcysyllte Aqueduct in North Wales. Outstanding features are the Trent & Mersey's 2897 yd/2649 m Harecastle Tunnel (both narrow and low) and the amazing Anderton Vertical Lift of 1875. This transfers craft between the canal and the River Weaver, 50 ft/15·2 m below. Connected with the coast at Glasson Dock, but otherwise isolated, is the long lock-free level of the Lancaster Canal. The heart of Manchester is pierced by the surviving stub of the Rochdale Canal and the Ashton, both lately restored and forming part of the Cheshire Ring. Some progress is being made towards eventual reopening of two lost trans-Pennine routes: the Rochdale and Huddersfield Narrow Canals, both very heavily locked. One inter-coastal line does survive: the Leeds & Liverpool Canal (see page 58).

The North East

One of the last strongholds of commercial traffic, this region offers great interest on that account rather than much natural beauty. Yorkshire Ouse, Aire & Calder Navigation, tidal Trent and Sheffield & South Yorkshire Navigation retain enough of their freight craft to give an impression of what water transport is all about. For pleasure boats, the Lower Trent demands a degree of care, taking note of tidal flows and the bore, known locally as an 'aegre'. All but the experts are advised to avoid the Trent below Keadby and the Humber Estuary. The Yorkshire Ouse, also difficult in its tidal reaches below Naburn Locks, is quietly pleasing; the River Ure even more so. Among all rivers of England, the Yorkshire Derwent is a jewel. The most idyllic portion upstream of Stamford Bridge suffers from disused locks whose future reinstatement is currently best described in diplomatic terms as a political hot potato! For the present, the 16 miles/25·7 km below Malton can be explored by motorised inflatable or other form of portable craft. It is well worth travelling far to achieve this feat.

Following page: The days of more leisurely boating – so greatly loved by the late Victorians and Edwardians – are recalled in this very English scene on the River Wey Navigation at Godalming, Surrey. The nearby Farncombe Boat House still specialises in the hire of manually propelled craft – skiffs and punts – and boasts one of the largest collections in Britain.

Navigation Authorities

A multiplicity of bodies control the inland waterways of England and Wales, ranging from the British Waterways Board to Water Authorities, local authorities and private Trusts. In an attempt to present this information in simple form, the various navigations have been categorised according to the approximate maximum dimensions of craft which can travel on them. For detailed additional information readers should consult *The Shell Book of Inland Waterways*, by Hugh McKnight (David & Charles, 1977), or *Inland Waterways of Great Britain*, by L A Edwards (Imray, Laurie, Norie & Wilson, 1972.)

Waterways categorised by maximum dimensions

A   In excess of 70 ft length and 14 ft beam/21·3 m × 4·27 m

B   70 ft length × 14 ft beam/21·3 m × 4·27m

C   70 ft length × less than 14 ft beam/21·3 m × less than 4·27 m

D   Less than 70 ft length × 14 ft beam/less than 21·3 m × 4·27 m

E   70 ft length × 7 ft beam/21·3 m × 2·13 m

F   Length considerably less than 70 ft or beam considerably less than 14 ft/21·3 m × 4·27 m

Unless specifically detailed, distances include branches and their locks. The only derelict waterways included are those where active restoration is in progress with real prospects of reopening; or where some local boating is possible in spite of obstructions or disused locks.

Of a total of 3374 miles/5429·9 km of navigations listed, with 1587 locks, the British Waterways Board controls about half the distance: 1643·5 miles/2645 km, with 1304 locks. Navigations are listed alphabetically under British Waterways Board. The Waterways Authorities then appear in alphabetical order, followed by individual authorities, alphabetically.

British Waterways Board, Melbury House, Melbury Terrace, London NW1 6JX. Tel: 01-262 6711.

Aire & Calder Nav (A)	From Goole to Castleford, Castleford to Wakefield and Leeds, Knottingley to Selby and Pollington to Bramwith via the New Junction C	58·75 miles/94·6 km	22 locks	Navigable
Ashby Canal (E)	Marston, Coventry C to Snarestone, terminus	22 miles/35·4 km	1 stop lock	Navigable
Ashton Canal (E)	Manchester, Rochdale C to Dukinfield, Peak Forest C	6·25 miles/10 km	18 locks	Navigable
Birmingham Canal Nav (E)	Birmingham to Wolverhampton, Dudley and Cannock (see map, page 37)	100 miles/161 km approx	155 locks approx	Navigable
Brecon & Abergavenny Canal (F)	Brecon to Pontymoile	33·25 miles/53·5 km	6 locks	Navigable
Bridgwater & Taunton Canal (F)	Bridgwater, River Parrett, to Taunton, River Tone	14·25 miles/22·9 km	6 locks, derelict	Partly navigable
Calder & Hebble Nav (D)	Wakefield to Sowerby Bridge, terminus	21·5 miles/34·6 km	39 locks	Navigable
Caldon Canal (E)	Stoke-on-Trent, Trent & Mersey C, to Froghall and Leek	20·25 miles/33 km	17 locks	Navigable
Chesterfield Canal (E)	West Stockwith, River Trent to Worksop, terminus	26 miles/42 km	16 locks	Navigable
Coventry Canal (E)	Coventry to Fradley, Trent & Mersey C	38 miles/61 km	13 locks	Navigable
Cromford Canal (B)	Ambergate to Cromford (isolated portion only)	5 miles/8 km	0 locks	Remaining 9 miles/14·5 km, Langley Mill to Ambergate, derelict
Erewash Canal (B)	Sawley, River Trent, to Langley Mill, terminus	12 miles/19·3 km	15 locks	Navigable
Fossdyke Canal (A)	Torksey, River Trent to Lincoln, River Witham	11·25 miles/18 km	1 lock	Navigable
Gloucester & Sharpness Canal (A)	Sharpness to Gloucester, River Severn	16·75 miles/27 km	2 locks	Navigable
Grand Union Canal Main Line (B)	Brentford, River Thames to Birmingham	135·4 miles/218 km	165 locks	Navigable. Beam reduced to less than 14 ft/4·27 m just south of Birmingham and then 7 ft/2·13 m at Camp Hill Locks, Birmingham
Grand Union Canal, Paddington Arm (B)	Southall to Paddington, Regent's C	13·7 miles/22 km	0 locks	Navigable
Grand Union Canal, Slough Arm (B)	Cowley Junction to Slough, terminus	5 miles/8 km	0 locks	Navigable
Grand Union Canal, Chess Branch (B)	Rickmansworth to Town Wharf, terminus	0·3 miles/0·5 km	1 lock	Navigable

Grand Union Canal, Wendover Arm (B)	Bulbourne to Tring Ford, terminus	1·5 miles/2·4 km	0 locks	Navigable
Grand Union Canal, Aylesbury Arm (E)	Marsworth to Aylesbury, terminus	6·25 miles/10 km	16 locks	Navigable
Grand Union Canal, Northampton Arm (E)	Gayton to Northampton, River Nene	4·7 miles/7·6 km	17 locks	Navigable
Grand Union Canal, Leicester Section (E)	Long Buckby to Foxton Bottom Lock	23 miles/37 km	18 locks	Navigable, includes 1·5 mile/2·4 km Welford Arm
Grand Union Canal, Leicester Section (B)	Market Harborough, via Foxton to Sawley, River Trent	48·5 miles/78 km	42 locks	Navigable, partly comprises River Soar
Huddersfield Broad Canal (D)	Cooper Bridge, Calder & Hebble Nav to Huddersfield, terminus	3·25 miles/5·2 km	9 locks	Navigable
Kennet & Avon Canal (C)	Reading, River Thames to Hanham Lock, Bristol Avon	86·5 miles/139 km	105 locks	Substantial sections navigable; remainder being restored. River Avon is category (A)
Lancaster Canal (B)	Preston to bottom of Tewitfield Locks, terminus, and to Glasson Dock, River Lune	44·4 miles/71·5 km	7 locks	Navigable; the 14·5 miles/23·3 km Northern Reaches to Kendal are mainly derelict
River Lee (A)	Limehouse Basin, Regent's C to Hertford	27·5 miles/44·3 km	21 locks	Navigable
Leeds & Liverpool Canal (D)	Leeds, Aire & Calder Nav to Liverpool Docks	127 miles/204·4 km	91 locks	Navigable; Wigan Junction to Liverpool is category (B)
Leeds & Liverpool Canal, Leigh Branch (B)	Wigan to Leigh, Bridgewater C	7·25 miles/11·7 km	2 locks	Navigable
Leeds & Liverpool Canal, Rufford Branch (B)	Lathom to Tarleton, River Douglas	7·25 miles/11·7 km	8 locks	Navigable
Leeds & Liverpool Canal, Stanley Dock Branch (B)	Main Line, Liverpool to Stanley Dock, River Mersey	0·25 miles/0·4 km	4 locks	Navigable
Llangollen Canal (E)	Hurleston, Shropshire Union C to Llantysilio, terminus	46 miles/74 km	21 locks	Navigable; draught only 2 ft/0·61 m, upper 6 miles/9·7 km
Macclesfield Canal (E)	Hall Green, Trent & Mersey C, to Marple, Peak Forest C	26 miles/41·8 km	13 locks	Navigable
Montgomeryshire Canal (E)	Welsh Frankton, Llangollen C, to Newtown, terminus	35 miles/56·3 km	26 locks	Mainly derelict, but subject to restoration work
Oxford Canal (E)	Oxford, River Thames, to Hawkesbury, Coventry C	78 miles/125·5 km	43 locks	Navigable
Peak Forest Canal (E)	Dukinfield, Ashton C, to Whaley Bridge, terminus	14·5 miles/23·3 km	16 locks	Navigable
Pocklington Canal (D)	Cottingwith, Yorks Derwent, to Pocklington	9·5 miles/15·3 km	9 locks	Mostly navigable, restoration nearing completion
Regent's Canal (B)	Paddington, Paddington Arm, to Limehouse, Rivers Lee and Thames	8·5 miles/13·7 km	13 locks	Navigable
Regent's Canal, Hertford Union (B)	Bethnal Green to Old Ford, River Lee	1·25 miles/2 km	3 locks	Navigable
Ripon Canal (D)	Oxclose Lock, River Ure, to Ripon, terminus	2·25 miles/3·6 km	3 locks	The upper two locks are derelict
River Severn (A)	Gloucester, Gloucester & Sharpness C, to Stourport, Staffs & Worcs C	42·2 miles/68 km	6 locks	Navigable; additionally, the Severn is navigable, Gloucester to Sharpness, although hazardous
Sheffield & S Yorks Nav (D)	Keadby, River Trent, to Sheffield, terminus	43 miles/69·2 km	29 locks	Navigable; River Trent to Doncaster is category (A) and there are plans to upgrade much of the remainder
Shropshire Union Canal (E)	Autherley, Staffs & Worcs C, to Nantwich	39 miles/62·8 km	29 locks	Navigable
Shropshire Union Canal (B)	Nantwich to Ellesmere Port, Manchester Ship C	27·6 miles/44·4 km	17 locks	Navigable; beam, Nantwich to Chester is reduced to 13·25 ft/4·03 m
Shropshire Union Canal, Middlewich Branch (E)	Barbridge to Middlewich, Trent & Mersey C	10 miles/16 km	4 locks	Navigable

Staffordshire & Worcestershire Canal (E)	Stourport, River Severn, to Great Haywood, Trent & Mersey C	46 miles/74 km	43 locks	Navigable
River Stort (C)	Rye House, River Lee, to Bishop's Stortford, terminus	13·75 miles/22·1 km	15 locks	Navigable
Stourbridge Canal (E)	Stourton, Staffs & Worcs Canal, to Black Delph, Birmingham C Nav	5·25 miles/8·4 km	20 locks	Navigable; a 1·25 mile/2 km branch also leads to Stourbridge
Stratford-upon-Avon Canal, Northern Section (E)	Lapworth, Grand Union C and Stratford C, Southern Section, to King's Norton, Worcester & Birmingham C	12·25 miles/19·7 km	20 locks	Navigable; for Southern Section see National Trust
Trent & Mersey Canal (C)	Derwent Mouth, River Trent, to Burton-on-Trent	16·5 miles/26·6 km	6 locks	Navigable
Trent & Mersey Canal (E)	Burton-on-Trent to Preston Brook, Bridgewater C	77 miles/124 km	70 locks	Navigable; permitted beam, Croxton aqueduct, Middlewich to Preston Brook is 9 ft/2·74 m
River Trent (A)	Shardlow, Trent & Mersey C, to Gainsborough	68·5 miles/110·2 km	13 locks	Navigable; on the Nottingham C section, Nottingham, locks are smaller, although still within category (A)
River Ure (D)	Swale Nab, Yorks Ouse, to Ripon C	8 miles/12·9 km	2 locks	Navigable
River Weaver (A)	Weston Point Docks, Manchester Ship C, to Winsford, terminus	20 miles/32·2 km	5 locks	Navigable; a connection is made with the Trent & Mersey C via the Anderton Lift, category (B)
Witham Navigation (A)	Lincoln, Fossdyke C, to the Wash	36·5 miles/58·8 km	3 locks	Navigable
Worcester & Birmingham Canal (E)	Gas Street Basin, Birmingham, Birmingham C Nav, to Worcester, River Severn	30 miles/48·3 km	58 locks	Navigable

Anglian Water Authority, Diploma House, Grammar School Walk, Huntingdon PE18 6NZ. Tel: Huntingdon (0480) 56181.

River Ancholme (A)	South Ferriby Sluice, River Humber, to Bishopbridge	19 miles/30·6 km	2 locks	Navigable; upper 2·5 miles/4 km is category (B)
River Cam (B)	Bottisham Lock to Pope's Corner, River Great Ouse	6·7 miles/10·8 km	1 lock	Navigable; see also Conservators of the Cam
River Cam, Reach and Burwell Lodes, Swaffham Lode, Wicken Lode (F)	All branches of the lower Cam	7 miles/11·3 km approx	2 locks	Navigable; but shallow in places
River Glen (F)	From the River Welland to Tongue End	11·5 miles/18·5 km	tidal gates	Navigable; craft over 30 ft/9·1 m will have difficulty in turning at the end
Kyme Eau (Sleaford Nav) (F)	From the River Witham to Sleaford, terminus	12·25 miles/19·7 km	derelict	Navigable for portable craft only; the lower 1·5 miles/2·4 km is, however, category (B)
River Lark (B)	From the Great Ouse near Ely to Judes Ferry, terminus	13 miles/21 km	1 lock	Navigable; a further 10 miles/16 km to Bury St Edmunds is possible for portable craft.
River Nene (C)	Northampton, Grand Union C, to the Wash	91·5 miles/147·3 km	38 locks	Navigable; downstream of Peterborough, category (A)
River Great Ouse (C)	Bedford to the Wash	75 miles/120·7 km	16 locks	Navigable
River Little Ouse (Brandon River) (A)	Brandon Creek, Great Ouse, to Brandon Staunch	13 miles/21 km	0 locks	Navigable; former locks upstream of Brandon now inoperable

River	Route	Distance	Locks	Notes
River Stour (Suffolk) (F)	Sudbury to Harwich	35·5 miles/57 km	derelict	Navigable for portable craft, the tidal estuary, Harwich to Cattawade being category (A)
River Welland (F)	Deeping St James to the Wash	24·25 miles/39 km	1 lock	Navigable; Spalding to the Wash is category (A)
River Wissey (A)	Ten Mile River, near Denver, River Great Ouse, to Stoke Ferry, terminus	10 miles/16 km	0 locks	Navigable

Severn-Trent Water Authority, Abelson House, 2297 Coventry Road, Sheldon, Birmingham B26 3PR. Tel: Birmingham (021) 743 4222.

River Idle (A)	West Stockwith, River Trent, to Bawtry, terminus	11 miles/17·7 km	1 lock	Navigable

Southern Water Authority, Guildbourne House, Worthing, Sussex BN11 1LD. Tel: Worthing (0903) 205252.

River Adur (A)	Shoreham-by-Sea, English Channel, to Bines Bridge, terminus	11 miles/17·7 km	0 locks	Navigable; tidal throughout
River Arun (C)	Littlehampton, English Channel, to Pallingham, terminus	25·5 miles/41 km	0 locks	Navigable; tidal. Connection is made with the Wey & Arun C, derelict
River Brede (F)	Rye, River Rother, to Brede, terminus	8 miles/12·9 km	1 lock	Navigable
River Medway (A)	Maidstone to Tonbridge, terminus	15·2 miles/24·5 km	9 locks	Navigable; see also Medway Ports Authority
River Ouse (Sussex) (A)	Newhaven, English Channel, to Hamsey Lock, Lewes, terminus	9·5 miles/15·3 km	0 locks	Navigable; tidal throughout
River Rother (Kent) (F)	Rye Harbour, English Channel, to Bodiam, terminus	16·2 miles/26·1 km	1 lock	Navigable
Royal Military Canal (F)	West Hythe, terminus, to Iden Lock, River Rother, Rye (not operable), terminus	19 miles/30·6 km	0 locks	Navigable by light craft only; partly owned by the National Trust

Thames Water Authority, Nugent House, Vastern Road, Reading RG1 8DB. Tel: Reading (0734) 593333.

River Thames (A)	Teddington to Inglesham, terminus	124·7 miles/200·7 km	44 locks	Navigable; one of the locks is on the River Kennet in Reading

Welsh Water Authority, Cambrian Way, Brecon, Powys, Wales, LD3 7HP. Tel: Brecon (0874) 3181.

River Dee (A)	Chester Weir to the coast at Point of Air	19·7 miles/31·7 km	0 locks	Navigable; tidal throughout. Chester weir can be passed on suitable tides. See also Cheshire County Council and Chester City Council
River Wye (A)	Beachley Point, Severn Estuary, to Tintern, terminus	11·5 miles/18·5 km	0 locks	Navigable; an open river, managed by WWA. More than 100 miles/161 km is available for advanced canoeists

Wessex Water Authority, Techno House, Redcliffe Way, Bristol BS1 6NY. Tel: Bristol (0272) 25491.

River Frome (A)	Poole Harbour to Wareham, terminus	7·7 miles/12·4 km	0 locks	Navigable; tidal. Craft over 30 ft/9 m cannot turn round in Wareham
River Parrett (D)	Bridgwater to Oath Sluice, present terminus	9 miles/14·5 km	0 locks	Navigable; restoration of 6·5 miles/10·5 km of upper river and the Westport C is possible

Yorkshire Water Authority, West Riding House, 67 Albion Street, Leeds LS1 5AA. Tel: Leeds (0532) 448201.

River Derwent (Yorks) (F)	Malton, terminus, to Barmby-on-the-Marsh, Yorks Ouse	38 miles/61·2 km	6 locks	Navigable, Stamford Bridge to the Ouse; locks above are derelict but may be restored, the upper

				23·5 miles/37·8 km being suitable for small craft
River Don (A)	Goole, Yorks Ouse, to Fishlake Old Ferry, Sheffield & S Yorks Nav	12·25 miles/19·7 km	0 locks	Navigable
River Wharfe (A)	Yorks Ouse to Tadcaster, terminus	9·25 miles/14·9 km	0 locks	Navigable

Barking and Ilford Navigation Company (1961) Ltd, c/o Younghusband and Stephens and Company Ltd, London Road, Barking, Essex. Tel: 01-594 5393

River Roding (A)	Barking Creek, River Thames, to Ilford, terminus	1·7 miles/2·7 km	0 locks	Navigable; tidal doors at entrance

Beaulieu Estate, Harbour Master, Buckler's Hard, Hampshire. Tel: Buckler's Hard (059 063) 200.

Beaulieu River (A)	Stone Point, Solent, to Beaulieu, terminus	8 miles/12·9 km	0 locks	Navigable; tidal throughout

Beverley Corporation, Municipal Offices, Beverley, East Yorkshire. Tel: Beverley (0482) 882255.

Beverley Beck (D)	Grove Hill, River Humber, to Beverley, terminus	0·75 miles/1·2 km	1 lock	Navigable

British Transport Docks Board, PO Box 1, Kingston House Tower, Bond Street, Hull HU1 3ER. Tel: Hull (0482) 27235.

River Humber (A)	Trent Falls, Yorks Ouse and River Trent, to Grimsby, North Sea	36 miles/58 km	0 locks	Navigable; tidal throughout
River Trent (A)	Gainsborough to Trent Falls, Rivers Ouse (Yorks) and Humber	22·25 miles/35·8 km	0 locks	Navigable; tidal throughout. See also British Waterways Board

British Transport Docks Board, Dock Offices, Stanhope Street, Goole, N Humberside DN14 5BB. Tel: Goole (0405) 2691/5.

River Ouse (Yorks) (A)	Trent Falls, Rivers Humber and Trent, to Skelton railway bridge	10 miles/16 km	0 locks	Navigable; tidal throughout. See also Ouse & Foss Nav and Linton Lock Commissioners

Chelmer & Blackwater Navigation Ltd, Little Baddow, Danbury, Essex. Tel: Danbury (024 541) 2025.

Chelmer & Blackwater Navigation (D)	Heybridge, tidal River Blackwater, to Chelmsford, terminus	13·8 miles/22·2 km	13 locks	Navigable

Cheshire County Council, County Hall, Chester CH1 1SF. Tel: Chester (0244) 602424.

River Dee (A)	Farndon, terminus, to Ironbridge	3·5 miles/5·6 km	0 locks	Navigable; see also Welsh Water Authority and Chester City Council

Chester City Council, Town Hall, Chester CH1 2HN. Tel: Chester (0244) 40144.

River Dee (A)	Ironbridge to Chester weir	6·5 miles/10·5 km	0 locks	Navigable

Colchester District Council, Town Hall, Colchester CO1 1PJ. Tel: Colchester (0206) 76071.

River Colne (A)	Colne Point, North Sea, to Colchester, terminus	11 miles/17·7 km	0 locks	Navigable; tidal throughout

Conservators of the River Cam, The Guildhall, Cambridge CB2 3QJ. Tel: Cambridge (0223) 58977.

River Cam (B)	Bottisham Lock to Cambridge	7·5 miles/12 km	2 locks	Navigable

Dart Harbour & Navigation Authority, The Old Post Office, South Embankment, Dartmouth TQ6 9BH. Tel: Dartmouth (080 43) 2337.

River Dart (A)	Kingswear and Dartmouth to Totnes, terminus	10·25 miles/16·5 km	0 locks	Navigable; tidal throughout

Dartford & Crayford Navigation Commissioners, 26 Lowfield Street, Dartford, Kent. Tel: Dartford (32) 20630.

Dartford & Crayford Nav (A)	River Thames to Dartford with branch from Crayford to River Darenth	3·5 miles/5·6 km	1 lock	Navigable

Devon County Council, County Hall, Topsham Road, Exeter EX2 4QD. Tel: Exeter (0392) 77977.

Grand Western Canal (C)	Lowdwells, terminus, to Tiverton, terminus	11 miles/17·7 km	0 locks	Navigable

Dover District Council, Brook House, Dover CT16 1RL. Tel: Dover (0304) 206184.

River Stour (Kent) (A)	Pegwell Bay, South Coast, to Fordwich, terminus	19·25 miles/31 km	0 locks	Navigable. Suitable for smaller craft only above Sandwich

Driffield Navigation Commission, Enquiries to Yorkshire Water Authority.

Driffield Navigation (D)	Aike, River Hull, to Great Driffield, terminus	11 miles/17·7 km	6 locks	Lower part nav. restoration planned

River Hull (A)	Struncheon Hill Lock, Driffield Nav, to River Humber	20 miles/32·2 km	0 locks	Navigable; tidal throughout

Exeter City Council, Municipal Offices, Civic Centre, Exeter EX1 1JJ. Tel: Exeter (0392) 77888.

Exeter Ship Canal (A)	Turf Lock, Exe Estuary, to Exeter, terminus	5 miles/8 km	3 locks	Navigable

Fowey Harbour Commissioners, Albert Quay, Fowey, Cornwall. Tel: Fowey (072 683) 2471.

River Fowey (A)	St Catherine's Point to Lostwithiel	7 miles/11·3 km	0 locks	Navigable; tidal throughout

Great Yarmouth Port & Haven Commissioners, 21 South Quay, Great Yarmouth, Norfolk. Tel: Great Yarmouth (0493) 55151.

Norfolk & Suffolk Broads (A)	The Rivers Yare, Bure, Ant, Thurne and Waveney and connections, linked with the North Sea at Great Yarmouth and Lowestoft	127 miles/204·4 km	1 lock	Navigable

Hampshire County Council, The Castle, Winchester SO23 8UJ. Tel: Winchester (0962) 4411.

River Hamble (A)	Hamble to Botley	7·5 miles/12 km	0 locks	Navigable; tidal throughout

Linton Lock Commissioners, c/o M D Oakley, 1–3 Wheelgate, Malton, Yorks. Tel: Malton (0653) 3639.

River Ouse (Yorks) (D)	Widdington Ings to Swale Nab	9·7 miles/15·6 km	1 lock	Navigable. See also British Transport Docks Board and Ouse & Foss Nav

Lower Avon Navigation Trust, Gable End, The Holloway, Pershore, Worcestershire. Tel: Pershore (038 65) 2517.

Lower Avon River (C)	Tewkesbury, River Severn, to Offenham, Upper Avon	27 miles/43·5 km	8 locks	Navigable

Manchester Ship Canal Company, Ship Canal House, King Street, Manchester M2 4WX. Tel: Manchester (061) 872 2411.

Manchester Ship Canal (A)	Eastham, River Mersey, to Manchester	36 miles/58 km	5 locks	Navigable. Pleasure craft must comply with stringent regulations

Manchester Ship Canal Company, Preston Brook Marina, Preston Brook, Runcorn WA7 3AF. Tel: Aston (092 86) 671.

Bridgewater Canal (B)	Castlefield Junction, Rochdale C, Manchester, to Runcorn, terminus	28 miles/45 km	0 locks	Navigable. Now abandoned beyond Runcorn Top Lock
	Water's Meeting, Stretford, to Leigh, Leeds & Liverpool C	10·75 miles/17·3 km	0 locks	Navigable

Market Weighton Drainage Board, Waterloo Buildings, Pocklington, Yorks. Tel: Pocklington (075 92) 2115.

Market Weighton Canal (B)	River Humber to Sod House Lock	6 miles/9·7 km	1 lock	Not fully navigable, but improvements being made

Medway Ports Authority, High Street, Rochester, Kent ME 1PZ. Tel: Medway (0634) 403731.

River Medway (A)	Sheerness, Thames Estuary, to Maidstone	27·5 miles/44·3 km	1 lock	Navigable. Tidal below Allington Lock. See also Southern Water Authority

Mersey Docks and Harbour Company, Dock Office, Liverpool L3 1BZ. Tel: (051) 236 1520.

River Mersey (A)	Garston to Liverpool	5·5 miles/8·9 km	0 locks	Navigable

Middle Level Commissioners, March, Cambs PE15 8AF. Tel: March (035 42) 3232.

Middle Level Navigation (F)	A series of drainage channels connecting River Nene with River Great Ouse	80 miles/129 km approx	7 locks	Navigable. Maximum length is 46 ft/14·02 m

National Trust, Canal Office, Lapworth, Solihull, Warwickshire. Tel: Lapworth (056 43) 3370.

Stratford-upon-Avon Canal (Southern Section) (E)	Lapworth, Grand Union C and Stratford C Northern Section to Stratford, River Avon	13 miles/20·9 km	36 locks	Navigable

National Trust, Dapdune Lea, Wharf Road, Guildford, Surrey GU1 4RR. Tel: Guildford (0483) 61389.

River Wey and Godalming Navigations (C)	Weybridge, River Thames, to Godalming, terminus	19·5 miles/31·4 km	16 locks	Navigable

North Cornwall District Council, Municipal Offices, Priory Road, Bodmin, Cornwall PL31 2AD. Tel: Bodmin (0208) 2216.

Bude Canal (A)	Bude Sea Lock to Rodd's Bridge, terminus	1·25 miles/2 km	1 lock	Navigable.

North Walsham & Dilham Canal Company Ltd, Ebridge Mills, North Walsham, Norfolk.

North Walsham & Dilham Canal (F)	River Ant (Broads) to Honing Lock, derelict	2·25 miles/3·6 km	0 locks	Navigable. Originally 4 locks to Swafield Bridge, 7·25 miles/11·7km

Ouse & Foss Navigation Trust, Guildhall, Yorks. Tel: York (0904) 54544.

River Foss (A)	Blue Bridge, York, Yorks Ouse, to Monk Bridge, terminus	1·25 miles/2 km	1 lock	Navigable. Originally 11·5 miles/18·5 km with 8 locks
River Ouse (Yorks) (A)	Goole to Widdington Ings	41 miles/66 km	1 lock	Navigable. See also British Transport Docks Board and Linton Lock Commissioners

Port of Bristol Authority, Port Offices, St Andrew's Road, Avonmouth, Bristol BS11 9DQ. Tel: Avonmouth (027 52) 3681.

River Avon (Bristol) (A)	Hanham Lock, Kennet & Avon C, to Avonmouth, Severn Estuary	13 miles/21 km	2 locks	Navigable

Port of London Authority, World Trade Centre, London, E1. Tel: 01-476 6900.

River Thames (A)	The Estuary to Teddington	64·5 miles/103·8 km	1 lock	Navigable. Richmond Lock is worked only at low water. Tidal throughout

Port of Preston, Dock Offices, Watery Lane, Preston PR2 2XE. Tel: Preston (0772) 726711.

River Ribble (A)	Preston to Irish Sea	20 miles/32·2 km	0 locks	Navigable; tidal throughout

Port of Tyne Authority, Berwick Street, Newcastle-upon-Tyne NE1 5HS. Tel: Newcastle (0632) 25541.

River Tyne (A)	Hedwin Streams to Tynemouth, North Sea	19 miles/30·6 km	0 locks	Navigable; tidal throughout

Queen's Harbour Master, HM Naval Base, Devonport, Devon. Tel: Plymouth (0752) 53740.

River Tamar (A)	Weir Head, Morwellham, terminus, to Plymouth, South Devon coast	19 miles/30·6 km	0 locks	Navigable; tidal throughout

Rochdale Canal Company, 75 Dale Street, Manchester M1 2HG. Tel: Manchester (061) 236 2456.

Rochdale Canal (B)	Castlefield Junction, Manchester, Bridgewater C, to Dale Street, Manchester, Ashton C	2 miles/3·2 km	9 locks	Navigable; originally 33 miles/53 km.

Sedgemoor District Council, The Priory, St Mary Street, Bridgwater, Somerset TA6 3EL. Tel: Bridgwater (0278) 4391.

River Parrett (A)	Bridgwater to the coast at Bridgwater Bay	25·25 miles/40·6 km	0 locks	Navigable; tidal throughout

South Hams District Council, Follaton House, Plymouth Road, Totnes, Devon. Tel: Totnes (0803) 864499.

River Salcombe (A)	Salcombe, South Devon coast, to Kingsbridge, terminus	6 miles/9·7 km	0 locks	Navigable; tidal throughout

South Lakeland District Council, PO Box 18, Stricklandgate House, Kendal LA9 4QQ. Tel: Kendal (0539) 24007.

Lake Windermere (A)	The largest area of water in the Lake District	10·5 miles × 1·25 miles/16·9 km × 2 km		Navigable

Southwold Borough Council, The Harbour Master, Town Hall, Southwold, Suffolk. Tel: Southwold (050 272) 3384.

River Blyth (A)	From the East Coast near Southwold to Blythburgh, terminus	7 miles/11·3 km	0 locks	Navigable; tidal throughout

Sunderland Borough Council, Town Hall and Civic Centre, Sunderland SR2 7DN. Tel: Sunderland (0783) 76161.

River Wear (A)	Wearmouth Bridge, Sunderland, to Chester-le-Street, terminus	10·4 miles/16·7 km	0 locks	Navigable; tidal throughout

Surrey County Council, County Hall, Penrhyn Road, Kingston-upon-Thames, Surrey. Tel: 01-546 1050.

Basingstoke Canal (C)	West Byfleet, River Wey Nav, to east end, Greywell Tunnel, North Warnborough, Hants, terminus	31 miles/49·9 km	29 locks	Currently being restored in conjunction with Hampshire County Council

Tees and Hartlepool Port Authority, Queen's Square, Middlesbrough. Tel: Middlesbrough (0642) 41121.

River Tees (A)	Hartlepool Bay, North Sea, to Fardean Side Ford, terminus	24 miles/38·6 km	0 locks	Navigable; tidal throughout

Upper Avon Navigation Trust, Avon House, Harvington, Worcestershire. Tel: Evesham (0386 870) 526.

Upper Avon River (B)	Offenham, Lower Avon to Alveston, terminus	20·5 miles/33 km	9 locks	Navigable. Plans have been made to create a Higher Avon Nav, Alveston to Warwick, linking with the Grand Union C. See also Lower Avon Trust

Upper Mersey Navigation Commission, Runcorn, Cheshire. Tel: Runcorn (092 85) 73089.

River Mersey (A)	Garston to Warrington	18·6 miles/29·9 km	0 locks	Navigable. See also Mersey Docks and Harbour Company

Westminster City Council, London, SW1.

Grosvenor Canal (A)	Chelsea, River Thames, to near Ebury Bridge, terminus	0·5 miles/0·8 km	1 lock	Navigable

West Sussex County Council, County Hall, Chichester. Tel: Chichester (0243) 85100.

Chichester Canal (A)	Birdham Pool, Chichester Harbour, to Casher Lock, terminus	0·6 miles/0·9 km	1 lock	Navigable. Originally part of the Portsmouth to Arundel canal route

Witham Fourth District Internal Drainage Board, 47 Norfolk Street, Boston, Lincolnshire. Tel: Boston (0205) 65226.

Witham Navigable Drains (F)	A series of waterways from the River Witham, Anton's Gowt Lock	59 miles/95 km	3 locks	Navigable, but sometimes closed during the winter

Waterways having no navigation authority

River Alde (Ore) (A)	Shingle Street, East Coast, to Snape, terminus	21 miles/33·8 km	0 locks	Navigable; tidal throughout
Coniston Water (A)	Lake District	5·25 miles × 0·5 miles/8·5 km × 0·8 km		Navigable
River Crouch (A)	Holliwell Point, Foulness, East Coast, to Battlesbridge, terminus	17·5 miles/28·2 km	0 locks	Navigable; tidal throughout
River Deben (A)	From the East Coast to Melton Bridge	11 miles/17·7 km	0 locks	Navigable; tidal throughout
Ullswater (A)	Lake District	7·5 miles × 2 miles/12 km × 3·2 km		Navigable

Commercial Craft

Two decades ago, freight craft were to be encountered on a large number of Britain's waterways. From the wide beam short boats of the Leeds & Liverpool, to the River Wey's West Country barges and the ubiquitous pairs of family-operated narrow boats, they played a useful economic rôle and immeasurably enhanced the ambience of the routes over which they traded. But such smaller vessels were doomed: with payloads less than 100 tons and often as little as 20 tons, they

The world of the narrow boat. Although trading craft are now virtually extinct, their passing was a gradual process and they were reasonably commonplace until the late 1960s. Some of the traditions are perpetuated by enthusiast owned craft, maintained in fine condition with all the former glory of painted decoration and polished brasswork. Photographed between 1964 and 1969. Top left: detail of a castle panel on a water can, painted about 1945 by Frank Jones, a celebrated canal artist from Leighton Buzzard on the Grand Union. Top right: the drabbest of Black Country waterways were enlivened by arrival of a Thomas Clayton tanker boat. The firm specialised in the transport of tar until its closure in 1966. Centre left: the last of the working boat horses, with decorated harness, at Farmer's Bridge, Birmingham. Centre right: heavily shaded sign writing on a joey (day) boat used for rubbish disposal in Birmingham. Bottom: winter dusk on the Grand Union at Rickmansworth, Hertfordshire.

were only kept working as a result of extremely low pay and excessive hours. Now, apart from notable exceptions largely run by enthusiasts, they have vanished, and the waterways world is greatly the poorer for their passing.

No one who has ever woken at 2 o'clock on the Grand Union Canal, to hear the throb of diesel engines and witness the sight of glowing headlamps as a convoy of laden narrow boats glided through the frosty night, can but realise that our canals have lost a virile and essential element of their character.

Rarely in England and Wales is there encouragement for waterways freight to compete on equal terms with road and rail; and the required modernisation of the track is now so far behind the advances of Continental Europe, that one despairs for our rivers and canals ever entering that kind of transport system. But, in certain areas, traffic lingers, more through its intrinsic economic value and good sense than because of any Government policy that waterborne freight is civilised transport. Some 267 miles/430 km of British Waterways' navigations in England and Wales are designated 'Commercial', with a further 507 miles/816 km owned by various other authorities and still carrying commercial traffic. These include waterways of the North East, rivers such as the Thames, Trent, Severn and Weaver, the mighty Manchester Ship Canal and estuaries navigated by coastal craft. According to 1974 figures compiled by the Inland Shipping Group of the Inland Waterways Association, they then accounted for an annual freight tonnage figure in excess of 50 million.

One breakthrough of the early 1970s was the introduction of barge carrying ships, of types widely used in America and in Europe. Examples that went into service in Britain include BACAT (Barge Aboard Catamaran) and LASH (Lighter Aboard Ship). With respective capacities of 140 tons and

435 tons, individual barges could navigate inland waters in trains propelled by push tug or tug. On reaching the sea terminal, they were loaded aboard a mother ship using the ship's own lifting mechanism, and then made their way across the sea to be unloaded on to the waterways of another country. The concept was particularly well suited to an island like Britain and all seemed set for our waterways to consequently compete on equal terms with those of our European neighbours. The experiment foundered through the refusal of dockers to handle the craft!

Given attitudes like these, coupled with a widespread Government lack of interest in investment and creation of new or improved waterways, Britain's inland water transport prospects look bleak. The pleasure boater or yachtsman may unthinkingly applaud the decline, preferring rivers and canals to exist for his sole benefit. But such an attitude is dreadfully shortsighted. Already operating at a large annual deficit and faced with a maintenance backlog calculated at tens of millions of pounds, it is unrealistic to visualise a future for most waterways where there is no financial contribution from transport interests. France, Germany, Holland, Belgium and many other overseas nations regard inland waterway transport as vital on a variety of grounds: not least the saving in precious stocks of fossil fuel. By the time this truth dawns on Britain's politicians, it may well be too late to reverse the trend. And once we led the world in commercial rivers and canals!

As a reminder of the colourful craft that plied our waterways in the recent past, these two pages are devoted to pictures of specific examples. Some can still be seen in trade, while the majority of types are preserved by enthusiast owners or in boat museums. For further illustrations, see *Canal and River Craft in Pictures*, by Hugh McKnight.

Thundering down the tidal Trent: an empty motor barge.

Top left: *clusters of Yorkshire Keels and steam tugs await completion of repairs to Ferrybridge Lock on the Aire & Calder Navigation in the summer of 1895.* Above: *modern 210-ton coal barges en route to Ferrybridge C. Power Station, where a 'barge tippler' can handle 1000 tons per hour.* Left: *a square-rigged Humber Keel on the River Trent, circa 1900. They continued trading under sail until 1949.* Below: *a collection of Bridgewater Canal steam tugs at Runcorn, Cheshire, about 1910.*

Voluntary Restoration

It is a peculiarly British trait that having devised the most advanced waterways system then in use, by the middle of the 19th century many canals were already falling into decay as victims of the railway age. This process continued until after the Second World War and was halted and later directly reversed by the intervention of the Inland Waterways Association and supporting bodies.

This remarkable story begins in 1949 when C D Barwell purchased the nearly derelict Lower Avon Navigation from Tewkesbury to Evesham and formed a charitable trust to put the works back into good order. The job was completed by 1965. During this period, the Southern Stratford Canal's 13 miles/21 km and numerous disused narrow locks were transferred from Government ownership to the National Trust. Between 1961 and 1964 the line was completely rebuilt under the direction of David Hutchings, using volunteer, prison and Services labour. The cost was £56 000 compared with £119 000 that had been proposed as the amount for properly closing (but not eliminating) the waterway. It had thus been conclusively proved that restoration could be cheaper than closure and the psychological impetus that resulted for further waterway rebuilding was considerable.

Throughout the 1960s various local bodies of canal restorers went into action, gaining expertise and sharing experience. They were banded together in 1970 under a national organisation, the Waterway Recovery Group, formed by Graham Palmer and closely allied to the Inland Waterways Association. Two years earlier, 600 unpaid workers

had converged on Manchester's disgracefully derelict Ashton Canal; in a weekend of torrential rain they cleared 2000 tons of junk from the channel. When a similar exercise was repeated in 1972, by which time official restoration work was also in progress, 950 volunteers removed a further 3000 tons of rubbish, their efforts estimated to be worth between £15 000 and £20 000! The Ashton and adjoining Peak Forest Canals were once more opened to traffic in 1974.

Highly sophisticated in their work methods and equipment, members of the Waterway Recovery Group own a sizeable fleet of vehicles, mechanical grabs, pumps and other devices which are made available for use on sites all over Britain. Lorries, cranes, towpath railways and other machinery is hired for the larger working parties.

In addition to waterways already mentioned, work has been completed or is now in progress on navigations including the following: Droitwich, Thames & Severn, Basingstoke, Grantham, Wey & Arun, Stourbridge, Dudley, Kennet & Avon, Pocklington and Montgomeryshire Canals; and on the Rivers Derwent (Yorkshire) and Great Ouse. Some tasks like the Wey & Arun and Thames & Severn face formidable difficulties. But so did the Basingstoke (within sight of completion following purchase by local authorities) and Shakespeare's Avon, reopened in 1974 (see page 67).

The turmoil of smoke, heavy plant, blazing fires and ardent amateur navvies gathered for a large scale working party is a stirring sight that signals the return of a decaying asset to fill a useful rôle in the life of the community. With the exception of some local enthusiasts in Sweden, the waterways recovery movement is unique to the British Isles. No credit is due to the various official bodies who have allowed a situation to develop whereby private citizens are prepared to restore publicly-owned water highways, often at considerable personal cost.

There are few derelict canals in Britain which do not attract their share of would-be restoration groups. Some of the problems are of huge proportions, constructional as well as financial. The Thames & Severn and Stroudwater Canals (abandoned 1927 and 1954 respectively) would offer a superb cruising route through the Cotswolds and create a direct link between the Thames and Severn. One major task facing the voluntary Stroudwater, Thames & Severn Canal Trust is 3817 yd/3490 m Sapperton Tunnel. Right: a party of enthusiasts prepare to spend a day's underground exploration. Four sections of roof have collapsed, one of them preventing a passage even by portable craft. Below: some of a group of 600 weekend volunteers clear a lock in the Brookwood Flight on the Basingstoke Canal, Surrey. Purchased by the Surrey and Hampshire County Councils, this 31 mile/50 km navigation is being completely restored with a likely reopening date of 1981.

The Leeds & Liverpool Canal

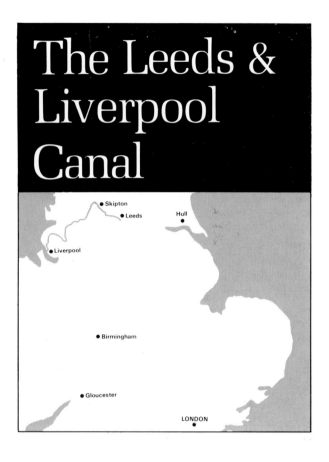

From the Aire & Calder Navigation in Leeds to Liverpool and the River Mersey (via Stanley Dock).
Distance 127 miles/204·4 km.
Locks 105, including those on the Leigh, Rufford and Stanley Dock Branches.
Maximum craft dimensions 62 ft length × 14·25 ft beam × 4 ft draught × 8 ft headroom/18·9 m × 4·34 m × 1·22 m × 2·44 m. On the Main Line, from Lock 21, Wigan, to Liverpool and on the Leigh and Stanley Dock Branches, length may be increased to 72 ft/21·95 m.
Navigation authority, fees, opening times British Waterways Board (see page 45) from which a cruising licence must be purchased. The majority of locks are worked by boat crews, although keepers supervise the operation at certain points. In recent years special keys have been necessary to release some of the many swing bridges and lock paddles. Together with a special long-throw windlass (lock handle), these are available from British Waterways at the Leeds, Wigan and Stanley Dock entry points.
Time to navigate Minimum, about five days, although the surrounding area is so full of interest that more time should be allocated if possible.
Maps and charts Nicholson's Guides to the Waterways, 1 North West (see Bibliography, page 231).

Hire craft Plenty of firms are based on the central portion of the canal. For details, consult the *IWA Inland Waterways Cruising Guide*, or refer to the British Waterways Board.

The Trans-Pennine Waterway

The Leeds & Liverpool Canal is arguably the most important man-made navigation in England. Offering a wide beam route from Yorkshire, county of wool, to Lancashire and its cotton mills, it has a strength and grandeur that matches in every way the rugged landscape of the Pennines across which it flows. Authorised in 1770, it progressed slowly under the charge of several eminent engineers, including James Brindley, Robert Whitworth and James Fletcher, and was not opened throughout until 1816. While locks and bridges were designed to admit craft of 14 ft/4·27 m beam, structures east of Wigan allowed only the passage of 62 ft/18·9 m long barges – the famous short boats like that illustrated on pages 14 and 15. Loading up to 45 tons, they were first horse drawn, subsequently steam powered (the steamers remained in service until the mid-1950s) and finally diesel propelled. Traffic persisted throughout, until a decade after the Second World War and more locally until the early 1970s. Even now, the occasional short boat load will be encountered.

Lock chambers, bridges, aqueducts, embankments and tunnels are of Titanic proportions, using massive and well dressed stone blocks. Two features – the Bingley Five Rise Locks and the Burnley Embankment are numbered among the Seven Wonders of the Waterways. Best of all, the Leeds & Liverpool Canal is served by magnificent surroundings: their beauty is obvious enough in the rolling dales around Skipton; less so, perhaps, in the solid mill towns that mark the waterway's progress out of Leeds and through Wigan to Liverpool. (Yes, Wigan may sound an extraordinary choice of cruising ground or the objective of a holiday excursion, but the experience is fascinating, nevertheless!) Virtually the only drawback of the Leeds & Liverpool Canal is its prosaic name. 'Trans-Pennine Waterway' offers a much more realistic idea of the delights in store.

Leeds is unlikely to gain an award for being

Opposite: top: *moorland cruising on the Leeds & Liverpool Canal at Gargrave*. Below: *a winter stoppage for repairs to an aqueduct.*

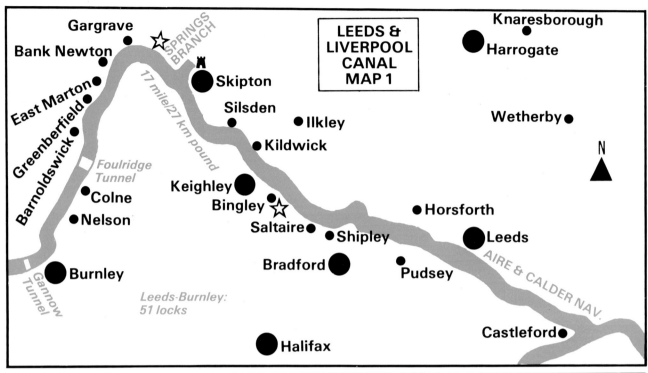

LEEDS & LIVERPOOL CANAL MAP 1

Knaresborough
Harrogate
Gargrave
Bank Newton
SPRINGS BRANCH
Skipton
East Marton
Silsden
Greenberfield
Ilkley
Barnoldswick
Kildwick
Wetherby
17 mile/27 km pound
Foulridge Tunnel
Keighley
Colne
Bingley
Horsforth
Nelson
Saltaire
Shipley
Leeds
Gannow Tunnel
Burnley
Bradford
Pudsey
AIRE & CALDER NAV.
Leeds-Burnley: 51 locks
Halifax
Castleford

N

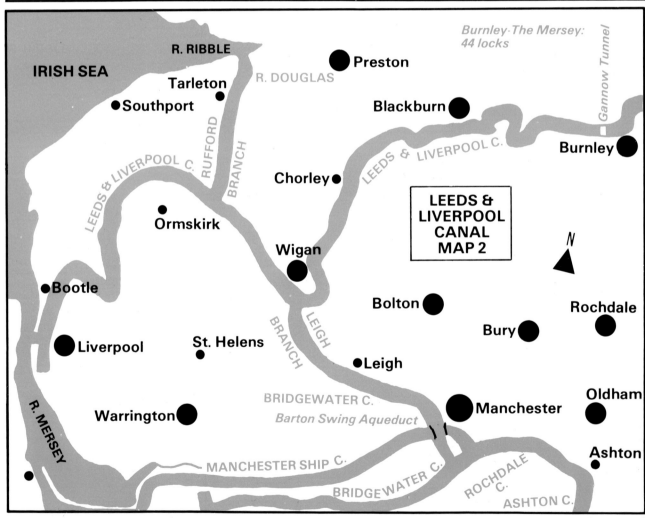

LEEDS & LIVERPOOL CANAL MAP 2

Burnley-The Mersey: 44 locks
R. RIBBLE
IRISH SEA
Preston
R. DOUGLAS
Tarleton
Gannow Tunnel
Southport
Blackburn
Burnley
RUFFORD BRANCH
LEEDS & LIVERPOOL C.
LEEDS & LIVERPOOL C.
Chorley
Ormskirk
Wigan
Bootle
BRANCH
LEIGH
Bolton
Rochdale
Liverpool
St. Helens
Bury
Leigh
BRIDGEWATER C.
Oldham
R. MERSEY
Warrington
Barton Swing Aqueduct
Manchester
Ashton
MANCHESTER SHIP C.
BRIDGEWATER C.
ROCHDALE C.
ASHTON C.

N

anyone's favourite city. In making a changeover from a 19th-century milltown to 20th-century industrial leader, many buildings of character have been lost. Quite the best approach is via the Aire & Calder Navigation to the beginnings of the Leeds & Liverpool at the back of City Station. Former basins serve partly as car parks, although pleasure craft moorings introduce a touch of colour. The intended eternal existence of the waterway is emphasised in its buildings, among them a blackened stone canal office and decayed warehouses. Amid all the urbanisation, tree-clad slopes are seen in the distance as the canal climbs up the Aire Valley. Several pairs of 2-rise and 3-rise locks will be encountered in the 15 miles/24 km to Bingley.

At Kirkstall are the ruins of a 12th-century Cistercian abbey in parkland, with an excellent folk

December night in Skipton, at the junction with the Springs branch which passes through the town and beneath the walls of the castle.

museum nearby, displaying exhibits illustrating local life and industry of the last three centuries. While only 6 miles/9·7 km beyond Leeds, the little village of Rodley retains its own appealing identity, with stone houses lining the waterfront, several Yorkshire keel barges converted into houseboats and a group of swing bridges. Such opening spans must be operated for the passage of a boat and although obviously quicker to pass than locks, they materially increase required travelling time.

Past the British Waterways Board maintenance yard at Apperley Bridge, with 2-rise staircase, the old mill town of Shipley is reached. Originally, the 3 mile/4·8 km Bradford Canal climbed through 10 locks until its closure in 1922. Saltaire is an extraordinary example of a mid-19th-century 'new town', laid out by mill owner Sir Titus Salt when he removed his mohair and alpaca works from Bradford into a country setting. The great mill is still in production, examples of its woollen wares being

available in a shop close to the navigation.

After the seven arched Dowley Gap Aqueduct, spanning a lovely wooded reach of the Aire, the famous town of Bingley comes into sight. Stone chimneys are clustered on the steep banks of the valley, as the canal leaps upwards: first is a 3-rise lock staircase, with a lift of 30 ft/9·1 m, followed by the monumental Bingley 5-rise, climbing 59 ft/18 m over a distance of 320 ft/97·5 m. Their operation is slightly complicated, but if common sense is allowed to prevail, few difficulties will be encountered. In any event, a keeper is generally on hand to assist. A plaque commemorates construction of the locks in 1774, an early date for such enterprising canal engineering in Britain, although a similar structure on the Canal de Briare at Rogny, France, had by then been working for more than a century (see page 110). Extensive pleasure boat moorings extend for a long distance beyond the top chamber, an indication that the level pound to come provides easier boating than the locked reaches towards Leeds.

East Riddlesden Hall, a 17th-century manor house, owned by the National Trust, is conveniently close to Granby swing bridge, No. 197A.

Negotiating Niffany swing bridge on the outskirts of Skipton. Careful watch must be kept for road traffic.

About 1 mile/1·6 km from the canal, at Keighley Station, steam trains of the Keighley & Worth Valley Railway offer a 5 mile/8 km excursion to Haworth and the Brontë Country. We are now on a 16 mile/25·7 km level running from Bingley to Gargrave. Here is some of the best moorland scenery, with sheep grazing in hilly, stone-walled fields, frequent farm swing bridges and several pleasant agricultural villages. One of these, Silsden, has several hire craft yards, stone warehouses and useful shops. Another, Kildwick, is a charming place of waterside cottages packed tightly together as protection from the cold winter winds. Clustered on the side of a hill, a main road passes under the canal through a high vaulted tunnel; all around are magnificent moorland views.

Skipton, northernmost point of the waterway, is among the finest canal towns in England. Gateway to the Yorkshire Moors, it supports a thriving market. The 770 yd/704 m Springs Branch passes beneath the towing walls of Skipton Castle, built between the 14th and 17th centuries and now open to the public. On the wharf is the Barge Inn and a boatyard, while town attractions include quality shops and one outstanding small restaurant, *Le Caveau de la Bastille*. Individual mention of eating places is generally outside the scope of this book, but the author so enjoyed his dish of braised venison one icy December night that this French establishment in the cellars of the former town prison had to be included. Close to the castle,

Messrs George Leutt's corn mill dates back to the year 1200 and welcomes visitors.

Moving on into open country and the Yorkshire Dales National Park, Gargrave village and its six locks is noted for huge beech trees. Locally produced gifts may be purchased in a craft shop housed in a converted barn. Here, the River Aire, boulder-strewn and fast-flowing, finally leaves the canal, which climbs through six locks. The waterway is now at its very best, with moss-grown walls and small farm houses. Scenery is exceptionally wild, as the navigation describes a series of amazing loops, clinging tenaciously to the contours. These reaches provide some of the most pleasing towpath walks in England. Moored boats at East Marton mark a return to civilisation with the cosy Cross Keys Inn and an unusual bridge comprising two arches, stacked one on top of the other. The 250 mile/402 km Pennine Way footpath follows the towpath for a short distance. Three locks at Greenberfield, with evidence of a former staircase and approach channel, replaced in 1820, introduce the 6 mile/9·7 km summit level, with water supplies carried from a series of reservoirs.

Passing through Barnoldswick and Salterforth, the 1640 yd/1500 m Foulridge Tunnel is entered. Lacking any towpath, a steam tug was put into service in 1880 and timed traffic lights were installed in the mid-1950s. Now, it is left to boat owners to ensure that no wide beam craft are approaching from the opposite direction. No account of Foulridge seems able to avoid mention of the cow which swam from one end of the tunnel to the other in 1912 and was revived with brandy.

The border between Yorkshire and Lancashire marks the end of spectacular scenery and the beginning of a series of industrial towns that will be encountered from time to time all the way into Liverpool. But despite this trend, cruising interest is maintained. Seven pleasing locks skirt a reservoir as the canal descends into Barrowford, shortly followed by Nelson, Brierfield and Burnley. Nowhere is open country lacking on the hilltop horizon and the back-handed compliment that such towns are easy to escape from is none the less true! At one time, Burnley was a centre of coal mining and the problems of subsidence affect the canal to this day. Yorkshire Street, in the town centre, is crossed by an aqueduct and then follows an extraordinary mile/1·6 km long embankment carrying the waterway at rooftop level through streets of little slate covered houses. Should the banks ever burst, an appalling scene of desolation would result. Gannow Tunnel, 559 yd/511 m closes the view of this rather dreary area.

Dejected countryside with numerous swing bridges accompanies the navigation along a lock-free level to the old cotton town of Blackburn and its six locks. As if to make amends for the spoiled landscape, Blackburn is progressively creating parkland by the canal, where a high embankment and aqueduct spans the River Darwen. Much better

Yorkshire stonework at Shipley that characterises the eastern part of the Leeds & Liverpool. Everything is built on a massive scale and bridges, mills and warehouses although now slightly decaying, seem to have been constructed to last for ever.

things are in store on the run to Whittle-le-Woods and the Johnson's Hillock flight of seven locks. Little more than a stub remains of the 3 mile/4·8 km Walton Summit Branch, part of whose course was obliterated by the M6 motorway. Until 1857, a 5 mile/8 km horse tramway connected its terminus with the southern end of the Lancaster Canal in Preston.

The next 12 miles/19·3 km to Wigan is mostly fairly rural, except for the brief intrusion of Chorley and the M61 motorway bridge. Travellers should revel in the peace of this pound, for, at a sharp right turn begins a series of 23 locks, tumbling down to the distant grimness of Wigan. It is well worth pausing (perhaps at one of several public houses) to await arrival of another boat whose crew can share the labour of lock working. Because of their sheer number, they can be rather tiring. The fortunate may receive aid from a British Waterways man (this cannot be relied upon). Another possibility is to secure a 'huffler', one of a band of able-bodied

characters aged between 12 and 70, who will appear from nowhere and, for a substantial gratuity, speed you through. In accepting such a service, you will be helping to perpetuate an ancient tradition! It is difficult when surveying the grassy surroundings of the upper locks to appreciate that until the mid 1960s the whole area was a conglomeration of pit-waste heaps, the blackened ground contorted into a fair representation of a moonscape. Lock 85, by the power station (which received coal supplies by short boat until 1972) is a good place to go shopping, for there is a fine covered market similar to those found in many French cities. Here, the Leigh Branch forks

Bingley Five Rise locks are one of the highlights of the British waterways system. Designed by John Longbotham and built by local stonemasons in 1774, they overcome a change in level of 59 ft/18 m, one chamber directly connected with the next. The entire complex is a pleasing mixture of stone and timber, with little footbridges, post and rail fencing and stone-lined overflow weirs.

to the left and across extensive wastelands to join the Bridgewater Canal in Leigh. This is the most usual route for inland waterway craft unless they wish to reach the Mersey and Irish Sea at Liverpool.

Back on the Main Line, two final locks and the

BWB maintenance yard and canal offices are sited close to the famous Wigan Pier. In fact, this is nothing more than a raised section of towpath, named with music-hall humour, from which excursion steamers ran public trips in the early years of the present century. Departing from Wigan, the waterway forms an alliance with the River Douglas in a wooded valley. Until its disuse in the final decade of the 18th century, the Douglas was navigable, through eight locks, to the Ribble Estuary. Its usefulness vanished with creation of the canal and the 7·25 mile/11·7 km Rufford Branch, leaving the Main Line at Burscough. Eight locks take the navigator through fertile farmland and past Rufford Old Hall, a 15th-century timber-framed house with a Folk Museum. At the final lock, Tarleton, is a boatyard. Beyond, the tidal Douglas provides a route to the Ribble and the Irish Sea. For craft making a coast-to-coast passage, this is perhaps preferable to working down to Liverpool.

The final 25 miles/40·2 km are agreeable if unspectacular in the early stages. From Scarisbrick the coast lies just 4 miles/6·4 km to the north west and the seaside resort of Southport with vast sandy beach and many other attractions should be visited, especially if you have children on board.

Lydiate, Aintree, home of the Grand National, and Litherland introduce a progressively more urbanised area. Youngsters in the docklands of Bootle are a real hazard and vandalism is a problem facing anyone sufficiently unwise to leave a boat unattended, even for a short while. The last 440 yd/402 m of canal into the heart of Liverpool has been obliterated, a threat that confronts some other city canals where land values are high. Half a mile/ 0·8 km before the present terminus, the short Stanley Dock Branch falls through four locks. Passage through to the Mersey is best secured in advance by telephoning British Waterways on 051 207 2449 and the Mersey Docks and Harbour Board on 051 236 1520. A ship lock into the river is available 24 hours a day. This area was the setting for the Inland Waterways Association's National Rally of Boats in 1968, when the western part of the Leeds & Liverpool appeared to be under direct threat of closure. The author well remembers arriving via the Manchester Ship Canal and the Mersey in a round-bilged canal tug which rolled violently in the chop of the tideway.

Liverpool is the second largest port in Britain, with 7 miles/11·3 km of docks. Regular ferries leave the Pier Head for Wallasey and New Brighton, a seaside resort on the opposite side of the Mersey. It is a proud and lively city, the only one in Britain to have built two cathedrals in the 20th century. The greatest need of the canal at its western end is more pleasure craft, for use is currently light. As a trans-England route for motor yachts, the Leeds & Liverpool deserves to be better known.

Deep in the heart of Liverpool's dockland, members of the Inland Waterways Association introduce a touch of colour to the district at a National Rally of Boats.

Shakespeare's Avon

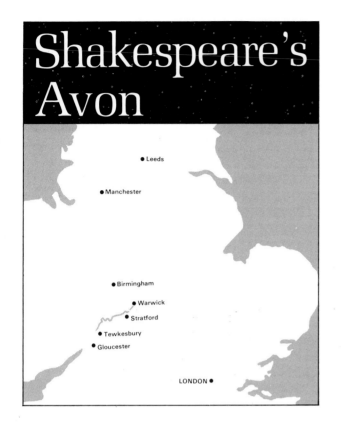

14·00 h to 16·00 h in the winter with closure on certain days. Volunteer lock keepers are in charge of other locks during summer peak periods. There are no keepers on the Upper Avon. The speed limit on the Lower Avon is 10 mph/16 kph (and should generally be much less) and on the Upper Avon is 4 mph/6·4 kph.

Time to navigate   It is not uncommon for cruiser hirers to complete the Avon–Severn–Worcester & Birmingham–Stratford Canal circle in a week. This is much too rapid for proper enjoyment and indeed such attempts encourage speeding. Shakespeare's Avon alone accounts for a minimum of two to three days.

Maps and guides   *Gateway to the Avon*, official handbook on navigation of the Lower Avon, LANT.

The Upper Avon Navigation, guide by David Hutchings and David Higgins, UANT.

Hire craft   Cruisers may be chartered on the Avon and adjoining waterways. For details, consult *The Canals Book* or the *IWA Inland Waterways Cruising Guide* (annually). Additionally, passenger boats and rowing craft are based on the river in Stratford.

Evening cruising on the Lower Avon upstream of Tewkesbury.

From   Tewkesbury, River Severn to Stratford-upon-Avon, junction with the Stratford Canal, and beyond, to Alveston.

Distance   47·5 miles/76·4 km. The river comprises the Lower Avon Navigation, Tewkesbury to Offenham and the Upper Avon Navigation, Offenham to Alveston.

Locks   17.

Maximum craft dimensions   Lower Avon: 70 ft length × 13·5 ft beam × 4 ft draught × 8·75 ft headroom (with beam up to 10 ft; 9 ft with beam of 6 ft or 8 ft with beam of 12 ft)/21·34 m × 4·11 m × 1·22 m × 2·67 m headroom (with beam up to 3·05 m; 2·74 m with beam of 1·83 m or 2·44 m with beam of 3·66 m).

   Upper Avon: 70 ft length × 13·5 ft beam × 3·5 ft draught × 10 ft headroom/21·34 m × 4·11 m × 1·07 m × 3·05 m.

Navigation authorities, fees, opening times   Lower Avon Navigation Trust and Upper Avon Navigation Trust (see pages 50 and 52). Annual or short term LANT licences may be purchased from keepers at Tewkesbury or Evesham Locks. Similar arrangements are in force for the Upper Avon, although advance application to the UANT office is preferred. Some of the Lower Avon locks are manned by keepers and are open from 9·00 h to 13·00 h and 14·00 h to 21·00 h or dusk, mid-March to mid-October and from 10·00 h to 13·00 h and

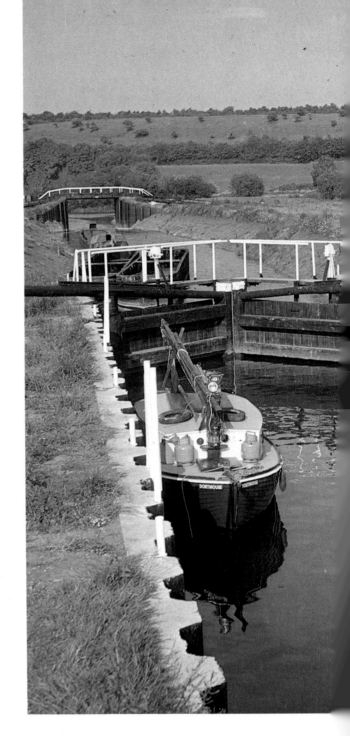

Shakespeare's Avon. Right: *George Billington Lock is the first of the remarkable new chambers constructed by the Upper Avon Navigation Trust to be encountered upstream of Evesham. It was built for a mere £5000 during a six week period in 1969.* Far right: *Bidford-on-Avon's lovely 15th-century stone bridge; the foundations of the present navigation arch were lowered considerably during the restoration.* Bottom right: *at Evesham Lock the Lower Avon Navigation Trust built this modern and stylish keeper's cottage in 1972. One of the few totally satisfactory waterways buildings of recent years, it spans a weir channel.*

A River Reborn

As well as being an archetype among English river navigations, the Avon is remarkable for the fact that it now exists as a waterway at all. Originally created by William Sandys between 1636 and 1639, the Upper Avon above Evesham had succumbed to dereliction by the early 1870s. During the Second World War, the section between Evesham and Pershore similarly declined. Then, in 1949, three years after the formation of the Inland Waterways Association at a time when restoration by volunteers was a totally untried idea, the Lower Avon Navigation was bought by C D Barwell. In the years to 1965, the entire river was returned to full working order at a cost of nearly £78 000, largely through the use of unpaid enthusiasts. At the same time, the Southern Section of the Stratford-upon-Avon Canal, having been transferred from British Waterways' ownership to the National Trust, was rebuilt between 1961 and 1964. The project manager for this task was the dynamic David Hutchings, who two centuries earlier would have been a great canal builder in the style of Brindley or Telford. It was time to consider reopening the Upper Avon, so mending a broken link in the chain of waterways through Worcestershire and Warwickshire.

After lengthy preliminary surveys and discussions with a variety of interested authorities, not all of them helpful, construction of the Upper Avon Navigation began in May 1969. Nine completely new locks and associated weirs had to be built and massive quantities of mud and rock removed from the river bed. By extensive use of volunteers, prisoners and the Royal Engineers, 16 miles/25·8 km of navigation were added to the network, with a suitably impressive opening ceremony by HM Queen Elizabeth the Queen Mother in June 1974, almost exactly a decade after she had performed a similar function on the Southern Stratford Canal. Most of the £300 000 cost was raised from private

sources, including £120 000 from one single waterways enthusiast.

Not content with this remarkable achievement, David Hutchings and his colleagues are now turning their attention to the Higher Avon, in the expectation of being able to create a navigation from Alveston to join the Grand Union Canal in Warwick. This will be a totally new waterway, requiring Parliamentary powers to construct seven locks and lengths of artificial canal in the 10 miles/16 km concerned. A 1978 estimate of the cost, using proven UANT methods, is £500 000, a fraction of the sum that would be required by a normal navigation authority. When completed, the

Higher Avon will provide the missing link in a system of broad beam rivers and canals between the Thames and the Severn.

The Lower Avon

The river leaves the Severn at the splendid old abbey town of Tewkesbury, where the backs of shops and houses in the long main street produce a pleasing jumble of waterside gardens. The LANT lock house is a modern building raised on piles; beyond it, the severe Victorian brickwork of the Borough Flour Mills is a reminder of an ancient activity serviced by river barges over many centuries. King John's bridge, with five low and

narrow arches, provides the least clearance of all Avon crossings. A broad reach extends through meadows and the little village of Twyning to an M5 motorway bridge, with 980 ft/299 m Bredon Hill dominating the view on the right. In Bredon itself is a huge 14th-century timber-built tithe barn, owned by the National Trust. Strensham Lock has a resident keeper, the last until Evesham.

At Eckington is a medieval stone bridge, set amid banks with pollarded willows and little evidence of 20th-century development. After an acute bend, known as the Swan's Neck, Nafford Lock is reached. Here, the chamber is spanned by a swing bridge carrying a footpath. Pershore Lock is situated

One of the Lower Avon's unusual diamond-shaped locks.

close to the town centre and features a diamond-shaped chamber, converted from an early turf-sided lock. The town is a great centre of fruit production. Its mill received grain supplies by barge until 1972, while the single gate of an old flash lock or navigation weir remained as a time-consuming impediment to boats until 1956. Another example, at Fladbury, lasted until 1961.

The mill house at Wyre Lock, also diamond-shaped, now serves as a LANT club. Further locks at Fladbury and Chadbury are surrounded by prosperous orchards and market garden cultivation. In Evesham, in addition to boatyard facilities, are rowing boats and tripping craft with expanses of public parkland making excellent use of the riverside setting. There is little now to be seen of the former great abbey, but Evesham is remembered in the history books for its battle of August 1265 when Simon de Montfort was defeated by Henry III's son Edward. A good range of convenient shops will supply most needs and indeed it is worth realising that no further towns of any size will be passed until Stratford. After negotiating the keeper-controlled lock at Evesham with its unusual house, the preserve of the Upper Avon Navigation Trust is entered at Offenham. Here, the whole character of the waterway alters and the navigator cannot fail to appreciate that he is about to embark on a journey of adventure and discovery.

The Upper Avon

There is a rather special quality about the Upper Avon structures. Lock chambers are variously built of second-hand steel piles or concrete blocks; gates were obtained from the abandoned Runcorn Flight of the Bridgewater Canal, London's disused Surrey Canal and from the former Thames Conservancy. Thames paddle gear, mounted sideways, has been adapted to open gates; gate paddle gear was supplied on especially favourable terms by a Sheffield foundry whose owner is an enthusiastic waterways user. Steel piping has been used for bridge railings and mooring stages above and below locks. The total effect, while lacking the clean lines of expensively dressed stonework or the 'smartness' of water authority installations, is rugged, tough and efficient.

Everywhere, there are constant reminders of the personalities and benefactors who made this rebirth possible. George Billington Lock recalls a young man who offered his life savings of £5 000 for the lock to be built in a mere six weeks shortly before his death. Robert Aickman Lock commemorates the founder of the Inland Waterways Association. In the tangled undergrowth beside the ruins of Harvington Mill, a single baulk of timber was discovered caught in the branches of a willow tree: this was the remains of a lock gate which had survived almost a century of utter dereliction. A track leads to the home of David Hutchings, UANT Project Manager, who runs the Trust from a converted railway station. At Marlcliffe, a steep bank of exceptionally hard clay rises from the water. This material presented great problems during dredging operations, and massive excavators retired from the scene, defeated.

Bidford is a very pretty stone village, where a riverbank meadow attracts masses of parked cars and picnickers throughout the summer. A 15th century bridge of nine arches has a navigation passage through one of the smaller openings, right of the central, largest arch; here the foundations had to be deeply excavated to provide sufficient draught for boats, as water levels are much lower than in the days of the old waterway. William Shakespeare is recorded as having enjoyed drinking sessions at the Falcon Inn, now a deserted building. E and H Billington Lock, at Barton village, was constructed in six weeks, as was Pilgrim Lock (paid for by the Pilgrim Trust). The chamber is lined with 40 000 hollow concrete blocks, all laid by hand and flooded no fewer than three times while work was in progress! A fine view of the Avon valley can be

Above: *volunteers prepare steel piling for use on a new Avon lock. The restoration relied heavily on such enthusiastic help.*

Below: *Queen Elizabeth the Queen Mother arrives by boat in Stratford during the official reopening of the Avon, 1974.*

Architect David Hutchings who master-minded rebuilding of the Upper Avon, seen at Harvington.

Springtime in Stratford-upon-Avon, where the river is constantly alive with small craft. Until 1964 this reach was totally disconnected from the network but may now be joined either by navigating from the Severn or via the Southern Stratford Canal.

Beyond a railway bridge, the final Stratford Lock is reached, its 11·5 ft/3·5 m rise and fall (twice that of other Avon locks) replacing the former 2-rise staircase of Lucy's Locks. The new works suddenly began to collapse into the chamber during its building, a situation solved by erecting a series of steel bracing arches over the top. On the glittering day of the Avon reopening, HM Queen Elizabeth the Queen Mother, having landed at Weir Brake by helicopter and cruised upstream aboard narrow boat *Jubilee*, unveiled a monument recording the restoration. The occasion, enlivened by the attendance of boats from all over England, was futher enhanced by a suitable verse composed by Sir John Betjeman and delivered by the Poet Laureate himself.

Stratford-upon-Avon is very much Shakespeare Town, with its curiously dated Memorial Theatre. One of the less publicised attractions is a fine motor museum. Public gardens surround the broad expanse of Bancroft Basin, where the restored Southern Stratford Canal provides a waterway link with the Avon. Numerous boats of all kinds congregate on the river, whose chief focal point is the slender spire of Holy Trinity church.

Beyond Sir Hugh Clopton's 15th-century road bridge and the red brick bridge of the Stratford & Morton Horse Tramway, the Avon flows to Alveston weir, present head of navigation. Beyond, Warwick and the Grand Union Canal beckon and it seems improbable (in view of the waterways restoration record of this part of Warwickshire) that boats will not be able by 1990, to use this route as part of a voyage across England.

seen from a hilly road running into Welford-on-Avon, where two former locks have been replaced by the single W A Cadbury Lock. A winding reach leads to Binton Bridges, noted for being the last place in England visited by both Captain Scott and the poet Rupert Brooke before their respective deaths abroad.

Luddington is a village on the outskirts of Stratford. The upper of two original locks had a completely circular chamber. Weir Brake Lock, last of the new works to be constructed, threatened to place the restoration scheme in jeopardy, for funds had by this time become exhausted and operations ceased for a while until additional donations were forthcoming.

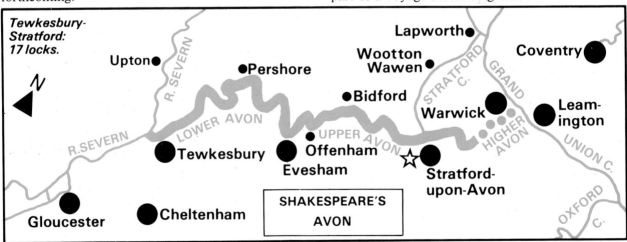

Tewkesbury-Stratford: 17 locks.

SHAKESPEARE'S AVON

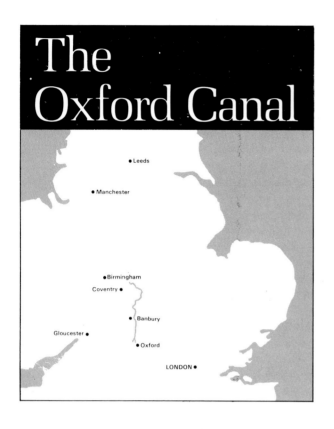

The Oxford Canal

From The Thames at Oxford to Hawkesbury, junction with the Coventry Canal.

Distance 78 miles/125·5 km.

Locks 43.

Maximum craft dimensions 72 ft length × 7 ft beam × 3 ft 3 in draught (3 ft 6 in, Napton to Hawkesbury) × 7 ft headroom/21·9 m × 2·13 m × 0·99 m (1·06 m, Napton to Hawkesbury) × 2·13 m.

Navigation authority, fees, opening times British Waterways Board (see page 45) from which a cruising licence must be purchased. All locks are operated by boat crews, with some supervision at flights like Claydon and Napton. At the time of writing, craft are requested not to work locks during hours of darkness and, depending on water shortages, lock times have been restricted in recent years; local information should be sought.

Time to navigate During the long daylight hours of summer, provided there are no restrictions on lock opening, the canal can be navigated in three days; but a rather longer time can be spent to advantage.

Maps and charts *Nicholson's Guides to the Waterways: 1 South East. Ladyline Cruising Guide: 2 Oxford Canal.* (See Bibliography, pages 231–2).

Hire craft There are numerous firms offering narrow beam cruisers on the Oxford Canal and adjoining waterways. Additionally, the Oxford Canal is included in the itineraries of firms operating pairs of hotel boats with professional crew and catering. Full details appear in annual directories such as *The Canals Book*, and the *IWA Inland Waterways Cruising Guide* (see Bibliography, page 232), or may be obtained on application to the British Waterways Board.

Narrow Canal to the Midlands

The Oxford Canal has been selected for detailed description not only because it is a particularly tranquil and rural navigation but also because it represents a peculiarly English type of waterway – the narrow beam canal. Many hundreds of miles of 18th and early 19th-century freight routes were constructed with locks and bridges just large enough to admit narrow boats laden to 25 tons. Commercial traffic lasted – amazingly, it now seems – until the early 1960s on the southern part of the Oxford Canal and 1970, north of Braunston. In most other parts of Europe, such small-scale canals would long since have been enlarged or become totally disused. Survival of the Oxford and similar routes is now assured through their new-found leisure rôle.

Intended to provide a transport link between the Coventry Canal coalfields and the Thames, the Oxford Canal was designed by James Brindley and authorised in 1769. Building began at the northern end and had reached Brinklow when Brindley died in 1772. Within six years boats arrived in Banbury,

Mellow brickwork at Claydon Top Lock, beginning of the Oxford Canal's remote summit level.

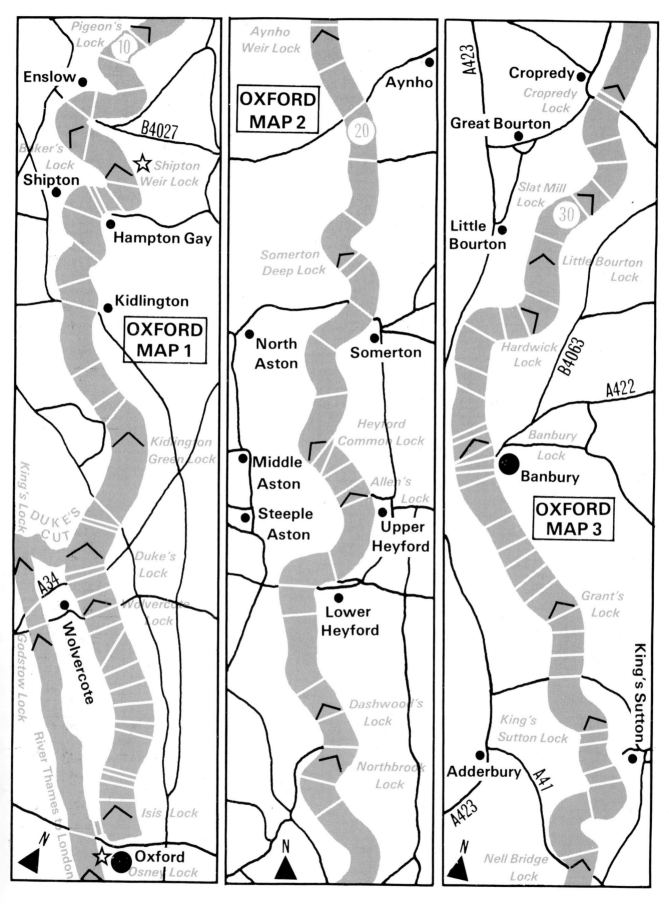

OXFORD MAP 2

OXFORD MAP 1

OXFORD MAP 3

Pigeon's Lock

10

Enslow

Baker's Lock

B4027

Shipton Weir Lock

Shipton

Hampton Gay

Kidlington

Kidlington Green Lock

King's Lock

DUKE'S CUT

A34

Duke's Lock

Wolvercote Lock

Wolvercote

Godstow Lock

River Thames to London

Isis Lock

N

Oxford

Osney Lock

Aynho Weir Lock

Aynho

20

Somerton Deep Lock

North Aston

Somerton

Heyford Common Lock

Middle Aston

Allen's Lock

Steeple Aston

Upper Heyford

Lower Heyford

N

Dashwood's Lock

Northbrook Lock

A423

Cropredy

Cropredy Lock

Great Bourton

Slat Mill Lock

30

Little Bourton

Little Bourton Lock

Hardwick Lock

B4063

A422

Banbury Lock

Banbury

Grant's Lock

King's Sutton

King's Sutton Lock

Adderbury

A41

A423

Nell Bridge Lock

N

but it was not until 1790 that the final link was created with the Thames. Throughout its long history, the waterway was controlled by an independent company until nationalisation in 1948. Today, during the summer months, the locks generally witness the passage of a greater number of pleasure boats than they ever did commercial craft at the height of the canal's prosperity.

The Southern Oxford Canal   There are two ways of entering the canal from the Thames. Either, from a point upstream of Osney Lock, where a cut passes close to Oxford railway station and under a swing bridge (normally open for boats, but if not, station staff will operate the span), or from upstream of King's Lock, via the Duke's Cut. The first alternative includes two canal locks and almost the only length of urban cruising on the Oxford, as navigation passes through the northern suburbs of the city. For as far as the village of Cropredy, the canal closely follows the course of the River Cherwell.

Initially, bridges and cottages are mostly of

First encounter with a narrow lock produces a feeling of total disbelief, for no other country in Europe has chambers a mere 7 ft 2 in/2·18 m wide. Yet it is this 18th-century intimacy that provides canals such as the Oxford with their undeniable charm. Local materials were used to construct this keeper's pretty cottage at Little Bourton Lock near Banbury. Further south structures are generally of stone.

Cotswold stone, emphasising that at the time of the canal's construction local materials were used wherever possible. But, by the time Banbury has been reached, the majority of structures are in red brick. An outstandingly pretty reach lies beyond the wooden bascule bridge in Thrupp village: from here until Shipton Lock the wider course of the canal is explained by the fact that the original bed of the diverted Cherwell was used for the navigation. White water lilies flourish in the shade of mature trees and the remains of an old ford will be seen by Shipton church. Shipton Lock has an unusual diamond-shaped chamber: like that at Aynho Weir Lock, this marks a junction with the Cherwell and the shallow rise and fall nevertheless passes a similar quantity of water downhill to compensate for water usage at locks downstream. Between Shipton and Baker's Locks, the deep water of the Cherwell offers many delightful moorings beneath ancient willow trees. All around, the countryside is particularly beautiful in high summer, with a good network of footpaths providing access to nearby villages. Some 2·5 miles/4 km west of Shipton lies the massive Blenheim Palace, birthplace of Sir Winston Churchill, who is buried in Bladon churchyard.

A regular succession of locks situated in peaceful countryside takes the canal to Somerton, where there is an unusually deep rise and fall of 12 ft/3·7 m. Little drawbridges with few villages close to the water lead to the important market town of Banbury, whose waterfront, while convenient for the excellent shops, is rather run down. One of the last traditional narrow boat repair yards and operated by a Mr Herbert Tooley, has a rustic dry dock here. Locks increase in frequency through Little Bourton and the Civil War battle settlement of Cropredy to the Claydon flight of five, at the top of which is a fine complex of stables and other former maintenance buildings in red brick.

Now begins an extremely winding 11 mile/17·7 km summit level to Marston Doles lock, a mere 5 miles/8 km distant, if following a straight line between the two points. The approach to the large Fenny Compton marina is memorable for a long and narrow section, the site of two tunnels, opened out between 1868 and 1870. A further series of

---

Utter peace on the lonely Summit Level at Fenny Compton. Although a pair of former tunnels at this point were opened out as long ago as 1868–70, the name 'Fenny Tunnel' persists to this day. The charming cast iron 'roving' bridge transfers the towing path from one bank to the other.

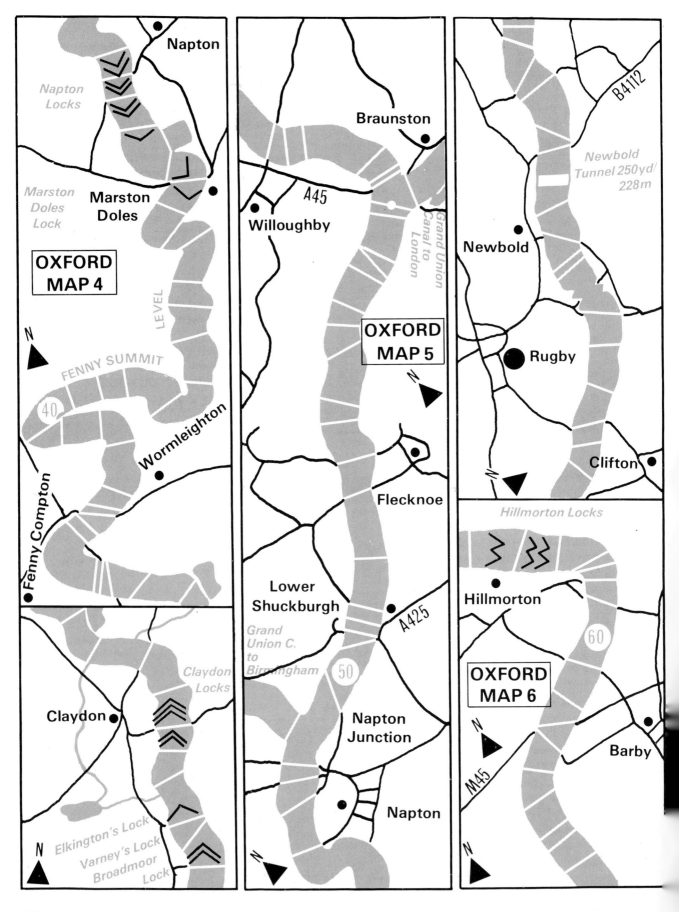

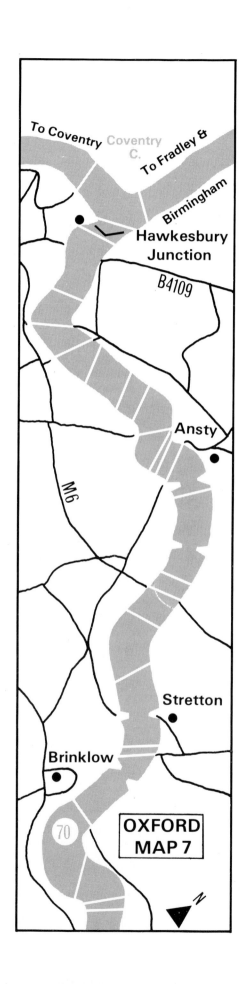

locks lower the canal towards the hill village of Napton, where a restored windmill beckons the navigator. From lock 14, a footpath leads to Holt Farm with its useful food and canal souvenir shop. Beyond the flight, Napton Junction marks the beginning of a 5 mile/8 km section, shared by Oxford Canal and Grand Union Canal, the latter leading through a multitude of wide locks built during 1930s' improvements, past Warwick to the Stratford Canal and Birmingham. The Oxford regains its separate identity again at Braunston, one of England's premier canal villages, noted for the large Ladyline marina and several other yards specialising in narrow boat hire, building and repair.

The Northern Oxford Canal Heading northwards from Braunston Junction, the remaining 24 miles/38·6 km of the Oxford Canal are no longer a winding route around the contours of the Warwickshire countryside; during the 1830s, a more direct line was constructed resulting in reduction of the distance by no fewer than 14 miles/23 km. Frequently, there are signs of the original loops, their entrances spanned by elegant cast iron towpath bridges. Until the late 1960s, this part of the waterway remained busy with coal-laden working boats and the navigation retains a more purposeful appearance than its 200-year-old southern section.

Agricultural scenery leads to three locks at Hillmorton on the outskirts of Rugby. Duplicated, side by side, they are often very busy with hire craft, for two leading fleets are based here, with others in the vicinity. Beyond a pair of aqueducts and the Rugby arm is Newbold village, with two public houses in the lane which leads down to a wooded approach to a tunnel 250 yd/229 m long, equipped with towpath. For several miles a main line railway keeps close company with the canal through Brinklow to the edge of Ansty. By this point the suburbs of Coventry introduce a somewhat urbanised landscape, with power station cooling towers, old colliery tips and the ceaseless noise of traffic on the M6 motorway. The journey ends at Hawkesbury Junction, a group of brick cottages with stop lock, iron bridge over an acute hairpin turn and tiny public house. Gone are the clusters of narrow boats which once made Hawkesbury a leading boat people's centre. The city of Coventry lies 5·5 miles/8·9 km away, via the Coventry Canal; cruise in the opposite direction for the Birmingham & Fazeley and Trent & Mersey Canals.

Scotland

Fishing boats on the Caledonian Canal at Corpac beneath the slopes of Ben Nevis.

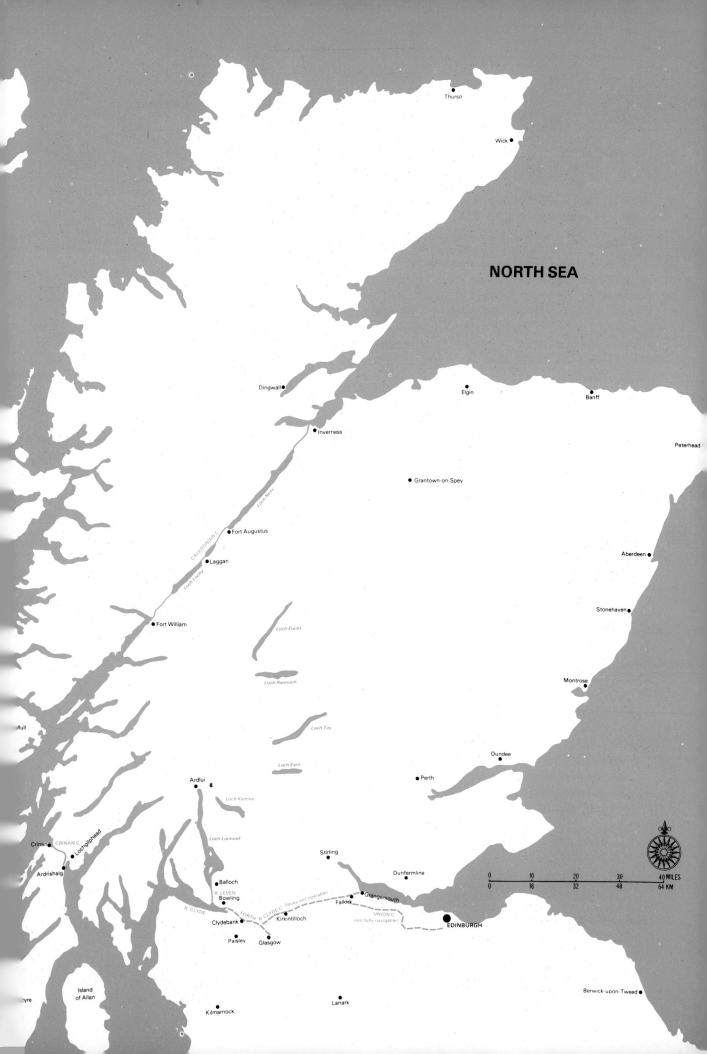

Waterways in Scotland

The topography of Scotland is not conducive to creation of an inter-connected system of canals. Apart from the Caledonian Canal (page 86), the short Crinan Canal and the natural inland navigation available on Loch Lomond, none of the former waterways remain in fully operational condition, although there is still limited scope for boating in light craft on the Forth & Clyde and Union Canals. For the present, the navigation authority is the British Waterways Board, although current plans for Scottish devolution may bring administrative changes in the near future.

Crinan Canal

From   Ardrishaig on Loch Gilp to Crinan on the Sound of Jura.
Distance   9 miles/14·5 km.
Locks   15, 88 ft length × 20 ft beam × 9·5 ft draught × 100 ft headroom (clearance beneath overhead power lines)/26·8 m × 6·09 m × 2·89 m × 30·48 m. Considerably larger craft may reach the non-tidal basins above sea locks at each end of the waterway.
Navigation authority   British Waterways Board, Canal Office, Ardrishaig, Strathclyde. Tel: Ardrishaig 210. Dues for the passage are payable at the harbour office.
Opening times   normally 6.30 h – 20.30 h or dusk. There is no through navigation on Sundays, although craft may enter the terminal basins at any time and any state of the tide.

Used almost exclusively by sea-going pleasure craft, the Crinan obviates a long passage round the Mull of Kintyre. Opened in 1809, it provides very considerable scenic attractions, especially at Crinan, where a series of locks, hotel, lighthouse and cottages overlook the Western Isles. The coast to coast journey takes 4½ to 6 hours, features *en route* including a narrow rocky length along the shores of Loch Crinan, the Bellanoch lagoon and rugged forest at the short summit.

Forth & Clyde Canal

From   the Clyde at Bowling (west coast) to Grangemouth on the Forth Estuary.
Distance   35·25 miles/56·7 km.
Locks   39, all now derelict, except for the sea lock

A weired and useless lock on the Forth & Clyde Canal in Glasgow.

The Union Canal's magnificent Avon Aqueduct, dating from the early 19th century.

providing access to Bowling Harbour. When fully operational, the canal admitted boats of 69·5 ft length × 19·7 ft beam × 8·5 ft draught × 65 ft headroom/21·2 m × 6 m × 2·6 m × 19·8 m.

Navigation authority British Waterways Board, Old Basin Works, Applecross Street, Glasgow, G4 9SP.

Until 1962, the Forth & Clyde Canal was one of the most valuable routes for yachtsmen in Britain, providing a safe, rapid and very attractive passage from Glasgow and the Clyde to the east coast. That it was closed to traffic as recently as 1962 remains scandalous, for at that time it was regularly used by fishing, cargo and pleasure vessels. Initial excuse for the closure was the saving of £160 000 which would have been necessary for the construction of an opening bridge on a section of the Glasgow to Stirling road. Other opening bridges have since been replaced by low culverts, the locks converted to weirs and maintenance reduced. But in its present state the canal continues to cost much in annual upkeep, with little return in terms of amenity value or indeed revenue from boats. About 1 mile/1·6 km at Grangemouth has been filled in, but the rest remains largely intact. Reopening is by no means impossible. Boating in light craft and canoes can be recommended, especially on the 16 mile/25·8 km summit level. In Glasgow, the 1790 aqueduct over the River Kelvin is a monumental work in stone: four arches reaching a height of 70 ft/21 m carry the navigation for 400 ft/122 m. A flight of locks in Falkirk, admirably landscaped by the local authority, mark the junction with the Union Canal, all connection having been broken since the Union's eleven locks were closed in 1933 and subsequently obliterated.

Union Canal

From the head of a former flight of locks

The breathtakingly beautiful Sound of Jura, seen from the little village of Crinan, comprising hotel, lighthouse, locks and cottages.

connecting with the Forth & Clyde Canal in Falkirk to Port Hopetoun, Edinburgh.

Distance 30 miles/48 km.

Locks None remain and culverting of several road bridges means that the waterway is now suitable only for light craft that can be portaged.

Navigation authority British Waterways Board, Canal House, Station Road, Broxburn, Lothian. Tel: Broxburn 2578.

One of the now decimated canals of the Scottish Midlands, the Union provides peaceful boating with a reasonably good standard of maintenance, although some parts may be thickly weeded. Outstanding features are a 696 yd/636 m tunnel at Falkirk, and a series of remarkable aqueducts dating from the canal's completion in 1822. These are the Avon, 810 ft/247 m long, 86 ft/26 m high, with 12 arches; Almond, 420 ft/128 m long, 76 ft/23 m high, with five arches; and Slateford, 500 ft/152 m long, 75 ft/23 m high, with eight arches. A cruising restaurant boat, *Pride of the Union*, operates from the Bridge Inn, Ratho, Lothian.

Loch Lomond

Situated north of Glasgow and the Clyde, Lomond is the second largest lake in Britain and has long been popular with boating people. Its 24 miles/39 km with a width of up to 5 miles/8 km make it suitable for sailing and motor cruising, with short or long term hire craft available, especially in Balloch, at the southern end. A rail link from Glasgow connects with paddle steamer services from late

Passenger paddle steamer Maid of the Loch *makes a journey down Loch Lomond, Britain's second largest lake. Excursions are timed to connect with trains between Glasgow and Balloch Station.*

May to early September. Boats drawing up to 3 ft/ 0·9 m can navigate the River Leven, 8 miles/13 km from the Clyde at Dumbarton to Balloch, depending on tidal conditions. Spectacular scenery and attractive moorings at Luss, Tarbet and Ardlui, make Loch Lomond the worthy object of an excursion for all waterways enthusiasts.

The Caledonian Canal

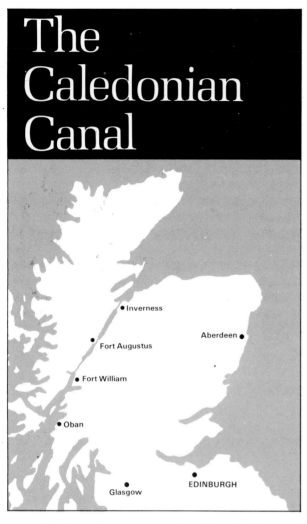

From Corpach, near Fort William on the west coast through the Great Glen to Inverness and the east coast.

Distance 60·5 miles/97 km.

Locks 29.

Maximum craft dimensions 150 ft length × 35 ft beam × 13·5 ft draught × 120 ft headroom/45·7 m × 10·7 m × 4·11 m × 36·6 m. Craft up to 160 ft/48·8 m length may pass, provided their draught is less than 9 ft/2·74 m.

Navigation authority British Waterways Board, Canal Office, Clachnaharry, Inverness IV3 6RA. Tel: 0463-33140. Charges for through passages of the canal are levied at the western entrance, and operate on a sliding scale: the cost, one way, for a pleasure boat 23 ft to 39·3 ft/7 m to 12 m overall, is £24.15 (1978). Locks are manned, winter and summer, from 8.00 h to 17.00 h.

Time to navigate The commercial fishing craft passing from coast to coast can complete a journey through the canal in a little over a day, during summer, but require longer in the winter. A speed restriction of 6 mph/9·7 kph is in force in the canal sections.

Charts Obtainable from the canal office. Alternatively, *Admiralty Chart 1791*.

Hire craft Several firms have fleets of weekly hire cruisers based on the waterway, while there are also cruising hotel boats and day excursion vessels. Details may be obtained from the canal office.

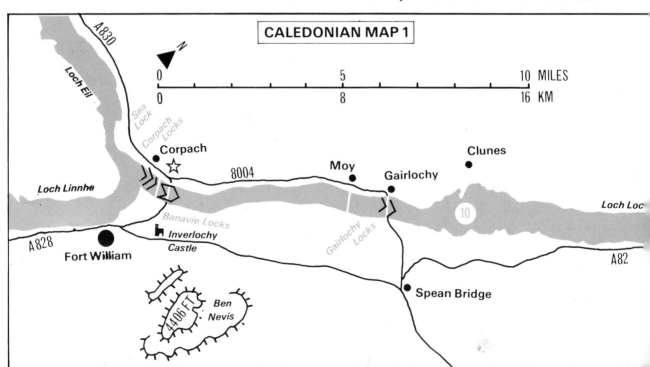

Journey Through the Highlands

The Caledonian is Britain's only large scale coast to coast waterway capable of passing virtually every category of large pleasure vessel. Of great value in avoiding the difficult journey round the north coast of Scotland, it was designed by Thomas Telford and opened to navigation in 1847. Throughout, the scenery is superb, following a chain of natural lochs across the Great Glen and passing two outstanding features: Britain's highest mountain, the 4418 ft/1347 m Ben Nevis; and the legendary Loch Ness whose waters are over 700 ft/213 m deep. Mechanisation of all locks has brought increased efficiency and although the canal has suffered from certain engineering problems in recent years, the condition of the works is generally very good. Everything about the Caledonian – scenery, equipment and atmosphere – is rather similar to Sweden's Göta Canal, with which Telford was also closely concerned.

Entry at the western end of the waterway is via Loch Eil, a beautiful length of water with the town of Fort William near its head, in the shadow of Ben Nevis. A sea lock at Corpach, with lighthouse at its approach, leads to busy commercial wharves visited by ships discharging at a wood-pulp mill. Shortly, a spectacular series of eight locks (Neptune's Staircase) lifts the canal to its course close to the banks of the River Lochy. There is a useful rail link from Banavie station to the centre of Fort William, an attractive grey stone tourist centre with excellent shops. Eight miles/13 km of canal lead past a twin-leaf, iron swing bridge at Moy to a pair of locks at Gairlochy and the 9 mile/14 km Loch Lochy, whose shores are thickly planted with conifers.

A further short canal with two locks at Laggan includes an impressive cutting at the waterway's summit level which opens out into Loch Oich, 106 ft/32 m above sea level. This is the shallowest of the Caledonian's lakes and care must be exercised in keeping to the buoyed channel. On the western shore are the ruins of Invergarry Castle, destroyed after the Battle of Culloden, and providing a focal point in this area of dramatic Highland scenery. Artificial navigation begins once more at Aberchalder, this time a 5 mile/8 km cut with single locks at Cullochy and Kytra and a 5-chamber staircase falling through Fort Augustus to Loch Ness. The fort takes its name from William Augustus, Duke of Cumberland, and since the middle of the last century has been an abbey school run by Benedictine monks. Arguably, the locks are the leading feature of the town and their banks are generally alive with tourists watching boats pass through.

Loch Ness, 23 miles/37 km long, never much over 1 mile/1·6 km wide and reaching a greater depth than any part of the North Sea, is a romantic

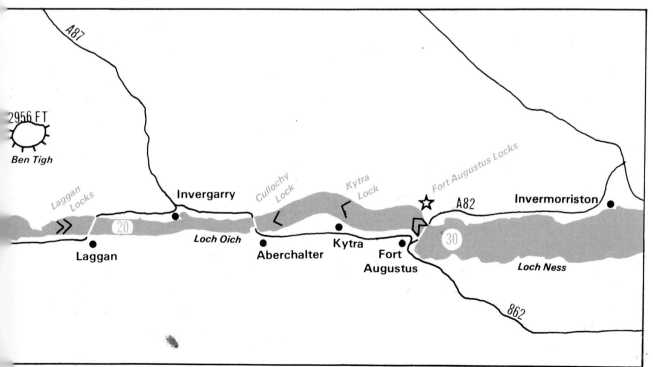

Scenes on the spectacular Caledonian Canal. Above: one of the rugged timber-built fishing vessels which are prime commercial users of the waterway, descends the four-lock staircase at Muirtown, Inverness. Right: a hire cruiser at Fort Augustus Locks. Loch Ness lies beyond the swing bridge. Below: occupying a commanding site on the shores of Loch Ness is Urquhart Castle, an important stronghold of the Great Glen.

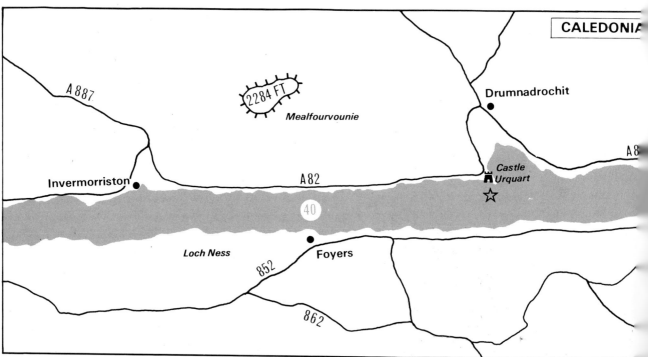

stretch of water that deserves respect from small craft navigators. Since the 7th century there have been reports of lurking sea monsters, and evidence obtained in recent years from observation stations manned throughout the summer indicates that there is a reasonable possibility that some species of creature has been successfully breeding in the depths since Loch Ness was separated from the sea in the last Ice Age. One convenient and appealing mooring where craft can anchor is in the bay by Urquhart Castle (north west shore); the ruins are open to the public and are pre-16th century. Passenger cruises run from Inverness across the loch aboard British Waterways' powerful tug *Scott II*. An ill-fated attempt on the world water speed record by John Cobb in 1952, is

Opposite page: *a sailing cruiser prepares to begin a journey through the Caledonian Canal at Corpach.* Below: *choppy seas on the wide waters of Loch Ness.*

commemorated by a memorial cairn on the west shore between Invermorriston and Urquhart Castle.

Loch Ness narrows at its north east end, passes a lighthouse via a buoyed channel and changes its identity to Loch Dochfour, a small lake at the head of the River Ness and the final 6 miles/9·7 km of canal to Inverness and the North Sea. Further locks occur at Dochgarroch (one), Muirtown (a staircase of four), Clachnaharry (one) and the sea lock which provides access to the Beauly Firth. Inverness, capital of the Highlands, is an important touring centre with many historical associations and at least one first rate hotel – the Caledonian – whose Scottish roast beef can be unreservedly recommended. The trans-Scotland voyage ends at Clachnaharry, a village typical of all maritime canal terminals, where seaweed, tides, lighthouses and the smell of salt water provide an unusual contrast with the world of inland navigations. The sea lock can operate for four hours either side of high water.

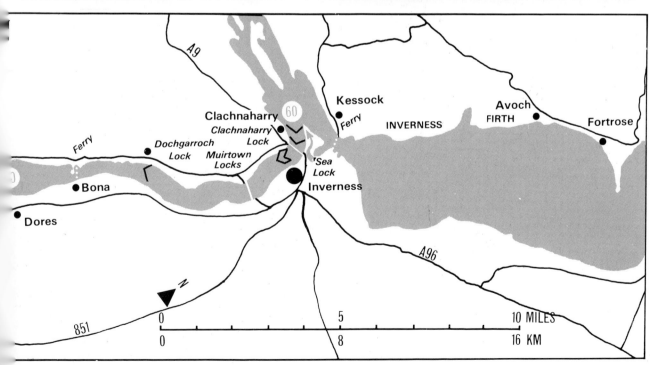

The Waterways of Ireland

By the middle of the last century, Ireland boasted a comprehensive network of inland navigations that was surprising for a country with few industrial areas and where the economy was almost totally based on agriculture. Down the backbone of the island, the Shannon provided a useful trade route between Lough Allan and the estuary beyond Limerick (see page 99). Alternative links between the river and Dublin were created by the Grand Canal and the Royal Canal, the former making a connection with the south coast at Waterford via the Barrow Line. North of the Shannon and across the border with what is now the province of Northern Ireland, the short lived Ballinamore & Ballyconnell Canal (see page 101) forged a link with the Fermanagh lakes: Upper and Lower Lough Erne; and from the southern tip of the Upper Lough, the now disused Ulster Canal ran for 45 miles/72 km through 26 locks to connect with Lough Neagh, this line being abandoned in 1931. From Neagh, the Newry Canal and Newry Ship Canal provided access to the east coast, the upper 18·5 miles/30 km lasting until 1939. Finally, the Lower Bann Navigation made an outlet from Neagh to the north coast near Coleraine, a function which it continues to fulfil. Thus, at its height of prosperity (1859–69, during the short life of the Ballinamore & Ballyconnell Canal), the Irish waterways system provided transport from north coast to south and from the Irish Sea to the Atlantic.

The contraction mostly occurred before the current interest in pleasure cruising and tourism and it was not until fairly recently that serious consideration was given to restoration of the former links. Until more stable political times, little progress is likely to be made in resuscitation of the cross-border route; and although abandoned as late as 1961, it seems unlikely that the Royal Canal will be reopened for many years, for it duplicates the line of the Grand Canal and boating use would need to be of sizeable proportions to justify the great expense of repairs.

Commercial traffic lasted longest on the Shannon and the Grand Canal system. More than 40 motor vessels were in use on these waters when all services were withdrawn by the national transport authority, *Coras Iompair Eireann*, in 1959. Examples of these rugged steel barges will still be seen either on maintenance duties or in private ownership. Those of the latest design, mostly constructed during the 1920s, were 62 ft/18·9 m long on a beam of 13 ft/4 m, with open tiller steering position and a massive 16 hp single

A Bolinder-powered maintenance barge on the Grand Canal at Tullamore.

Working through Spencer 2-rise lock on the Barrow Line produces an impressive flood of water.

One of the maintenance barge skippers at work on the Grand Canal near Tullamore.

cylinder Bolinder semi-diesel engine. When one of them sank under tow in the tail race canal at Ardnacrusha in 1951, it remained totally submerged for three years. When finally raised, it was put back into service with the original engine which was first installed in 1912; she remains operational to this day!

Rural Ireland is one of the most remote, beautiful and friendly corners of Western Europe. Visitors from abroad are given astonishing hospitality of a kind that surprised and delighted the writer. Short of diesel fuel and miles from a conventional source of supply, he experienced the utmost difficulty in persuading a farmer to accept payment for ten gallons! The Irish bar, centre of social life, offers the basis for memorable evenings during a cruise.

The vivid green of the countryside, melancholy succession of ruined buildings from thatched cabins to castles and stately homes, thriving donkey-cart transport and happy acceptance of a philosophy which dictates that what can be postponed until tomorrow might as well wait until the day after that … these are integral to the Irish life style.

Regulations relating to the import of yachts from abroad are few, hire cruisers are widely available and the Irish Tourist Board appears to operate on the assumption that visitors to their country should be helped to enjoy their holiday in every way possible. It is a pity that such an attitude does not prevail in some of the other European nations.

Grand Canal

From the Shannon at Shannon Harbour to James' Street Harbour, Dublin and the Irish Sea.

Distance 79·4 miles/127·8 km, with several branches: (1) the Circular Line or Ringsend branch, from the main line near James' Street Harbour to the tidal River Liffey and thence Dublin Bay, 3·75 miles/6 km; (2) the Edenderry branch, 1 mile/1·6 km; (3) the Milltown feeder at Robertstown, 2 miles/3·2 km.

Locks 36, of which 5 are staircase pairs. There are 8 on the Circular Line. 61 ft length × 13 ft beam × 4·5 ft draught × 9 ft headroom/18·59 m × 3·96 m × 1·37 m × 2·74 m.

Navigation authority Coras Iompair Eireann, Heuston Station, Kingsbridge, Dublin 8. Tel: Dublin 771871.

A small payment for use of locks may be made to keepers at several key points. Locks are generally manned and are open from 5.00 h to 21.00 h, March to October; and from 7.00 h to 21.00 h, November to February.

Map and guide *Guide to the Grand Canal of Ireland*, Inland Waterways Association of Ireland, 1975, from Terence Mallagh, 2 Clonskeagh Road, Dublin 6.

Cruiser hire One firm is based on the canal at Tullamore; otherwise, Shannon-boats can be used. Details from the Irish Tourist Board, Baggot Street

Bridge, Dublin 2. Tel: Dublin 65871.

A passage of the Grand Canal offers a fascinating insight into Irish rural life. Much of the route passes above the level of tracts of bogland, where turf is either cut with *slanes* (long spades) and carried off by donkey cart for domestic fuel use, or otherwise by large machines to feed the power stations whose cooling towers frequently dominate the otherwise totally agricultural scenery. Leaving the Shannon at Shannon Harbour, a slumbering village grouped around the ruins of the former Georgian canal hotel and one of a series of five between here and Dublin, the waterway arrives at the first 2-rise staircase lock at Belmont. Operation is similar to English wide beam locks, and the *racks* (paddles) are both large and efficient.

Stone accommodation bridges and small aqueducts bear exquisite name and date plaques, and there are several ruined castles on the canal bank, including Ballycowan, near Rahan and Shra, near Tullamore. Here, the sizeable town has a small harbour. Further peat bogs extend for many miles, the turf trains sometimes crossing the navigation on lift bridges.

Edenderry is connected with the main line via a branch canal and in spite of the attractive landscaped moorings in the village centre, care should be exercised in keeping meddlesome urchins off the boat. This problem will also be experienced in Dublin to an alarming degree; so much so, that a passage through the city should, if possible, be timed to coincide with school hours!

Lowtown, a hamlet standing rather higher than the surrounding terrain, marks the start of the Grand Canal's Barrow Line and the 2 mile/3·2 km Milltown Feeder. Water and diesel supplies are somewhat infrequent, but here the established method of replenishing drinking tanks is to pump direct from the canal which is crystal clear. Rumour has it that the Guinness brewery in Dublin draws its water from this same source. Robertstown is a well known canal village, where the classical passenger boat hotel serves in part as a waterways museum. Each summer a canal fête (*festa*) is held, with horse drawn barge trips and general merriment.

Some of the canal's best scenery begins around Landenstown, with tree lined reaches and cuttings through rock. Eventually, Dublin is reached, its outer suburbs rather unkempt, although the city centre is a most beautiful place of Georgian terraces fronting the leafy banks of the waterway. Ireland's capital is in no way representative of the rest of the country, for it is a bustling and lively town with good hotels and restaurants and a feeling of prosperity that is often lacking elsewhere.

Barrow Navigation

From Lowtown on the main line of the Grand Canal to the Barrow Estuary at St Mullins Sea Lock.
Distance 70 miles/112·7 km.
Locks 32, of which 3 are staircase pairs. Dimensions are the same as for the Grand Canal (see page 95), although draught downstream of Carlow may be reduced to 2·5 ft/0·76 m in a dry summer.
Navigation authority as for the Grand Canal, opening times being the same.
Map and guide *Guide to the Barrow*, Inland Waterways Association of Ireland, 1977, from Terence Mallagh, 2 Clonskeagh Road, Dublin 6.
Cruiser hire See Grand Canal, page 95.

Anyone intent on discovering an almost completely deserted waterway amid outstanding scenery could do no better than to head for the Barrow. Here, the pioneering spirit is alive and flourishing and until very recent times the lock keepers would stare in near disbelief at the approach of a boat!

The upper 28 miles/45 km comprise a canal to Athy; thenceforth the canalised River Barrow runs to the sea. Stone mile markers are deeply incised in totally misleading Irish miles, the characters sometimes being carved in reverse! At Monasterevan is a delightfully spiky iron bascule bridge, surmounted by a large grooved winding wheel. Close by, an 11·5 mile/18·5 km branch with three locks, ran to Portarlington and Mountmellick, but has been impassable since the late 1950s. Signs of former commercial barge wharves will be seen in the malting town of Athy, beyond which some really exciting river reaches follow, often with unguarded weirs close to the lock cut entrances.

Ruined mill houses, rusting drawbridges and banks of golden gorse and crimson fuchsia accompany the navigator through to Carlow. Here, the old castle was reduced to ruins by an early 19th-century doctor's over enthusiastic use of gunpowder while converting the structure into a lunatic asylum. The river has become sufficiently wide for competitive rowing, with an annual regatta in early summer.

Opposite, top: care should be exercised when approaching unguarded weirs like this Barrow Navigation example near Goresbridge. Below: the wide waters of Ulster's Lough Neagh. Photograph, Northern Ireland Tourist Board.

Little towns include Goresbridge and Graignenamanagh, set amid a landscape of meadows, wooded gorges and ancient stone bridges. Beyond the sea lock at St Mullins, the appropriate Admiralty charts should be consulted, while useful navigational notes are contained in the *IWAI Guide*. Experienced boaters can explore one of Ireland's finest rivers, the Nore, 10 miles/16 km between New Ross and Inistioge; and the River Suir from Cheek Point through Waterford to Carrick-on-Suir (25·5 miles/41 km). But it is emphasised that knowledge of tidal waters and possession of good ground tackle is essential.

Royal Canal

Duplicating the line of the Grand Canal between Dublin and the Shannon at Richmond Harbour, the Royal Canal ran for 90 miles/145 km through Maynooth, Mullingar and (via a branch) Longford with 56 locks. Never a thriving commercial concern, it lasted until the 1950s and was finally abandoned as recently as 1961. In his excellent travelogue of Irish waterways, *Green and Silver*, LTC Rolt describes a passage during the late 1940s. Its demise is particularly unfortunate, for the scenery is generally of a higher quality than the Grand. There are several fine stone aqueducts, and a number of staircase pair locks.

Lough Erne

From Belleek, western end of Lower Lough Erne to Belturbet, southern end of Upper Lough Erne.
Distance 52 miles/84 km.
Locks 1. Craft up to 112 ft length × 20 ft beam × 3 ft draught × about 9 ft headroom/34 m × 6·1 m × 0·91 m × about 2·7 m can navigate throughout the system, although draught and headroom can be increased considerably for all but a few sections.
Navigation authority Northern Ireland Department of Agriculture, Drainage Division, Howard House, 1 Brunswick Street, Belfast BT2 7GE. Tel: Belfast 30883.
Charts *Admiralty Charts 5082 and 5083*. Also a series of 34 maps with gazetteer, available from R F Ewart Esq., Secretary, Erne Charter Boat Association, Erne Marine, Bellanaleck, County Fermanagh. Tel: Florence Court 267.
Cruiser hire In 1978, there were about 74 craft available on Erne in Ulster and a further 15 based on the lough at Belturbet in the Republic. Details from the Erne Charter Boat Association, address above.

About one third of the area of County Fermanagh consists of Ulster's Lakeland, comprising Upper and Lower Loughs Erne and extending to about 300 miles²/777 km². Parts of the system reach into the Irish Republic, and for practical purposes there is little trouble in cruising across the border. The two lakes are joined at Enniskillen, where there is a single lock. Extremely remote and sparsely populated, the lakes are dotted with 154 wooded islands, some inhabited with wild goat and little else. Throughout, the fishing is excellent and is unlikely to be bettered anywhere in Europe. Among the maze of islands there are several short river navigations, including the Finn, Woodford and Erne. Lough Erne has much interest in the form of castles and ancient ecclesiastical monuments, although the chief attraction is its totally unspoiled and peaceful atmosphere.

Other Irish Waterways

Two further cruising areas are Ulster's Lough Neagh and the River Bann and Lough Corrib, close to the Atlantic Coast in Southern Ireland. Neither appear to have hire cruisers, although small craft can doubtless be chartered by making arrangements locally. Neagh extends to 153 miles²/396 km² of open water to the west of Belfast and offers good sailing. At its southern end, the Upper Bann extends to Portadown, while the north coast of Ulster can be reached via the Lower Bann Navigation through Coleraine to the sea at Portstewart. Total distance between these extremities is 63 miles/101 km. Maximum craft dimensions through five locks are 100 ft length × 18 ft beam × 6 ft draught (reduced to 4 ft when levels are low) × 13 ft headroom/30·5 m × 5·5 m × 1·83 m (reducing to 1·22 m) × 4 m. Good cruising facilities have been created, including a fine marina at Ballysally near Coleraine. Public cruises on Lough Neagh operate from Antrim.

Lough Corrib comprises a pair of connected lakes north of Galway, where the short Eglinton Canal once made a connection with the coast (closed in 1955). Covering 68 miles²/176 km², Corrib is scattered with numerous islands, thus creating one of Ireland's most beautiful cruising grounds. A tripping boat is based at Galway. During the 1850s, the 3 mile/4·8 m Cong Canal was constructed to link Corrib with Lough Mask, to the north. Failure by the engineers to adequately survey the terrain resulted in water supplies draining away through porous rock. Consequently, not a single boat was able to navigate through the four locks which remain an embarrassing testimony to this notable blunder!

The River Shannon

From Acres Lake, near Battlebridge, County Leitrim, to Limerick.

Distance 132 miles/212 km.

Locks 9.

Maximum craft dimensions 96 ft length × 19 ft beam × 4·5 ft draught × 16·5 ft headroom/29·3 m × 5·8 m × 1·37 m × 5·03 m. Headroom downstream of Killaloe is reduced to 13 ft/4 m with a 9·5 ft/2·89 m restriction at Ardnacrusha Locks. Two recently restored locks on the Lough Allen Canal at the extreme head of the Shannon have chambers with 74 ft/22·56 m length × 14 ft/4·27 m beam.

Navigation authority, fees, opening times Office of Public Works, 51 St Stephen's Green, Dublin 2. Tel: Dublin 767541. Payment is made direct to the lock keepers, no other form of permit being required. Keepers are on hand to work the locks at all reasonable times during daylight hours.

Time to navigate The few locks and considerable expanses of open water mean that the Shannon *can* be cruised from one end to the other in little more than two days at midsummer. Ideally, several weeks should be allocated and best of all, a couple

of months for exploration of all waterways within the Republic.

Maps and charts Nineteenth-century *Admiralty Charts 5078 and 5080* cover Loughs Ree and Derg, the only sections where considerable navigational care is required. *The Shannon Guide*, from Irish Shell Ltd, 20 Lower Hatch Street, Dublin 2, contains all necessary information on navigation and shore facilities.

Hire Craft Plenty of excellent modern cruisers, from two to eight berths, are available. The leading company, Emerald Star Line, St James's Gate, Dublin 8, Tel: Dublin 720244 and 780297, offers a choice of 150 craft based at either Portumna or Carrick-on-Shannon. Small open rowing/fishing craft can be hired at various towns and villages on the larger loughs.

Slowly Down the Shannon

Throughout this *Guide*, every opportunity has been taken to emphasise the need to travel slowly, lingering in the most delectable reaches and getting to properly understand the spirit of the place. Nowhere should this rule be applied more rigorously than on the gentle Shannon, for the lifestyle of Ireland is geared to a considerably slower pace than any other country in Western Europe. In this green land of saints, legends and notably friendly people, concentrate hard on abandoning British standards of activity and try to emulate the totally relaxed behaviour of the natives!

A waterside summer house at Rockingham, on the shores of Lough Key.

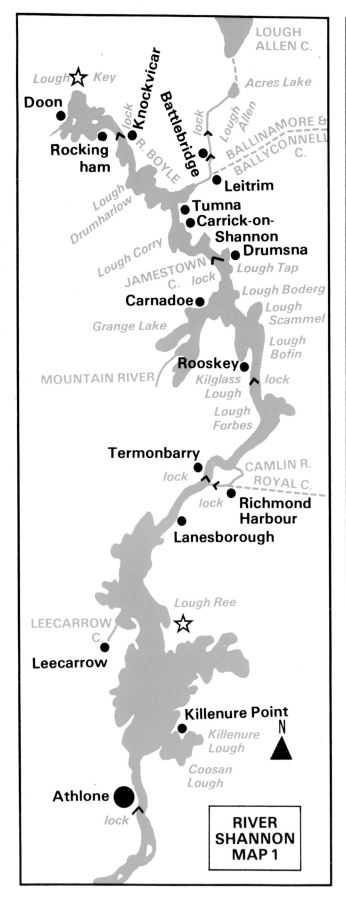

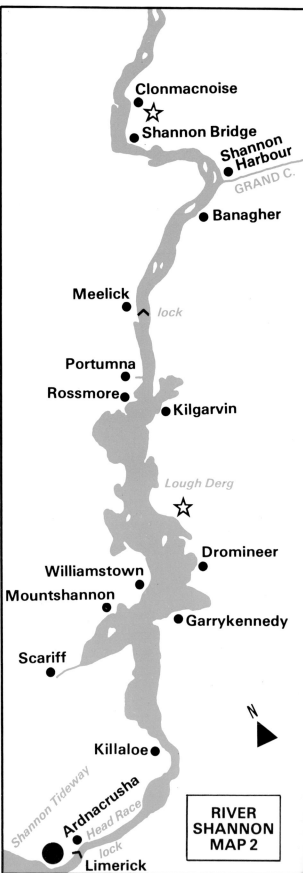

Although navigable in part since early times, the Shannon waterway was not created until the 1760s, with further lock improvements carried out under a work-creation scheme in the middle of the last century. During the 1950s and following the end of regular commercial barge traffic, there were serious plans to reconstruct numbers of opening-span bridges with low-level fixed structures. Subsequent large scale investment in boating and tourism has developed the river as an outstanding holiday attraction, although its sheer size and the under population of the surrounding countryside ensure that over crowding is unthinkable, in the present century at least.

The head of navigation on the Shannon after 1820 was Lough Allen, its third largest lake and situated a little south of the Ulster border. Here, shallows in the river bed were by-passed via the 4·5 mile/7·2 km Lough Allen Canal. The waterway remained until 1929 when Lough Allen's level was

raised in connection with the hydro-electric scheme at Ardnacrusha, downstream of Killaloe. Then, in 1977, creation of an amenity area on the shores of Acres Lake near the head of the canal, prompted its restoration, together with two locks. Thus, nearly 4 miles/6·4 km of cruising water has been added to the Shannon upstream of Battlebridge, where the river proper is joined.

Another derelict canal, whose future prospects are rather more uncertain, is the 38 mile/61 km Ballinamore & Ballyconnell, whose beginnings remain navigable from the Shannon to Leitrim. Opened in 1859 as a most useful connection with Upper Lough Erne across the Ulster border, it was a commercial failure and its 16 locks were derelict within ten years. The great advantages of restoration are obvious, but little serious consideration will be given to the question while the current uneasy situation lasts between North and South.

Running down the Shannon, the river shortly broadens into a very characteristic reed fringed lake at the lower end of which the River Boyle enters

---

Midsummer sunrise over Lough Derg at Williamstown.

from the west. Navigable for nearly 10 miles/16 km, this leads from the village of Tumna, through Lough Drumharlow, where it is essential to keep to the marked course. Further on, the narrow river widens again into Cootehall Lough, with moorings and all facilities available at a quay by the village bridge in Cootehall. Although shown as a considerable place on the map, in common with most Irish towns this is a tiny settlement; frequently, the only shop is combined with a bar and serves as the social centre for the district. Next comes Oakport Lough and beyond it Knockvicar (moorings at the quay) and a keeper's house for the lock which is situated 800 yd/732 m along a tree-lined towpath. The journey ends at Lough Key, perhaps the most beautiful lake on the entire Shannon system. Dotted with some 32 wooded islands and a fine little harbour on the west shore near the site of Rockingham House, a Regency mansion now demolished, this part of the lake has been developed as the Lough Key Forest Park. Several of the islands have ruined buildings, including a castle, an abbey and a church. The substantial remains of a Cistercian abbey can be visited in the town of Boyle, 1·2 miles/1·9 km from a mooring at Drum Bridge, while on the west shore is an excellent sandy bathing beach at Doon.

Returning to the Shannon, the town of Carrick is soon reached. Government aid in recent years has resulted in provision of extensive marina facilities, occupied in part by the leading cruiser hire firm, Emerald Star Line. Throughout the summer, this little town is busy with waterborne tourists and its shops obviously derive a major part of their income from the visitors.

A buoyed channel takes the navigator safely through Lough Corry, one of the frequent expanses of open water that alternate with winding sections of river set amid meadowland. Like most inland waters in Ireland, the coarse fishing is excellent, while trout may also be taken here. A permit is required for game angling. Craft may navigate up the original course of the Shannon to the bridge in Jamestown, a onetime royal borough with remains of fortified walls. The downstream line of the waterway now passes into the Jamestown Canal, with a single lock towards its lower end. On rejoining the river, one can travel upstream to a small harbour at the limit of navigation close to Drumsna.

Moving southwards, Loughs Tap and extensive Boderg soon follow, the latter providing the opportunity for a detour via Carnadoe to three beautiful lakes: Carnadoe, Grange and Kilglass, leading eventually to a mile/1·6 km of cruising

along the poetically named Mountain River. Surrounds vary from reed beds to rocky banks and the sense of utter isolation epitomises this lovely waterway. Back on the main line, the large Lough Bofin now follows. In windy weather a severe chop can build up and one safe mooring is the tiny harbour of Dromod on the east shore. Markers indicate the entrance, which is otherwise difficult to find on a rocky bank. The village lies at some distance across fields of bog cotton.

A bridge at Rooskey has an opening span to increase headroom from 11 ft/3·35 m to 18 ft/5·5 m. Three counties – Leitrim, Longford and Roscommon – meet at the Shannon. A lock must be negotiated beyond the town. The next lake is Lough Forbes, 2·5 miles/4 km in length, noted for its trout fishing. At the southern tip a junction offers a choice of routes. The right fork follows the Shannon through Termonbarry and its lock. The village is named after St Barry who lived in the 6th century; a stone weighing some 4 tons can be seen in the nearby church at Whitehall. Legend claims that this

Approaching the lock on the Jamestown Canal, one of the river's mid-19th-century improvements.

was miraculously transformed into a boat to enable the saint to cross the river! By taking the alternative left fork, the narrow Camlin River leads via a longer route to Richmond Harbour, terminus of the derelict Royal Canal (see page 98), where a lock and dry dock have been restored to use. The harbour itself is a fine basin lined with grey cottages and could again one day become the beginning of an additional route to Dublin. Cloondara Lock provides the means of rejoining the Shannon.

A long reach of river now follows to Lanesborough, crossed at one point by a light railway carrying turf (peat), used for fuelling the power station which stands near Lanesborough bridge. All facilities are available here, the departure point for the crossing of Lough Ree, one of the Shannon's great inland seas. About 18 miles/29 km long and covering 39 mile²/101 km², Ree should be treated with respect. Even in settled weather, sizeable seas can develop and in the event of engine failure there may be no one within sight to offer help. Using the Admiralty Chart, preferably up-

dated, navigation is not difficult if binoculars are used to locate markers. There are numerous islands, variously named in English and Irish: thus, Inch Macdermot is followed by Goat Island and Inch Eangh. Ecclesiastical ruins will be seen, especially on Inchcleraun. Safe moorings are rather few: the best are up a short canal in Lecarrow; Barley Harbour, opposite, on the east shore; a jetty at Hodson Bay, at the southern end; and the Porteena boatyard, in the Inner Lakes to the south east.

Arrival at the town of Athlone, beyond the southern end of Lough Ree, will be marked by a mild sense of achievement that the lake has been successfully crossed (the end to end passage is roughly equivalent in distance to the Dover to Calais Channel voyage!) The only place of any size on the Shannon above Limerick, Athlone lies midway between Dublin and the Atlantic coast at

The long traditions of Christian culture are visible every-where in Ireland. This Celtic Cross is on the shores of the middle Shannon at Clonmacnoise.

A lock keeper at his cottage door on the Barrow Line the Grand Canal. While boaters must sometimes expe to operate their own locks, help is usually available.

Cruising on the vast expanse of Lough Derg, a lake of wooded, rocky shores, tiny sheltered harbours and isolated moorings ensuring complete privacy.

ansport for turf being cut from the great bogs through
ich the Grand Canal passes. The material is the
instay of domestic and industrial fuel.

An Irish tinker family encamped on the canal banks.
Horse transport remains commonplace both among the
travelling people and in agricultural communities.

Galway. Every opportunity should be taken to replenish supplies at the shops and to experience the bustling provincial life. After negotiating Athlone Lock, 10 miles/16 km of peaceful river winds through flat meadows, with a clearly marked course past several large islands. A jetty facilitates a visit to the ancient monastic city of Clonmacnoise, founded on rising ground above the Shannon by St Ciaran in AD 548. Ruins include three high Celtic crosses, a pair of round towers, no fewer than eight churches, and several hundred early decorated tombstones. Five miles/8 km downstream is Shannon Bridge, a 16-arch structure with power station cooling towers and village street nearby.

Next port of call is Shannon Harbour, once a vital crossroads in the waterway network. On the east bank, the Grand Canal from Dublin enters the river at a sleepy village with ruined Georgian canal hotel, warehouses and associated buildings. The disused Ballinasloe Branch, closed in 1961, heads westwards for 14 miles/23 km. At Banagher, a sprawling village on the east bank, the remains of a former lock and canal, no longer necessary, can be seen by the fortified bridgehead. The river divides into a complex series of channels with large islands above Meelick Lock. Then, past further islands the road bridge of Portumna eventually comes into sight, with a span which must be opened for cruisers to proceed below. There is a good harbour at the end of a short canal, suitable for visiting the village and awaiting convenient time and conditions for launching off into the expanse of Lough Derg, beyond.

Probably more beautiful with its wooded shores than the more barren Ree, Lough Derg is 24 miles/39 km from north to south and its numerous mooring points and small harbours offer scope for prolonged exploration. Needless to say, navigation should be taken seriously, although during a decade of operation, the largest hire fleet operator on the Shannon has not yet been involved in a single serious insurance claim. Dozens of islands dot the surface of the lake, with moorings at Rossmore and Kilgarvan Quays. Further south, Williamstown is little more than a tiny jetty among the reeds on the west bank, while Dromineer, opposite, has a marina and sailing club grouped around the ruins of a castle. Beyond Youghal Bay, Garrykennedy is an attractive port of call, with a boat building yard. Almost opposite, Mountshannon has a long wall suitable for mooring, the usual village facilities and is a good starting point for a dinghy expedition to nearby Holy Island where the jetty does not allow cruisers access. Left to the sheep and wild birds, the island has a ruined chapel, ancient round tower and

a pretty summerhouse available for the free use of visitors wishing to camp there. Urbanised influences of a sort affect the rather scruffy little town of Scarriff, reached after 2 miles/3·2 km of cruising up a narrow, reed-fringed river. The broad southern end of Lough Derg gradually narrows at its approach to Killaloe, a little town with hotels, sailing clubs, fishing craft and tripping boats. During the writer's last visit, a travelling circus was encamped on the outskirts and the evident joy and wonder thus produced among the younger members of the community was heartening to witness in these sophisticated days of television and mass communication.

A lock and canal cut in Killaloe is used only when the flow under the river bridge is exceptionally strong: otherwise the short canal provides convenient moorings. For hire craft and boats which are not fully seaworthy, Killaloe is effectively the lowest limit of navigation. Below the town there is a sizeable man-made lake, followed by 7 miles/11 km of head race canal lead to the hydroelectric generating station of Ardnacrusha. Here, a 2-rise staircase lock, partly within the power station itself, offers a rise and fall of 110 ft/33·5 m, easily a record for the British Isles. Then comes the approach to Limerick, Ireland's fourth largest city. The area is affected by the tide and local advice should be sought before attempting a passage to or from the Shannon Estuary.

Above: *the local milkman makes his rounds at Killaloe.*
Opposite page: *an agreeable little harbour at Dromineer on Lough Derg.*

France

Day begins early for the French péniche families. On misty October morning, Goliath moves through dawn Montargis, Canal de Briare.

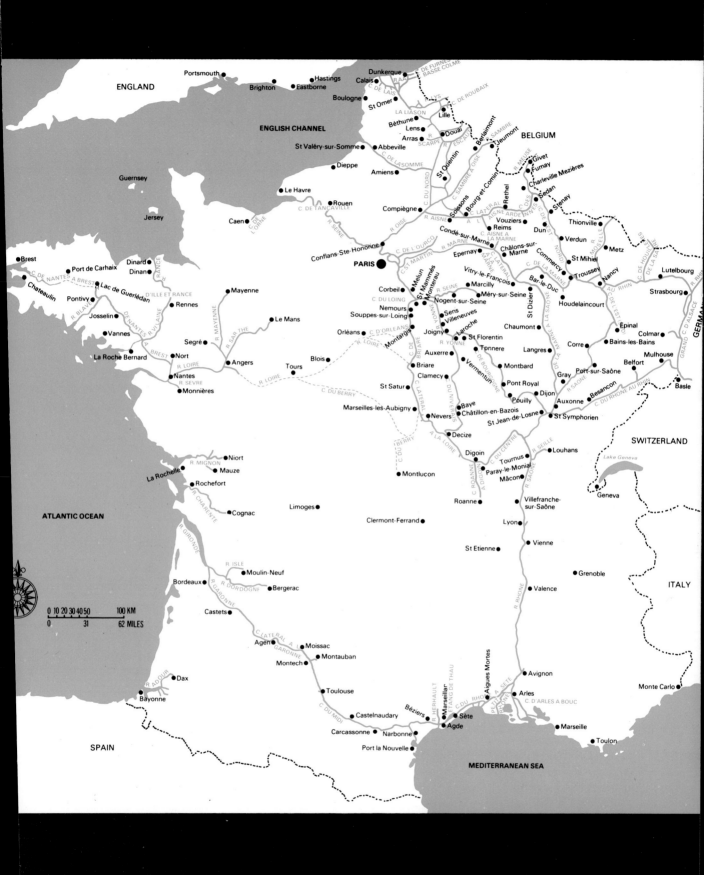

ENGLAND

Portsmouth

Hastings
Brighton Eastborne

Boulogne

ENGLISH CHANNEL

Dunkerque
Calais
St Omer
LA LIASON
Lille
Béthune
Lens
Arras Douai
St Valéry-sur-Somme Abbeville
Dieppe
Amiens

BELGIUM

Beaumont
Jeumont
Givet
Fumay
Charleville Mezières
Sedan
Stenay
Thionville
Metz
Lutelbourg

Guernsey

Jersey

Le Havre
Rouen
Compiègne
Caen
Conflans-Ste-Honorine
PARIS
Corbeil
Melun
Nemours
Souppes-sur-Loing
Orléans
Montargis
Blois
Tours
St Satur
Marseilles-les-Aubigny

Brest
Port de Carhaix
Dinard
Dinan
Chateaulin
Pontivy Lac de Guerlédan
Josselin
Vannes
La Roche Bernard
Nort
Nantes
Monnières

Mayenne
Rennes
Le Mans
Segré
Angers

St Quentin
Soissons Bourg-et-Comin
Rethel
Vouziers
Reims
Condé-sur-Marne
Châlons-sur-Marne
Epernay
Vitry-le-François
Marcilly
Méry-sur-Seine
Nogent-sur-Seine
Sens
Villeneuves
Joigny Laroche
St Florentin
Auxerre Tonnerre
Vermenton
Clamecy
Baye
Châtillon-en-Bazois
Nevers
Decize

Verdun
St Mihiel
Commercy
Troussey Nancy
Bar-le-Duc
Houdelaincourt
Chaumont
Langres
Corre
Montbard
Pont Royal
Pouilly
Dijon
Auxonne
St Jean-de-Losne St Symphorien

Strasbourg
Epinal
Colmar
Bains-les-Bains
Mulhouse
Port-sur-Saône Belfort
Gray
Besancon
Basle

SWITZERLAND

Niort
Mauze
La Rochelle
Rochefort
Cognac

Limoges

Clermont-Ferrand

Digoin
Montlucon
Roanne
Paray-le-Monial
Mâcon
St Etienne

Tournus Louhans
Villefranche-sur-Saône
Lyon
Vienne

Lake Geneva
Geneva

ITALY

ATLANTIC OCEAN

Bordeaux
Moulin-Neuf
Bergerac
Castets
Agen Moissac
Montauban
Montech
Dax
Bayonne
Toulouse

Grenoble
Valence

Avignon
Aigues Mortes
Arles
Marseillan
Marseille
Sète
Agde
Narbonne
Port la Nouvelle

Monte Carlo

Toulon

Béziers
Castelnaudary
Carcassonne

SPAIN

MEDITERRANEAN SEA

0 10 20 30 40 50   100 KM
0   31   62 MILES

109

History

France is a huge country: this fact becomes evident when driving from north to south. Even more so if travelling by water. There are about 7560 km/4700 miles of canal and river navigation, based on the three main river basins of the Seine, Rhine and Rhône. In Roman times some use was made of rivers in their natural state for transport, but it was not until the 17th century that serious attempts were made to improve river navigation and more important to construct canals, linking one river to another.

With the coming of the railway age, water transport continued to play an important part in freight movement, and with navigations largely under State control there was none of the inter-company rivalry which stunted canal development in Britain. The second phase of French waterways came with a period of standardisation and new construction in the latter part of the 19th century and the early years of the 20th. The story is currently being completed with creation of a large capacity network for 1350-ton Eurobarges, involving building of new commercial routes and the modernisation of existing links.

The first major canal to be engineered was the Briare, joining the Loire to the Loing, a tributary of the Seine. It is 54 km/33·5 miles long, was begun under Henry IV and completed after various delays some 38 years later in 1642. Its most outstanding engineering feature was a remarkable staircase of seven locks at Rogny, since replaced by separate chambers but preserved as an ancient monument. Shortly afterwards, in 1675, the Orléans Canal, now *déclassé*, was begun to improve connection between the Loire Valley and Paris.

By 1783, the Picardy Canal (later absorbed into the St Quentin Canal) had created a link between the Somme and the Oise. The greatest single navigation of this era was the legendary Canal du Midi (see page 140). By opening a route from Toulouse to a newly created seaport at Sète, it enabled interchange of craft across the Languedoc, between the Atlantic and the Mediterranean. This remarkable work, some 240 km/149 miles long, was begun in 1667 and completed in 1681, a year after the death of its pioneering engineer Pierre-Paul Riquet, Baron de Bonrepos. In spite of crossing a watershed in this dry, southern region of the country, the excellent system of feeder canals leading to its summit meant that the Midi has always enjoyed plentiful supplies. Its locks, aqueducts and single short Malpas Tunnel near Béziers remain substantially as designed, three centuries later. The fact that the locks are now being lengthened in an attempt to halt reduction of commercial traffic, speaks highly of the quality of the original enterprise. (See note on page 140.)

Throughout the 18th and 19th centuries new links and extensions were brought into operation, many of these being based on the concept that artificial waterways are more reliable than navigable rivers. Thus, the Canal latéral à la Garonne, opened in 1856, extended the Midi westwards from Toulouse towards Bordeaux and avoided an unsatisfactory length of the Garonne River. The Canal du Centre (1784–90) joined the Saône and the Loire and so brought into being the first water communication between the Mediterranean Coast and the Seine, via the River Rhône. The network had begun to spread its influence towards all corners of the nation.

The Canal du Bourgogne (Burgundy), heavily locked but still extremely attractive to pleasure boaters, offered an alternative way between the Saône and the Seine via the River Yonne. Although planned as long ago as the 16th century, it was not opened until 1832. A third line through the centre

An early 19-century print of the Canal de l'Ourcq in Paris.

of France is the Marne–Saône Canal, built between 1862 and 1907. Other important 19th century navigations are the Marne–Rhine Canal (1853), the Rhône–Rhine Canal (1833) and the Sambre–Oise Canal of 1839.

In 1879, at a time when waterways in Britain were fighting for their very existence and frequently admitted craft no larger than the 25-ton narrow boat, the French Government selected a standard size of lock dimensions. This *Freycinet* Act was to enable many routes to trade efficiently until the present day; it established a miminum size of barge, the 350-ton *péniche*, measuring 38·5 m length × 5·05 m beam × 2 m draught 126·3 ft × 16·5 ft × 6·5 ft, all locks being correspondingly larger. A few waterways that were smaller than these dimensions, such as the Canal d'Orléans and the Canal du Berry, lingered on with local sub-standard craft, and were eventually closed to traffic, unimproved.

The waterways of France advanced into the 20th century as well used commercial highways. Several important schemes for improvement of the Upper Rhine and the Rhône Navigation were halted by the Second World War. With hostilities ended, there was a considerable backlog of maintenance. One notoriously bad section was the Canal du Loing, much used by horse boats and motor barges, but thick with weed and badly in need of dredging. Lesser used routes, like the slightly sub-standard Canal du Nivernais, relied on an astonishingly varied range of lock machinery, cannibalised from various sources by the occupying forces to replace the 'sabotage' of the *Résistance*.

Development of selected French inland waterways since the War has been undertaken on a far-sighted and grandiose scale. A series of five-year plans has been instituted for the development of routes of *grand gabarit*, being those navigations capable of accommodating 1350-ton craft. (Traditionai 350-ton *péniche* routes are known as *petit gabarit*.) One of the most important schemes is for the creation of a 1350-ton barge North Sea – Mediterranean Waterway, whereby the much tamed and partly canalised Rhône to Lyon, the Saône to St Symphorien and the Alsatian branch to Mulhouse (following the line of the existing Rhône-Rhine Canal in the valley of the Doubs), will link with the Rhine. The central section remains to be created. A future plan envisages a large scale waterway between the Seine and the east of France. Since 1964 a section of 270 km/167 miles of the Moselle from its junction with the Rhine at Koblenz has been opened up, the works now having reached Neuves Maisons, near Nancy.

Huge investment is required for the massive size of the locks and other structures, while serious consideration is being given to the use of inclined planes, lifts and water slopes, such devices having been built on a smaller-scale experimental basis.

While the new and improved routes should undoubtedly generate massive quantities of freight, the majority of pleasure boatmen will prefer to navigate the older, smaller lines. Efficient and direct though they may be, the waterways of the latter part of the 20th century, with their concrete-lined channels and ceaseless traffic, do not compare with the beauty and more relaxed atmosphere of the water byways.

Routes Through France

Before examining in detail a selection of the most interesting waterways and those which offer the greatest potential to the pleasure boater, it is proposed to look briefly at the various regions of France and to describe their chief characteristics. When planning a cruise, all manner of circular routes present themselves. It is as well to remember, however, that France is a large country: what looks on the map like an agreeable two-week round trip can often be accomplished only in four or five weeks of civilised travel. As a very rough guide, the circle comprising Canal du Nivernais, River Yonne, part of the Seine, and the Canals du Loing, Briare and latéral à la Loire, has been completed by the author in a fairly hectic sixteen days. On another occasion, he crewed a large motor yacht from Majorca to St Dizier on the Canal de la Marne à la Saône via the Spanish Costa Brava and the Rhône in rather less than two weeks. Enjoyable though each experience was, double the length of time could profitably have been allocated. So, if at all possible, choose a less ambitious schedule and leave scope for being sufficiently idle to really soak up the unique atmosphere of rural France.

For convenience, the country can best be divided into five areas:

1. Waterways of the North West, including the Channel Ports and the Belgian border.
2. Routes of the Centre, from Paris and the Seine, through Burgundy to the Saône and Lyon.
3. The South, from Lyon via the Rhône to the Mediterranean and across Languedoc to the Atlantic Coast.
4. The East, from the Ardennes to Alsace, with connections to Belgium and Germany.
5. Brittany, a network formerly joined to the rest of the system via the Loire, but now isolated.

1. The North West

Visiting pleasure craft from Britain most often begin their association with French waterways at Calais, alternative entries being through the estuary of the Somme via the Canal Maritime or the Seine at Le Havre. Together with the surrounding countryside, the waterways of Northern France have a somewhat unjustified reputation for industrialism and lack of interest. True, this is not an area where one would necessarily choose to hire a cruiser for a fortnight's holiday (even if this was possible), but for a visiting motor yacht in transit, there is much of interest.

Assuming that Paris is your goal (with perhaps the more distant objective of Burgundy and the Mediterranean), you will leave the Channel coast via the Canal de Calais and a short section of the River Aa (36 km/22 miles). The route is agreeable enough, with green countryside, plenty of family-operated *péniches* and all the signs that this part of France is a thriving commercial nation, whose economy has made great advances in the last two decades. At Watten, a series of canals generally grouped under the title of La Liason, head eastwards for 123 km/76 miles. This is a busy thoroughfare, modernised to accommodate trains of barges propelled by pusher tugs. Many of the bankside towns have been left at a slight distance by removal of loops on the old navigation. Wash from freight traffic is considerable and substantial fenders are required for mooring up. There are six large electrically operated locks, where craft are marshalled over a public address system. Obviously in such conditions some knowledge of French is more than helpful. Until 1967, a pair of vertical lifts similar to those connecting the River Weaver with the Trent & Mersey Canal raised and lowered craft 13 m/43 ft at St Omer. They have now been replaced by a modern lock.

The most direct route towards Paris now lies along the busy Canal du Nord, completed in 1965, and using part of the route of the old Canal de la Somme. There are two tunnels in the 95 km/59 miles, that at Ruyaulcourt being 4350 m/4757 yd long, and 19 locks. A further seven locks mark progress down the rather industrialised River Oise. This wide river is heavily used by commercial traffic, and everywhere there are reminders of the battles of the First World War. Each slight hump in the terrain has its own military cemetery. The 1918 Armistice was signed in Compiègne. A further 104 km/64 miles of the Oise brings us to the Seine at Conflans-Ste-Honorine.

These larger commercial navigations, while presenting no real problems for small pleasure craft, are not suitable for the timid boater. But given a reliable engine and a healthy respect for large and powerful barges, little harm should result.

A variety of other routes is available, including the pleasant River Sambre into Belgium, and, as a north–south alternative to the Canal du Nord the Canal de St Quentin. Here, the enduring memory is of a pair of tunnels, Bony (5670 m/6200 yd) and Lesdins (1097 m/1200 yd). Tugs powered by overhead electric cables haul themselves along on an underwater chain, and long trains of craft (*râmes*) are formed for the passage.

2. Routes of the Centre

Four alternative ways may be taken between the Seine and the Saône. Each offers some of the most beautiful waterway scenery in France. They are described in detail on pages 126–139.

3. The South

Easily the most popular pleasure boating region of France, with sizeable hire fleets operating throughout the Midi (see pages 140–151).

4. The East

With frontiers to both Belgium and Germany, this part of France shows that waterways are international. For this reason, the canalised Upper Rhine (Grand Canal d'Alsace) is described in the German Section, page 172. And the outstandingly beautiful French section of the River Meuse is treated as a whole under Belgium, page 184.

Chief rivers of the region are the Meuse, Marne, Moselle and the Doubs, this last providing part of the route of the Rhône–Rhine Canal between the Saône and the Grand Canal d'Alsace. Without exception, all these waterways and the canals which link them are well suited to pleasure cruising, offering outstanding scenery, some interesting canal engineering and a wealth of delightful towns and villages.

Canal des Ardennes   It runs from the Canal latéral à l'Aisne at Vieux-Les-Asfeld to Pont-à-Bar, junction with the Canal de l'Est (Branche Nord, the canalised Meuse), 60 km/37 miles, 41 locks. An 11 km/7 mile branch leads to Vouziers. A most appealing navigation through pine woods and meadows with a flight of 27 locks grouped close together near the northern end. Traffic consists of *péniches* in moderate numbers.

The Marne and Canal latéral à la Marne   The river itself runs from the Seine at Alfortville, a short distance upstream of Paris, eastwards to Épernay, 178 km/110 miles. The course of the navigation continues via the Canal latéral to Vitry-le-François, 66 km/41 miles. The river line has 18 locks and various branches, with a further 15 locks on the canal. Attractive in the upper reaches (and less so as Paris is approached), the Marne is rather prone to low water levels in time of drought. In the Épernay district, famous for Champagne production, there are opportunities for visiting wine cellars.

Canal de la Marne au Rhin   It extends from Vitry-le-François, junction with the Canal de la Marne à la Saône and the Canal latéral à la Marne,

---

Pleasure boatmen must expect very heavy commercial traffic on the lower and middle Seine. These busy quays are at Rouen.

to Strasbourg, junction with the Rhine, on the Franco–German Border, 313 km/194 miles, with 154 locks and an inclined plane. Being an important geographical link, connecting the Seine and Rhine, commercial traffic is quite brisk and works are maintained in good condition. The waterway provides great contrasts of scenery, but easily the most enjoyable section is the final length through Alsace, where place names, architecture and terrain are decidedly more German than French. It would be difficult to find a more appealing navigation in the whole of France.

All locks are electrically operated and further evidence of modernisation can be found in the city of Nancy, where work on canalising the River Moselle was well advanced in 1977. When completed, navigation on the canal (now crossing the river on a large aqueduct) will cease for a distance. There are several tunnels, where craft are normally hauled either by electric tug or locomotive. The longest is at Mauvages, 4877 m/5333 yd.

High point of the canal is the inclined plane at Arzviller, some 60 km/37 miles west of Strasbourg. Here, in the densely wooded valley of the River Zorn, 17 locks have been replaced in truly dramatic fashion by a single caisson to overcome a change in levels of 44·5 m/146 ft. With a maximum capacity of 350 tons, this science-fiction device was opened in 1969 at a cost of 60 million francs. Apart from reducing navigation time for the section from 8½ hours to 20 minutes, the inclined plane acted as a small-scale prototype for planned works on the Rhine–Rhône navigation. A tripping boat, souvenir shop and guided tours indicate that the Arzviller plane is a leading attraction of the district.

At Moussey, the Canal des Houillères de la Sarre (Sarre Coalfields Canal) branches northwards, to terminate in Saarbrucken, across the German border. In 78 km/48 miles, and 30 locks, there is much heavy industry; the final part of the waterway is along the River Sarre.

River Moselle It stretches from Toul, near Nancy and over the German border, past Luxembourg and into the Rhine at Koblenz, 337 km/209 miles in total. Work is nearing completion on the improvement of the entire river to admit 1350-ton barges. In consequence, the French section is characterised by concrete banks and lacks the romantic appeal of the better known length through Germany. Huge quantities of barge traffic surge to and fro and the atmosphere is distinctly international (see also German section, page 156.)

Canal de l'Est (Branche Sud) In reality this is a continuation of the canalised Meuse, which has flowed south from Belgium and through the Ardennes. It extends from the Marne au Rhin Canal near Nancy to the River Saône at Corre, 147 km/91 miles, with 99 locks. Built as a result of the changed frontier which followed the 1867 war, the Canal de l'Est is composed of the canalised Moselle between Toul and Neuves-Maisons; then comes a Moselle lateral canal almost to Épinal; finally a heavily locked canal proper makes a connection with the Saône. There are plans to build a new navigation of *grand gabarit* between Charmes and Corre, while enlarging the capacity of the Moselle. This will form part of the projected 1350-ton barge capacity network.

The most attractive parts of the existing *Freycinet* line are the wooded reaches of the Moselle and the southern parts towards the Saône. A short branch connects with Épinal. Speed restrictions are rigorously enforced, lock keepers noting by telephone how long a boat takes between one point and another. On the summit savage fines will be imposed for exceeding 7 kph, (just over 4 mph).

Canal du Rhône au Rhin It runs from the Saône at St Symphorien to the Rhine (Grand Canal d'Alsace) downstream of Basle, 237 km/147 miles, 119 locks. Originally, the route continued northwards near the German border from near Mulhouse to Strasbourg, but since the opening of the Grand Canal d'Alsace, traffic has been diverted along this canalised section of the Rhine. Remaining parts of the former waterway are the branch to Colmar and a length between Rhinau and Strasbourg which offers pleasure craft a respite from the hectic activity and dull surroundings of the Alsace Canal. Much of the navigation is along the exceptionally fine River Doubs, a waterway of rocky, tree-covered cliffs. There are plans to create a new Eurobarge waterway between the Rhine and the Saône, an immense undertaking in view of the broken terrain.

Leaving the Saône, the Doubs is first encountered at Dôle, birthplace of Louis Pasteur. Scenically, this is one of the very finest of French waterways: it is also somewhat hazardous, with lock cuts commencing close to weirs. Great care is required in keeping to the channel, especially when moving downstream. The University town of Besançon has been important since Roman times. The birth place of Victor Hugo and the Lumière brothers (inventors of ciné-photography), it is now the centre of the French watchmaking industry.

Beyond a branch to Belfort, the summit level is reached, and Alsace is entered. Apart from French remaining the spoken language, the atmosphere is distinctly German, both as regards food and architecture. From Mulhouse to the Grand Canal d'Alsace, 13 km/8 miles of new large-gauge waterway provide an impression of how the entire route might eventually be. This concrete-lined channel through dull countryside offers no scenic attractions.

5. Brittany

The Brittany peninsula has a system of mainly interconnected rivers and canals that provide an ideal inland cruising ground as well as offering a useful short cut for sea-going craft between the Channel and the Atlantic. With the Loire no longer available as a link between Brittany and the main system of French waterways, and locks substandard to the *Freycinet* Act, commercial traffic is very light. Maintenance may sometimes be found inferior to normally accepted French levels, but is nevertheless good by British standards.

Brittany is a charming holiday region where specialities include sea food and crêpes (savoury pancakes in astonishing variety). The atmosphere, while French, is refreshingly different. Megalithic monuments frequently tell of a thriving ancient culture: more than 3000 prehistoric standing stones are clustered around Carnac, west of the Vilaine estuary. Architecture, especially in the rural areas is distinctive, with stone walls, thatch and exterior stairways. The influence of the Church is strong, numerous *pardons* or religious festivals when traditional costume is worn, being celebrated.

Hire cruisers are well established by French and British companies and water tourism has been Government aided with considerable enthusiasm.

The author's experience of the area was gained during the unprecedented drought of 1976, when many lengths of canal had been drained to provide water supplies for the farmers; while problems on such a scale are unlikely to recur, water levels can become low in summer in places.

Whereas most French canals are amply large for the majority of pleasure boats, and dimensions have not been given, this is not the case in Brittany. The majority of the system is available to boats not exceeding the following dimensions: 25 m length × 4·60 m beam × 2·40 m headroom × 1·60 m draught/82 ft × 15 ft × 7·8 ft × 5·2 ft. Further information may be obtained from the series of

Deep in the heart of the Brittany countryside, a hire cruiser approaches a railway viaduct over the River Vilaine upstream of Beslé.

Breton cruising guides published by M P Clavreux, 12, rue de Jammapes, 44000 Nantes.

River Vilaine and Canal d'Ille et Rance This is the direct route across the peninsula from St Malo to Pénestin on the southern coast, 240 km/149 miles, 63 locks. The construction of a barrage with a lock at Arzal, has produced a broad non-tidal navigation on the lower River Vilaine between the sea and Redon. These 48 km/30 miles pass through a wide valley with wooded, rocky shores in the lower reaches and open meadows towards Redon. There is ample scope for small sailing cruisers as well as motor craft. At the 17th-century ship building port of La Roche Bernard, a little harbour and marina offer all necessary facilities grouped around a rocky outcrop, just downstream of a remarkable suspension bridge whose deck is 49 m/160 ft above

the Vilaine. A leading hire cruiser base is situated here, convenient for a good shopping centre with busy market. Tripping boats make regular journeys upstream to Redon, the junction with the Canal Nantes à Brest. Another marina is established in the town basin.

Navigation continues along the canalised Vilaine, with 12 locks in the 89 km/55 miles to Rennes. Gravel barges constitute the main commercial traffic, with frequent small fishing punts. One good mooring, with a waterside restaurant, is at the village of Beslé. Rennes, capital of Brittany, is a large industrial city of great antiquity; over 1000 houses were destroyed in a fire of 1720. Now follows the Ille et Rance Canal, 85 km/53 miles with 48 locks to Dinan. Eleven locks are grouped in a flight near Hédé, otherwise they are regularly spaced throughout the route. After the old town of Dinan, with ramparts and a castle on a 75 m/246 ft high plateau, the estuary of the Rance is entered, 16 km/10 miles of water up to 1·5 km/1 mile wide, with waterside villages and sandy beaches. Tripping boats connect Dinan, Dinard and St Malo. A barrage across the Rance uses tidal power to generate electricity, and depending on how controls are operated, levels in the river above can fall by 1 m/3 ft in ten minutes!

Canal Nantes à Brest and River Blavet Since building the Guerlédan reservoir and dam in the Blavet Gorges near Mur-de-Bretagne (Central Brittany), the through route of the Canal Nantes à Brest has been closed. The western portion – Pont Coblant to Port Carhaix, 52 km/32 miles with

seven locks has been restored (1974–5), but can only be reached via the River Aulne Maritime from the sea near Brest. The main line of the route runs from the south west coast at Lorient via the Blavet Maritime and Canal de Blavet to Pontivy, 76 km/47 miles with 28 locks. Here, the Canal de Nantes à Brest is joined, running south east to Redon (111 km/69 miles, with 89 locks), and thereafter to Nantes (95 km/59 miles, with 18 locks.) The upper end of the waterway around Pontivy, while set in beautiful countryside, negotiates no fewer than 50 locks in 18 km/11 miles, and on this account is little used. One highlight of the route is the little town of Josselin, with an outstanding pinnacled castle rising sheer from the river Oust (open to the public).

Other waterways of Brittany The Loire is navigable from St Nazaire, through Nantes (here the Ducal Castle's attractions include an outstanding Museum of Breton life and art) and onwards for a further 85 km/53 miles to Bouchemaine. Sadly, the beauties of the Loire Valley with its châteaux are denied to all but the smallest craft; but canoes paddled by the intrepid are said to be able to reach Nevers via Tours, Orléans and Briare. Excursions from Bouchemaine that are possible for large craft are along the Rivers Maine and Mayenne to the town of Mayenne, (134 km/83 miles, 45 locks); and up the River Sarthe to Le Mans, (131 km/81 miles, 20 locks).

One last region deserves special mention: the Grande Brière, a strange area of 6000 hectares 13 200 acres of peat bog, marsh and pasture, north of St Nazaire and the Loire estuary. Intersected by drainage canals equipped with several locks, the Brière is noted for hunting and fishing. Special 9 m/29 ft barges known as *blins*, transport up to four tons of agricultural produce and reeds for thatching.

Below: *Josselin Castle, towering above the Canal Nantes à Brest.* Right: *a wooded reach of the River Vilaine near Redon.*

Commercial Craft

Above: *while a pleasure cruiser cautiously awaits its turn at a lock, an unladen* péniche *gathers speed on the Canal du Nivernais at Ravereau.*
Below: *the French barge family enjoys a good standard of living, often taking a small car with them on deck.*

Above: *a tight fit for* Francy *at Tannay Lock, Canal du Nivernais.*

Above : *an empty* péniche *looms up out of the autumnal rain and prepares to pass a pleasure cruiser on the Canal du Loing.*
Left: *a boatman on the Canal de Bourgogne whose face bears the signs of a lifetime's studied concentration.*
Below: *pushing ahead of it a wall of water, this barge on the Seine should be given a wide berth by pleasure traffic.*

Pleasure Cruising

(for a suitable rate of payment): these are some of the joys of discovering France in the most civilised way imaginable. The following three pages present a picture of typical family boating in a beautiful country.

A holiday on the French inland waterways offers much more than mere boating. Exploration of the countryside, discovery of new food in country town markets, delicious restaurant meals in even the sleepiest village, encounters with lock keepers who encourage you to plunder their vegetable gardens

Below: *an elegant hand-wound iron bascule bridge on the Canal du Nivernais which is opened for the passage of craft by the local lock keeper. Other waterways feature centrally-pivoted swing bridges and lifting structures where the whole deck rises parallel with the water.*

Above: *fishing nets on the banks of the Canal Rhône à Sète.*
Below, left: *entering one of a series of three short tunnels at the summit of the Canal du Nivernais.*
Below, right: *the pleasures of preparing fresh French beans purchased from a lock keeper.*

Above: *one of the delights of a French boating holiday is the food, whether taken in the form of a canalside picnic or,* below, *in a restaurant overlooking the River Vilaine.*

Above: *imprisoned aboard a motor yacht at the bottom of one of the massive Rhône locks.*
Below: *village shopping in France constitutes a daily highlight on a boating holiday.*

Architecture and Engineering

In the unlikely event of waking up on the banks of a totally strange canal and not knowing what country you were in, it would not take long to identify the place as France merely by observing the surroundings. The character and style of French waterways is an unmistakable amalgam comprising such diverse factors as lock machinery, keepers' cottages, aqueducts and bridges. For the greater part these structures are of the 19th century and although regional variations are present, state ownership of the navigations generally dating from their original construction displays a uniform character that changes little from Burgundy to Brittany, the Midi to Alsace.

Everywhere, much use is made of ironwork: lock gates, paddle gear, aqueduct railings, wall-mounted lock name and distance plates, swing and bascule bridges all use the material. Paint is not a product which appears to be much in favour, and where the sombre grey of the *Ponts et Chausées* (Bridges and Highways Department) is used, it is often faded to a matt finish or transformed to a smoothly rusted patina.

On the older, rural canals, the lock keepers themselves blend into the same gentle colours, the men dressed in the ubiquitous faded blue denims of the working people, their wives wearing restrained and much washed flowered dresses. On busier routes, keepers adopt an attitude of greater authority in line with their increased responsibilities and they may wear a cap marked with the initials P and C, denoting their employer. But even here, their bearing remains one of measured economy of effort. One area that offers scope for individual expression is the lock garden, where leading elements are carefully raked gravel, patches of coarse grass (hardly deserving the name of lawn), bright flowers in strategically placed white-washed car tyres and regimented rows of vegetables, surplus produce being sold to passing boats. Occasionally, these places suggest that gardening is an occupation superior to mere lock keeping and a riotous collection of painted wheelbarrows, well-heads, miniature windmills and even disused dinghies are filled with clusters of petunias, nasturtiums and tagetes (the well-named French marigolds).

Modernisation of the larger navigations has produced its own architectural vernacular: concrete and glass lock control cabins belonging more to the Space Age; and yet they still show characteristics that are undeniably French.

All this has resulted from an unconscious development, admirably suited to the slow-moving life of the waterways. For all the quiet charm of the rivers and canals of France, they are well maintained and efficiently run.

Rugged lock machinery will be seen in great variety. At the Écluse St Florentin on the Canal du Bourgogne, the determined lady keeper rotates a large iron wheel to open or close the gates.

Opposite: *the magnificent Briare Aqueduct at the junction of the Canal de Briare and Canal latéral à la Loire. The waterway is carried for 660 m/722 yd over the River Loire in an iron trough supported on stone pillars. It was designed by Eiffel (of Tower fame), opened in 1896 and replaced series of locks on each side of the river crossing. Ornamental detail is very fine, especially in the triumphant lamp standards at each end.*

Space Age technology of the French canals. The control cabin of a new lock on the River Moselle at Toul contrasts with the 13th-century cathedral of St Étienne.

Below and top right: a series of 17 locks in 4 km/ 2·5 miles on the Canal de la Marne au Rhin was replaced in 1969 by the St-Louis-Arzviller inclined plane. The restricted nature of this site in the steep-sided valley of the River Zorn was unsuitable for either a conventional vertical lift or a longitudinal plane (as at Ronquières, Belgium) – thus a traverse plane was installed to overcome a change in levels of 44·55 m/146 ft. Equipped with a single tank (there is provision for adding a second

one) 44 m/144 ft long, a 350-ton péniche can negotiate the structure in 20 minutes, representing a saving in time of eight hours compared with working through the original locks. During a 13-hour day, the incline can accommodate 39 barges. Electrically operated guillotine gates seal each end of the caisson, which filled with water weighs 850 tons. Apart from the speed of the operation, other advantages are reduced maintenance costs and the experience gained for possible future installation of similar inclines of greater capacity on the proposed North Sea – Mediterranean Canal, Lorraine and Alsace sections. (Photograph below, courtesy, Syndicats d'Initiative de St-Louis-Lutzelbourg.)

Above: *a unique alternative to locks, vertical lifts or inclined planes, is the Water Slope or 'Push Puddle'. After construction of a 1:10 scale model at Vennissieux, near Lyon, this* péniche-*sized example was built on the Montauban branch of the Canal latéral à la Garonne at Montech. Operation commenced in 1973. A concrete flume, 6 m / 19·7 ft wide and 540 m / 1772 ft long with a three per cent gradient, contains a wedge-shaped pool of water on which a barge floats. Either side, a pair of 1000 hp diesel-electric locomotives push a steel shield up the ramp; at the upper end, a submerging gate folds down below water, thus enabling the barge to enter the canal. Five conventional locks with a lift of about 14 m /* 50 ft *are by-passed in about ten minutes. Much data of possible use in construction of larger Water Slopes has resulted from the experiment.* Photograph, courtesy, David Edwards-May. Below: *a selection of graphically explicit signs which require little knowledge of French.* Left: *drinking water points do not occur very frequently, and craft with limited-capacity tanks should take every advantage to replenish them.* Centre: *the lock keeper has considerable powers to prevent interference from casual observers.* Right: *'Don't touch the bare electric wires', a stern warning at the entrance to Mauvages tunnel, Canal du Marne au Rhin, where towage is by electrically-driven tug.*

Paris to the Mediterranean

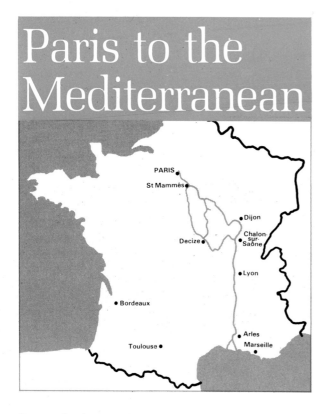

One of the most common requirements of yachtsmen passing through France is the selection of a route between the Capital and the Mediterranean Coast. But the waterways of Burgundy and the Rhône Valley are also very much worth cruising for their own sake. The navigations selected here offer a choice of four journeys, all starting on the Seine and meeting once more on the Saône. Nowhere is the rural character of France so admirably to be discovered. Apart from the use of privately owned craft, there are possibilities for hiring cruisers and for travelling some sections by hotel boat.

From Paris to the Mediterranean.

Distance, route 1, via the canal de Briare. River Seine, Paris to St Mammès, 89 km/55 miles. Canal du Loing, St Mammès to Châlette-sur-Loing, 49 km/30 miles. Canal de Briare, Châlette-sur-Loing to Briare, 56 km/35 miles. Canal latéral à la Loire, Briare to Digoin, 200 km/124 miles. Canal du Centre, Digoin to Chalon-sur-Saône, 112 km/70 miles. River Saône, Chalon-sur-Saône to Lyon, 143 km/89 miles. River Rhône, Lyon to Port-St-Louis-du-Rhône, 330 km/205 miles. Total distance: 979 km/608 miles.

Distance, route 2, via the Canal du Nivernais. River Seine, Paris to Monterau, 102 km/63 miles. River Yonne, Monterau to Auxerre, 108 km/67 miles. Canal du Nivernais, Auxerre to Decize, 174 km/108 miles. Canal latéral à la Loire, Decize to Digoin, 64 km/40 miles. Canal du Centre, Digoin to Chalon-sur-Saône, 112 km/70 miles. River Saône, Chalon-sur-Saône to Lyon, 143 km/89 miles. River Rhône, Lyon to Port-St-Louis-du-Rhône, 330 km/205 miles. Total distance: 1033 km/642 miles.

Distance, route 3, via the Burgundy Canal. River Seine, Paris to Monterau, 102 km/63 miles. River Yonne, Monterau to Laroche, 86 km/53 miles. Canal du Bourgogne, Laroche to St Jean-de-Losne, 242 km/150 miles. River Saône, St Jean-de-Losne to Lyon, 213 km/132 miles. River Rhône, Lyon to Port-St-Louis-du-Rhône, 330 km/205 miles. Total distance: 973 km/604 miles.

Distance, route 4, via the Marne River Seine, Paris to Alfortville, 7 km/4 miles. River Marne, Alfortville to Épernay, 178 km/111 miles. Canal latéral à la Marne, Épernay to Vitry-le-François, 67 km/42 miles. Canal de la Marne à la Saône, Vitry-le-François to Heuilley 224 km/139 miles. River Saône, Heuilley to Lyon, 250 km/155 miles. River Rhône, Lyon to Port-St-Louis-du-Rhône, 330 km/205 miles. Total distance: 1056 km/656 miles.

Locks, route 1: Seine, 9. Loing, 20. Briare, 32, Loire latéral, 31. Centre, 60. Saône, 6. Rhône, 12. Total: 170.

Locks, route 2: Seine, 10. Yonne, 26. Nivernais, 116, Loire latéral, 17. Centre, 56. Saône, 6. Rhône, 12. Total: 243.

Locks, route 3: Seine, 10. Yonne, 17. Bourgogne, 191. Saône, 11. Rhône, 12. Total: 241.

Locks, route 4: Seine, 0. Marne and Marne latéral, 33. Marne-Saône, 114. Saône, 14. Rhône, 12. Total: 173.

Maximum craft dimensions Almost all sections of the four routes are built to *Freycinet* dimensions at the very least and are often considerably larger. (38·5 m length × 5·05 m beam × 1·8 m draught × 3·4 m height above water/126 ft × 16·5 ft × 5·9 ft × 11·1 ft.) Exceptions are the central portion of the Canal du Nivernais (route 2) which will only pass 30 m length × 5·05 m beam × 1·2 m draught × 2·7 m height above water/98·4 ft × 16·5 ft × 3·9 ft × 8·8 ft; and the Canal du Bourgogne (route 3) where Pouilly-en-Auxois tunnel restricts headroom to 3·0 m at the centre, 2·2 m at the sides (9·84 ft and 7·21 ft).

Navigation authority, fees, opening times Enquiries should be made to Le Ministre de l'Equipment, Direction des Ports Maritimes et des Voies Navigables, 2e bureau, Boulevard St Germain, Paris 7. They will supply addresses of local canal offices if required. There is no general charge for cruising any of these waterways. (Fees are demanded at Pouilly-en-Auxois tunnel and the

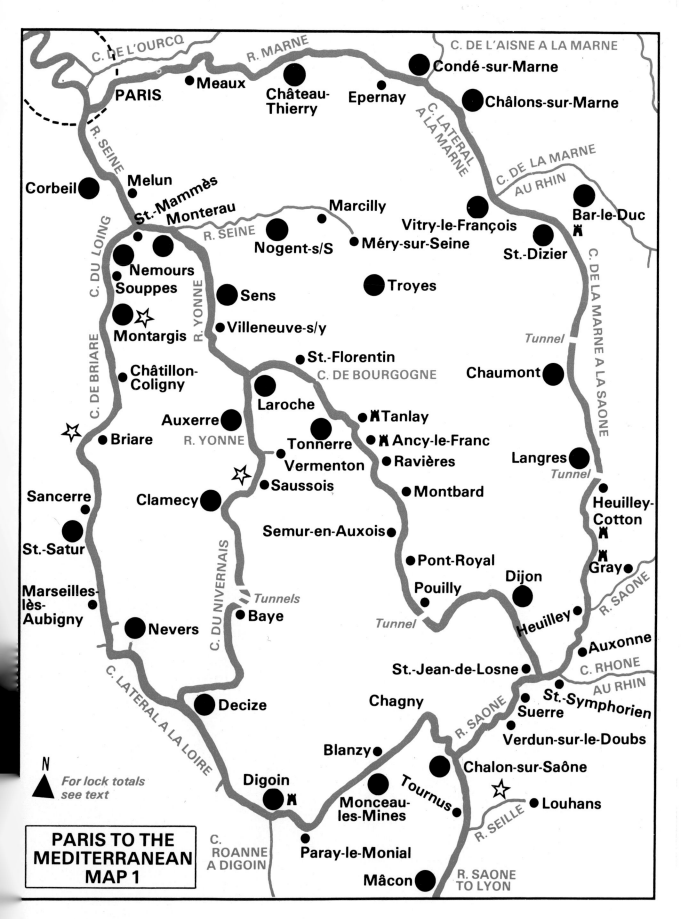

PARIS TO THE MEDITERRANEAN MAP 1

N
For lock totals see text

127

crossing at the Loire at Decize.) Apart from scheduled stoppages – *chômages*, for which lists can be supplied by the French Government Tourist Office, London – locks are open between 6·30 h and 19·30 h, April to September, with slightly reduced hours in the winter months. They are not available on the following public holidays: Easter Monday, 1 May, 14 July, 11 November and 25 December. Locks on the Canal de Bourgogne and the Canal de la Marne à la Saône have been closed on Sundays in recent years, but it is believed that this regulation has now been lifted. The Rhône locks are manned throughout the year between 5·00 h and 21·00 h

Maps and charts For all sections other than the Rhône, the maps contained in *Guide de la Navigation Intérieure* are more than adequate (see Bibliography). Large scale maps of many French waterways (especially useful on the rivers) are available from Journal de la Navigation, 29 Boulevard Henri-IV, 75 Paris 4.

Hire craft It has long been a source of amazement that there are very few hire cruiser companies operating on the French waterways. Several have been based on the Yonne, Canal latéral à la Loire and Canal du Nivernais in recent years, but at the time of writing there is some doubt as to which will continue in business. The British-owned Loire Line have a base in the area. Enquiries should be made through Blakes Holidays, Wroxham, Norfolk, or the French Tourist Office. The FTO will also be able to give advice on the availability of hotel boats which ply over parts of the routes described.

Route 1, via the Canal de Briare

River Seine In its lower reaches this is a mighty navigation with a huge volume of commercial traffic conveyed in single or grouped barges the size of small ships. Le Havre, at the mouth of the Seine, is an obvious entry to France, but not for the faint-hearted. The first lock is reached at Amfreville, 160 km/99 miles inland, although the tide can normally be discounted upstream of Rouen, 120 km/74 miles. The effect of *Le Mascaret*, a wave similar to the Severn bore, is most noticeable on spring tides. But we are mainly concerned here with the Middle Seine, upstream of Paris, 242 km/150 miles from the coast.

The Capital of France is an object lesson in the fullest use of inland waterways, not only for freight transport but also as a pleasure waterway. In spite of the frequently turbulent conditions caused by passing traffic, there are numerous cruisers,

houseboats and *bateaux-mouches*, trip boats. It is possible to make a 46 km/29 mile circuit of central Paris through 17 locks, via the Seine, Canal St Martin and Canal St Denis. There is certainly no better way of exploring this beautiful city than by water. Upriver, traffic by water, road, rail and air combines in a metropolitan cacophony, but as the 20th-century tower blocks are left astern and the banks become decorated with willows and a succession of charming *fin du siècle* houses, there is time to appreciate the surroundings. The few locks are extremely large, mechanised and sometimes confusingly placed immediately alongside un-guarded weirs, a problem most noticeable when travelling downstream.

Canal du Loing The Loing is a small river by French standards, but the waterway which winds in and out of its course along the southern edge of the Forest of Fontainebleau is remarkably attractive. One leaves the Seine and its ceaseless pusher tugs at St Mammès, a real canal town, with dozens of moored *péniches*, boatmen's wives deftly sculling steel dinghies on shopping expeditions and exciting establishments selling a bargeman's every need, from steel rope to green rubber boots. For as long as anyone can remember, the Loing has been shallower than most French canals of its size: consequently, the laden *péniches* grind painfully along, anxious to be first through the next lock. Progress can thus be slow. But the scenery is everything in compensation: white poplars festooned in mistletoe, damp flowery meadows,

lockside cafés and a succession of pleasing small towns.

Beyond the A6, Paris–Lyon motorway and the city of Nemours, lies Souppes-sur-Loing, well remembered by the writer when he arrived by motorcycle one warm May morning to buy stores, while the boat maintained her position in the procession through the locks. Quite typical of a small provincial French town, it excels in its fish shop. Earlier that same day, in a pre-breakfast summer mist, we had complimented a lock keeper near Cépoy on his beautiful and productive garden, on the location of his cottage at the foot of a wooded cliff and on his good fortune in general. 'Monsieur,' he replied, 'I have lived here these last 35 years, and I can think of nowhere else I would rather be.' We found little difficulty in agreeing with him.

Canal de Briare This 17th-century navigation (see page 110) is joined shortly before Montargis and a junction with the sadly abandoned Canal d'Orléans. On one occasion, a day's delay on account of an emergency lock stoppage enabled the author to become quite familiar with Montargis. During a subsequent journey the antics of a Belgian *péniche* intent on negotiating the lock and several hundred meters beyond it in reverse gear, provided the excuse for further exploration. There are remarkably good shops close by and several pretty side canals admirably placed for the townsfolk to attend to laundry on their back doorsteps.

The Briare is a rustic concern, reasonably busy with traffic, but bearing all the mellowness that would be expected of Europe's oldest major canal, completed in 1642. Improvements have been made during the intervening three centuries, most notable being the replacement, in 1890, of the staircase of seven locks at Rogny by more convenient separate chambers. The older route is beautifully preserved, if gateless, and is a considerable tourist attraction.

Canal latéral à la Loire Formerly the Canal de Briare descended to the level of the River Loire via four locks, crossing this broad expanse of water to join the Loire latéral on the far side. This posed navigational difficulties and so the magnificent Briare aqueduct with its 660 m/722 yd span was constructed in 1896 (see page 123). Operated on a one-way system, the *péniches* make such an exact fit that steering can be neglected, the boat families sometimes walking along the aqueduct towpath while the barges take themselves across!

During the writer's first passage of the latéral in 1968, two varieties of commercial vessel were still in use in addition to the *péniches*. These were expressively named *bâtards*, lumbering wooden boats converted to motor power and *berrichons*, ancient horsedrawn craft designed for the smaller locks of the disused Canal du Berry and loading about 100 tons. They represented the end of an era, all horseboats now having been pensioned off. A

A well-laden péniche *glides down the Canal du Loing near the forest of Fontainebleau.*

stable amidships was provided for the animals, while the boat family existed under a rudimentary canvas awning in the stern. One example, the *Sirdar*, made painful progress, 13 km/8 miles being rated good during a long day's work.

The latéral is not noted for spectacular surroundings, and it is something of a disappointment to discover that this part of the Loire is not that portion well known for a succession of magnificent *châteaux*. But for the canal enthusiast there are compensations, including three branches locking down to the Loire at St Thibault, Givry and Nevers. Although the river no longer carries traffic other than very local gravel dredgers, keepers are still to be found installed at cottages on the branches, seemingly employed in the ultimate sinecure. A noted bottleneck occurs at Guétin, where a 2-rise lock opens immediately into the trough of a substantial aqueduct over the River Allier. Regulations specify that descending craft have right of passage in the mornings, ascending boats in the afternoons. The arrangement is quite inflexible, even if no traffic is wishing to pass in one of the two directions. Additional problems and consequential delays are caused by the inability to refill the locks for an uphill boat until the previous entrant has edged its way over the aqueduct.

A connection is made with the Canal du Nivernais at Décize, via a short branch and impressive basin followed by a brief spell on the waters of the Loire itself. Here occurs one of the most outstanding examples of French bureaucratic idiocy to be encountered on the whole canal system. In years gone by, a pair of donkeys was stationed to tow unpowered boats over the river crossing. True to the letter of the regulation concerned, the donkeys are retained and a fee demanded of all the boats for the unrequired towage service! Another stone aqueduct over the Loire marks the junction of the latéral and the Canal du Centre at Digoin. Close by is the little used Canal de Roanne à Digoin, 55 km/34 miles, with ten locks.

Canal du Centre Because it passes the town of Montceau-les-Mines, this waterway suffers the popular reputation of being industrialised. That is, however, far from being true, although the coal mines did once account for much of the local freight. Lasting memories will be of mainly rural surroundings, the cultural highlights being the beautiful 18th-century *château* at Digoine, and the town of Paray-le-Monial. In the late 17th century, a nun named Marguerite-Marie witnessed a series of visions which eventually resulted in the devotion to the Sacred Heart. The *Basilique du Sacré-Coeur* is the chief attraction of the town which is a centre of

The 17th-century staircase of seven locks at Rogny, Canal de Briare, preserved as an ancient monument.

A hire cruiser works through the 2-rise lock at Guétin, while waiting barges lurk anxiously in the background.

pilgrimage. As elsewhere in France, electricity supplies are uncertain during stormy weather: the author was once able to produce a candle to illuminate the restaurant of a curiously old-fashioned hotel when the lights failed.

Locks ascend to the short summit level between Bois-Bretoux and Longpendu, and then fall towards the Saône. From this point they are automatically worked, unseen 'eyes' detecting approaching boats whose crews have merely to pull a string to activate gates and paddles. The last lock, on a new length of cut in Chalon-sur-Saône, rises and falls about 13 m/43 ft and is equipped with a guillotine gate.

River Saône Without any doubt, this is one of the glorious rivers of France. Limpid (in summer at least), interrupted by few locks, and presenting a panorama of willows, cows, gracious houses and marker posts, it runs all the way from Corre to Lyon, 375 km/233 miles. It is the ideal location for a leisurely cruise; equally, for British yachts bound for the Mediterranean, it signals the end of small locks and consequent delays. Being already an important trade artery, the Saône will receive even more traffic when future works create a 1350-ton barge route between the Rhône and the Rhine. Junctions are made with the Canal de l'Est (Branch Sud) at Corre; Canal de la Marne à la Saône at Heuilley; Canal de Bourgogne at St-Jean-de-Losne; Canal du Rhône au Rhin at St Symphorien; Canal

du Centre at Chalon-sur-Saône; and the Rhône in Lyon.

The upper Saône features a greater share of locks than downstream of St Symphorien, and mid-19th-century improvements have left a number of very long *dérivations*, or artificial cuts which reduce the distance through by-passing loops in the natural river course. Twice there are tunnels – St Albin (681 m/745 yd) and Savoyeux (643 m/703 yd) with one-way working and traffic lights. Some care is necessary in looking out for the lock cut entrances (marked with signboards), otherwise unwanted encounters with weirs could result. When river levels are high, certain locks can be by-passed in a downriver journey by shooting the weirs, the prevailing situation being explained by signal boards. Another navigational feature demanding care is a series of underwater training walls marked with stakes or beacons; these mostly occur below Mâcon.

Scenery tends to be hilly and wooded above Auxonne and rather flatter, through meadowland, below. Everywhere, sleek white Charollais cattle graze, fishermen slumber in their little punts or attend to drop nets suspended from rudimentary bankside cranes, and downstream of Mâcon vineyards accompany the navigation on and off all the way to the Mediterranean. Towns of interest are too numerous to mention in detail, those on the upper river including Corre, Gray and Pontailler. St Jean-de-Losne, junction of the Canal du Bourgogne, is a veritable boat people's town, where gatherings of flag bedecked *péniches* are held from time to

Cruising on the Upper Saône, where long lock cuts avoid loops of the natural river

On the waterways of Central France. Left: *lines of white poplars shade a canal lock cut on the limpid River Saône near Auxonne. The pleasure boat is Lord Harvington's splendid motor yacht* Melita, *which has travelled widely throughout Western Europe.* Right: *among the local people — barge families, shop keepers and anglers — who are encountered on a canal journey, greatest contact is with lock keepers. At manually worked locks it is normal for the boat crew to help with gates and paddles. Here, the keeper at Montargis, Canal de Briare, maintains a record of all craft passing through.* Below: *hilly country in Burgundy, as the Canal de Bourgogne climbs to its summit level at Pouilly Tunnel. These are the Pouillenay Locks, which form part of a succession of 51 in the 36 km/22 miles before the descent towards the Saône.*

133

time, photographs of the events decorating the walls of the local café. Chalon-sur-Saône is a busy port, remembered as the location of Nicéphore Niépce's pioneering photography in 1822, when a seven-hour exposure was necessary. Tournus, with its suspension bridge and magnificent abbey church of St Philibert, is good for antiques and basketwork. Downriver at La Truchère, the remote and charmingly rural River Seille offers 39 km/24 miles of cruising through four locks to Louhans, where the long arcaded main street is preserved as an historical monument. Passage takes a mere five hours or so and the only traffic likely to be encountered is one of a pair of gravel barges. Gravel is a leading freight of the Saône, being dredged from the riverbed as an aid to navigation in addition to its use as a building material. Indeed, study of the movement of gravel over waterways of central France is a fascinating subject, areas with plentiful supplies seeming to import quantities from elsewhere! Raked into intricate patterns and studded with flower-filled car tyres it is frequently the most prized element of a lock garden, receiving as much care as an English lawn.

Lyon, second city of France, marks the confluence of Saône and Rhône. Flourishing in Roman times, there are many relics from that era, including a well preserved amphitheatre. One traditional industry centres on silk, while gastronomic considerations make it a popular tourist attraction. There are good moorings on the Saône with quayside food and flower markets, outstanding formal gardens – *Parc de la Tête d'Or* – and a magnificent panorama from the square by the basilica of Notre Dame de Fourvière, reached via a funicular railway. At least a day should be allocated to sight-seeing before heading south into the fast running waters of the Rhône.

River Rhône 'The Rhône is not, strictly speaking, a river: it is an enormous torrent' is a much quoted description of this, the most powerful watercourse of France. When first visited by the author in 1957, it was a navigation that fully merited its reputation – the swirling blue-green glacier-fed water presenting serious hazards, with floods in winter and dangerously low levels in summer. The taming process between Lyon and the sea is now virtually complete, having been commenced in 1933 by the *Compagnie Nationale du Rhône*. Three objectives have been thus achieved: creation of a reliable navigation; irrigation of the surrounding countryside; and the generation of huge quantities of electricity. Eventually, the work is destined to continue upstream to the French frontier at Geneva.

If all has been carried out to schedule, by the time this book is in print, there should be twelve locks in operation, each 195 m/640 ft long and 12 m/39.5 ft wide. Canalisation has resulted in the creation of exceptionally long artificial cuts up to 29 km/18 miles in length.

In spite of these monumental improvements, the Rhône is not a waterway to be trifled with. Craft should be capable of making at least seven knots, especially if a return passage upstream is contemplated. Employment of a pilot, once essential, is no longer necessary, especially as the charge for this service has increased in direct proportion to the reduction in demand! But a good chart *is* required and can be obtained in Lyon or from Journal de la Navigation, 29 Boulevard Henri IV, 75 Paris 4.

Passenger cruise craft operate from Lyon, taking two days to reach Arles with an overnight hotel stop in Valence; there are also shorter day trips, details from the Lyon *Syndicat d'Initiative* (tourist office).

Prodigious daily distances can be achieved on the Rhône, the writer having once left Arles at 8·30 h aboard a powerful twin-screw motor yacht, arriving in Lyon at 11·00 h two days later, after a journey of 295 km/183 miles! For peace of mind, we found it best to follow a barge (surprisingly few in number and quick travelling). The result is that overnight moorings are dictated by lock closures and there is little opportunity for making stops at the many attractive towns en route.

The locks are a great experience: all have a rise and fall well in excess of 6 m/20 ft, that of St Pierre-de-Bollène lowering craft a staggering 27 m/89 ft. Mooring bollards rise and fall with the water level.

All the while, there is an atmosphere of the south, with arid banks, bleached buildings and terraces of vines, especially at L'Hermitage, opposite the harbour of Tournon. The *Mistral*, a fierce wind, sometimes blows without respite for days at a time, creating sizeable waves and conditions where the eyes water and photographs are hopelessy blurred. For much of the journey, ruined castles glare at each other across the river, emphasising a long history of conflict when the Rhône was a political boundary. Among these fortifications are Roquemaure and the Tour de l'Hers. The celebrated Palace of the Popes and the ruined bridge of Avignon are now by-passed by a canal section, but the town, perhaps above all others, is well worth a visit. Downstream is Beaucaire, terminal of the Canal Rhône à Sète, now reached via the Petit Rhône near Arles, (see page 151). There are moorings on the quay in Arles, a Roman capital

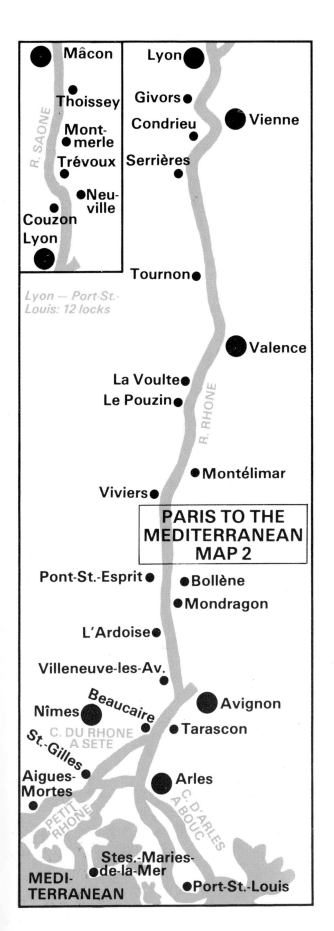

PARIS TO THE MEDITERRANEAN MAP 2

Mâcon

Lyon

Thoissey

Givors

Mont-merle

Condrieu

Vienne

Trévoux

Serrières

R. SAONE

Neu-ville

Couzon

Lyon

Tournon

Lyon – Port-St.-Louis: 12 locks

Valence

La Voulte

Le Pouzin

R. RHONE

Montélimar

Viviers

Pont-St.-Esprit

Bollène

Mondragon

L'Ardoise

Villeneuve-les-Av.

Beaucaire

Avignon

Nîmes

C. DU RHONE A SETE

Tarascon

St.-Gilles

Aigues-Mortes

Arles

C. D'ARLES A BOUC

PETIT RHONE

Stes.-Maries-de-la-Mer

MEDI-TERRANEAN

Port-St.-Louis

with ancient arena built for 21 000 spectators. From here, the Canal d'Arles à Bouc makes connections with the coast and the Étang de Berre. Until 1963, a continuation led to Marseille, but the huge Rove tunnel (7 km/4·3 miles) has suffered a collapse.

Passing along the east side of the Camargue, the Rhône finally reaches the Mediterranean at Port-St-Louis, where there is a single shallow lock, boat yard and little else. Beyond, the great sea shimmers in a heat haze, the world of inland boating comes to an end and the European yachtsman's playground welcomes the navigator.

Route 2, via the Canal du Nivernais

River Yonne The author's first encounter with the Yonne was in mid-October, when there were mists and golden foliage. A large but peaceful river, its speciality is a number of exceedingly large locks with sloping sides which demand constant attention if a descending boat is to avoid damage. Rudimentary weirs comprising a forest of wooden paddles are often situated alongside, with little or no lock cut to offer protection. Placid fishermen occupy punts and their stillness is such you almost expect them to be lightly covered with green moss.

Leaving the Seine at Montereau – here the Yonne is the larger of the two rivers – the first of several long *dérivations* (artificial cuts) is encountered at Courlon-sur-Yonne. The major place en route is Sens, a cathedral city which gave shelter to Thomas à Becket and now boasts thriving barge quays. One peaceful reach follows another until Laroche-St Cydroine, a busy railway town and junction with the Canal du Bourgogne. Finally, Auxerre is reached, dominated by the cathedral of St Etienne and two lesser churches. Here, there are narrow twisting streets of ancient houses, a selection of excellent restaurants and the technical end of the Yonne Navigation; for although the course of the river continues southwards, from this point it is known as the Canal du Nivernais.

Canal du Nivernais. There was a time during the mid-1960s when this delectable waterway was

Next page: *the French are a nation of ardent fishermen and unlike the majority of their British counterparts, are expert in cooking and eating coarse fish. Often, commercial traffic apart, little fishing punts are almost the only craft that pleasure boaters are likely to encounter. This peaceful scene is on the slow-running River Yonne.*

under serious threat of closure. For, although locks are of standard *Freycinet* dimensions to begin with, towards its summit they have never been enlarged. Traffic on that section had virtually ceased, and but for the establishment of the Saint Line hire fleet by Peter Zivy at Baye (now operating under new ownership) the line would almost certainly have been shut. Even now, the Nivernais is a delectable backwater, its locks chiefly worked by pensioners or the pregnant wives of men who supplement the family income with another job. Thanks to a remarkable internal telephone system, using brass-bound instruments of ancient vintage, locks are generally prepared in advance to greet the traveller. It is thus necessary to make known one's intention to moor up during the day. Before proper canalisation of the lower, Yonne, section, timber was floated downriver towards the Seine and Paris in rafts, manned by a body of men known as *les flotteurs*.

Only gradually does the Yonne achieve a metamorphosis into a lateral canal, and there are some glorious stretches of river including a dramatic section past rock pinnacles at Le Saussois, much used by trainee mountaineers. The builders of the Nivernais adopted an unusual method of supplementing income by planting the banks with fruit and nut trees, granting produce rights to lock keepers in respect of seven trees above and below each cottage.

At the approach to the busy little town of Clamecy, depending on water levels, navigators are given the choice of working through a lock or by-passing it completely by remaining on the river. Gradually the locks become more frequent and commercial traffic, such as it is, dies out altogether beyond Sardy where smaller dimensions remain as they were when the waterway was first opened in 1842. A long flight at Fussy leads to the summit level, with a bewildering array of gate and paddle opening equipment, some rare wooden gates (almost everywhere in France they are of iron or steel) and keepers who are among the most friendly and helpful to be encountered anywhere. One insisted on showing us a citation for wartime heroism bearing the signature of General Eisenhower.

Three tunnels and some stone lined cutting take the summit to Baye, with a long and beautiful water supply reservoir close to the canal. Now begins the gradual descent to the Loire latéral Canal at Decize, past plenty of villages and small towns, the epitome of rural France. This is a place of white poplars hung with mistletoe, secretive mansions among the trees and a total lack of any desire to hurry. The

Nivernais is well maintained in view of the tiny volume of traffic and can be thoroughly recommended. The Burgundy snails are highly prized, and there is a notice board erected alongside a lock at Crain: '*Défense absolue á ramasser les escargots!*' (Gathering of snails strictly forbidden.) This lock keeper was obviously determined to prevent Parisian hoards from plundering his supply!

Route 3, via the Canal du Bourgogne.

Canal du Bourgogne Following the courses of routes 1 and 2 from Paris via the Seine and Yonne, the Bourgogne is entered at Laroche, between Sens and Auxerre. Its most notable attribute is the quantity of locks − 191, which can result in water shortages after a dry summer. From the very start it is evident that the Bourgogne specialises in its own peculiarities of lock gear. At Laroche, a deep 2-rise chamber has gates activated by huge spoked iron wheels through which clanking links of chain are threaded; elsewhere, scissor-like levers achieve the same result. In addition to normal gate paddles, there are also *vannes de terre* equipped with a pointer indicating O (*ouverte*) or F (*fermé*). From a distance it is not possible to tell whether they are open or closed, but as it is accepted that only the keepers may touch them − and not infrequently they are left partly open to pass water supplies down the canal − the difficulty is largely theoretical.

Laroche has a large and noisy basin alongside a trading estate and a busy railway line, and is not particularly typical of this attractive valley of the River Armançon. But the little town of St Florentin is; built in terraces above the river, which the canal

A typically rural lock at Marigny-le-Cahouet, Canal du Bourgogne.

crosses on an aqueduct, there is a 17th-century church, lush allotment gardens and laconic fishermen perched on the edge of a sparkling weir. Among several *châteaux* within easy walking distance is a fine 16th and 17th-century example at Tanlay, and another at Ancy-le-Franc, a huge edifice on a square plan with a massive pink front door.

Montbard, noted for its connections with the 18th-century naturalist Georges Buffon, has a fortress, once home of the Dukes of Burgundy and – perhaps of greater interest to inland voyagers – a fine covered market close to the waterway. Moving southwards through the Côte d'Or, the country becomes increasingly hilly, locks occurring at frequent intervals, with a seemingly everlasting flight of 36 in 11 km/7 miles between Pouillenay and Villeneuve-sur-Charigny. Even though commercial traffic is light, this is not the impression you gain if a *péniche* is laboriously locking ahead! The lives of the lock keepers centre on enviable self sufficiency: great stacks of timber await the fires of winter; assorted livestock from chickens to goats and rabbits congregate on the locksides; vegetables and fruit are in abundance. Examples of this produce are pressed on the passing boatman for a fee.

A long narrows beyond the tiny port of Pont-Royal marks the gradual convergence of the busy A6 *autoroute* to the south. There is a fortified *château*, still more locks and the summit level is reached at Pouilly-en-Auxois. In the town square, the Hôtel de Commerce, an unassuming establishment, boasts one of the best kitchens at reasonable cost that the author has encountered. The other feature of note is a 3347 m/3660 yd tunnel, whose roof is so low that unladen *péniches* are placed in a partially sunken tank before being hauled through by a weird electric tug which draws current from unguarded overhead wires. Passage is to a strict timetable and pleasure boats are charged a fee whether or not they avail themselves of the tug. The tunnel was allegedly hewn by English prisoners during the Napoleonic wars: sealed inside the workings with regular food and the promise of freedom when the task was completed, few of these unfortunates lived to see their homes again.

The remainder of the journey through the gastronomic heartland of France includes the fine city of Dijon, famous (among much else) for mustard in variety and its brightly coloured roofs of Burgundian tiles. Experimental haulage of barges by electric mule was introduced in this area in the late 19th century, and similar diesel tractors were used until recent times by gravel boats from the

Saône. The river is reached at St Jean-de-Losne (see page 131).

Route 4, via the Canal de la Marne à la Saône.

Leaving Paris via the Marne (see page 113), the Marne à Saône is entered at Vitry-le-François. Opened as recently as 1907, calculations involving distances and locks to be operated make this the quickest route between Paris and the Saône. While such considerations are generally far removed from the author's priorities, it must be admitted that his only passage of the canal was accomplished by motor yacht in a mere four days: thus, although general characteristics are well remembered, there was little time for civilised observation. The skipper was frustrated by all locks being closed for May Day and even a fire in the port engine did not prevent him pressing on into the next evening in order to add a further pair of locks to the day's total!

Leaving Vitry-le-François, the waterway is never far from the Marne, but scenery does not achieve memorable heights until well past the industrial town of St Dizier. There follows a succession of somewhat grey little villages, with swing bridges at unusually frequent intervals and a railway which is often too close for comfort. Bayard has Gallo-Roman remains, while at Joinville the 16th-century *Château du Grand Jardin* is well worth a visit. At Condes is a 300 m/328 yd tunnel excavated through a hill below the town and very pretty views along the banks of the Marne, where springtime foliage displays a remarkable variety of greens. Langres is a partly fortified town of Roman origin, with ramparts providing a wonderful panorama over the Marne Valley. But it is best recalled by the writer on account of the steeply ascending approach road where he was flung from the pillion of the ship's motorcycle into the path of a following *camion*. Then comes the 4820 m/5271 yd Balesmes tunnel (one-way traffic according to a timetable); necessary delays to *péniches* has brought prosperity to the little village of Heuilley-Cotton at the far end. Wild garlic scents the tunnel cutting in spring and hilly meadows are filled with apple blossom.

Having now passed the summit level, the waterway begins its 43-lock descent to the Saône, following the appealing valley of the Vingeanne. There is a succession of *châteaux* to explore (Talmay, Beaumont, Rosières and Fontaine-François) and many pretty villages. The Saône (see page 131) is eventually reached at the *dérivation* d'Heuilley, midway between Gray and Auxonne.

Canal du Midi Route

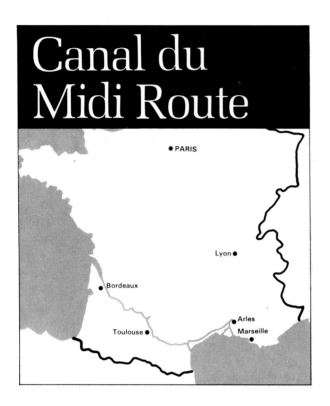

From Bordeaux to the River Rhône.

Distance 606 km/376 miles. This is the link from Atlantic to Mediterranean, and is formed by the following individual waterways:

River Garonne, Bordeaux to Castets, 57 km/35 miles; Canal latéral à la Garonne, Castets to Toulouse, 193·5 km/120 miles; Canal du Midi, Toulouse to Les Onglous, 240 km/149 miles; Étang de Thau, Les Onglous to Sète, 17·5 km/11 miles; Canal du Rhône à Sète, Sète to Beaucaire, 98 km/61 miles. Additionally, there are a number of branches, mentioned in the description of the journey.

Locks Castets to Toulouse, 53. Toulouse to Les Onglous, 101.

Maximum craft dimensions During 1978–85, all Canal du Midi locks and bridges are being enlarged and permitted draught increased to *Freycinet* standards. When completed, it will be possible to navigate a barge 38·50 m length × 5·05 m beam × 1·80 m draught (subsequently to be improved) × 3·70 m headroom/126·3 ft × 16·5 ft × 5·9 ft × 12·1 ft. But until work is finished, the sizes are 30 m × 5·05 m × 1·80 m × 3·50 m/98·4 ft × 16·5 ft × 5·9 ft × 11·4 ft. The rest of the route has already been enlarged to the *Freycinet* standard. At the time of going to press, there is some doubt as to whether the enlargement will be carried out after all.

Navigation authority, fees, opening times Enquiries should be addressed to Service de la Navigation, 2 port St Etienne, 31, Toulouse. Tel: 80–79–91. Like virtually every waterway in France, there is no charge for private craft. Tipping of lock keepers is perhaps best reserved for some special service, such as supplying water. Purchase of fresh vegetables or supplies is one method of conveying thanks. Otherwise tips will either be insultingly small or ruinous to the navigator! Locks are manned from 6.30 h to 19.30 h, April to September, with slightly reduced hours during the winter. There is a half hour break for lunch. In addition to published closures for maintenance (*chômages*), locks are shut on the following public holidays: Easter Monday, 1 May, 14 July, 11 November and 25 December.

Time to navigate With a maximum speed in the canals of 8 kph/5 mph, some 96 hours are required to complete the section Castets to Sète. Craft have been known to exceed this, but if that is one's intention, it is suggested that some alternative form of transport is selected. Ideally, three weeks can profitably be used between Bordeaux and the Rhône.

Maps and charts *Guide Blue Line*, published by Blue Line Cruisers (France) Ltd, Le Grand Bassin, BP 67, 11400, Castelnaudary, France, contains strip maps of all the Midi canals with commentary in French, English and German. *Guide de la*

Southern sunshine on the Canal latéral à la Garonne at the Écluse de Fontet, not far from the junction with the River Garonne. Pantiles and palm trees emphasise the Mediterranean quality of the waterway.

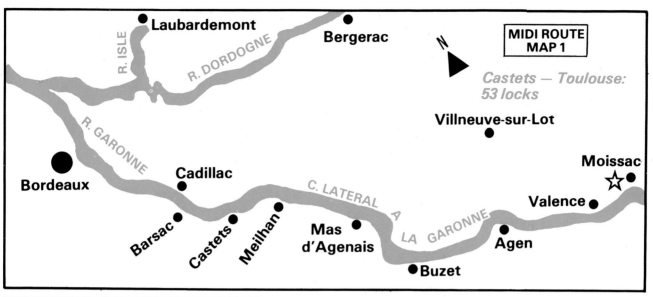

MIDI ROUTE MAP 1

Castets — Toulouse: 53 locks

Laubardemont

Bergerac

R. ISLE

R. DORDOGNE

Villneuve-sur-Lot

Moissac

Bordeaux

Cadillac

R. GARONNE

C. LATERAL A LA GARONNE

Valence

Barsac

Castets

Meilhan

Mas d'Agenais

Agen

Buzet

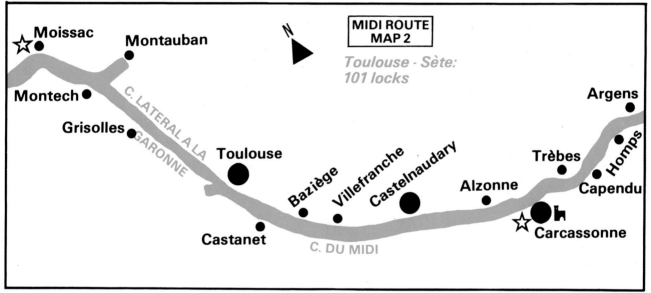

MIDI ROUTE MAP 2

Toulouse - Sète: 101 locks

Moissac

Montauban

Montech

C. LATERAL A LA GARONNE

Argens

Grisolles

Toulouse

Baziège

Villefranche

Castelnaudary

Alzonne

Trèbes

Homps

Capendu

Castanet

C. DU MIDI

Carcassonne

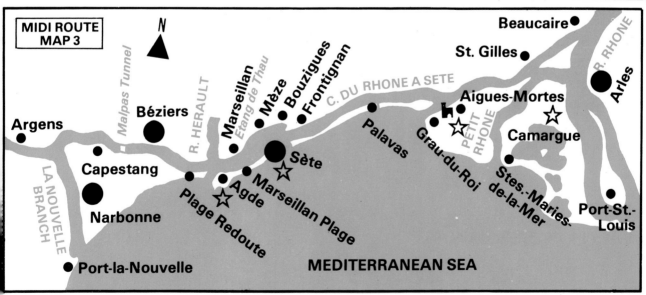

MIDI ROUTE MAP 3

Beaucaire

Malpas Tunnel

St. Gilles

R. RHONE

Marseillan

Étang de Thau

Mèze

Bouzigues

Frontignan

C. DU RHONE A SETE

Aigues-Mortes

Arles

Béziers

R. HERAULT

Palavas

Grau-du-Roi

PETIT RHONE

Camargue

Argens

Capestang

Sète

Marseillan Plage

Agde

Plage Redoute

Stes.-Maries-de-la-Mer

Port-St.-Louis

LA NOUVELLE BRANCH

Narbonne

Port-la-Nouvelle

MEDITERRANEAN SEA

Navigation Intérieure (see Bibliography) has excellent two-colour charts. For the surroundings of the waterway, the appropriate Michelin maps are invaluable (scale: 1/200 000).

Hire craft   The Midi is easily the best equipped area in France, with around 200 boats available for use between Castets and the Rhône. Development of this type of holiday began in 1969, when the first seven craft of Blue Line Cruisers were shipped to Bordeaux Docks and navigated in convoy to Toulouse amid great publicity. Three Englishmen were responsible: Michael Streat, John Humphries and Gerald Norman. The company is now part of the Guinness Group, and English bookings are handled by Blakes Holidays, Wroxham, Norfolk or direct from Blue Line Cruisers (France) Ltd, Castelnaudary, France. Other firms include Beaver Fleet, (bookings also through Blakes).

Several companies operate hotel boats in converted barges. For details of which services are available, contact the French Tourist Office.

The Canal Between Two Seas

Creation of the *Canal Royal*, as the Midi was originally known, is one of the most exciting stories in waterways history. Opened in 1681, the line features the world's first aqueduct navigable by ships, the first canal tunnel and a system of locks

Riquet is suitably remembered in his native town of Béziers.

A PIERRE-PAUL RIQUET
SA VILLE NATALE

and water supply that has operated successfully for three centuries without significant improvement. (Far reaching rebuilding works were commenced in 1978.) All this was brought about by Pierre-Paul Riquet, Baron de Bonrepos, who is suitably commemorated in monuments and street names throughout Languedoc.

As a collector of the salt tax, Riquet soon became familiar with the Midi countryside, yet it was not until 1665, when he was 61 years old, that the Royal Assent was granted by Louis XIV to put into operation his plan for building a canal between Toulouse and the Mediterranean. Some 64 km/40 miles of feeder canal was laid out in the Montagne Noire to conduct water supplies to the summit level, established east of Toulouse. This amazingly advanced system relied on collecting water from a series of small rivers, passing it through sluices, a tunnel and specially built reservoirs, and conducting it to the line of the navigation where it flowed in equal portions towards each distant sea.

With only limited experience of canal building to back up their theory, Riquet and his associates achieved wonders. The first ship was able to sail between the Atlantic and Mediterranean in 1681, just seven months after Riquet's death, when all was within a league of completion.

The canal prospered and next stage in development of the route came with the opening of the Garonne latéral Canal in 1856, providing 193 km/120 miles of more reliable navigation than was previously offered by the Garonne west of Toulouse. Apart from introduction of powered barges during the 1920s, little disturbed the efficient operation of the line until enlargement of the Canal Latéral to 350-ton barge *Freycinet* standards from 1971–6. This undertaking at a cost of 36 million francs, involved lengthening each lock at its tail, installing mechanisation and increasing the canal's depth. Some locks are worked by power under keeper control, while others are totally automatic. Priority for approaching craft is indicated by colour lights. When the way ahead is clear, a crew member twists a pole – the *tirette* – suspended over the canal. This prepares the lock and opens the gates. Once moored inside, another single lever activates paddles and gates, providing a 3-minute delay to clear the chamber before the gates close once more. The working boat people claim that more time is required to navigate the canal as a result.

In 1978, similar modifications were put in hand on the Midi itself. These are expected to be completed when Stage 1 comes to an end in 1985 at a cost of 220 million francs. Most of the multiple lock staircases will be replaced (the 4-rise staircase at Castelnaudary probably becoming a pair of single deep locks.) It is not yet known how the 7-rise series at Béziers will be treated. As all the original round-arched bridges must be replaced and the 300-year-old locks lengthened, to say nothing of the presumed abolition of at least some of the lock keepers and their charming cottages, the resulting effect on tourist appeal will be most unfortunate. With commercial traffic on this section having declined to a mere six regular boats by 1978, pleasure boating is easily the largest money earner. Whether these measures make economic sense remains to be seen. One hope is that for the first time the Midi will be used by 350-ton *péniches* from the rest of the Continental network, via the Rhône, instead of being restricted to local traffic as at present. (See note near the foot of page 140)

Voyage Through Languedoc

River Garonne   Entry from the Atlantic is via the wide estuary of the River Gironde, which changes its name to Garonne at Ambès, where the River Dordogne enters on the north bank and is navigable for large craft to Castillon, about 87 km/54 miles of tidal water. The buoyed channel ends at Libourne, after 42 km/26 miles. In the last century ten locks beyond Bergerac continued the navigation to Limeuil, 160 km/100 miles from the Gironde, but these have long been derelict. The upper waters, through limestone cliffs and the haunts of

prehistoric man are thus accessible only to canoeists. A tributary, the River Isle, similarly truncated, may now be cruised for 32 km/20 miles to the first of 40 derelict locks at Laubardement.

Boats entering France from the sea should halt in Bordeaux for customs clearance, this being most safely achieved by locking into the extensive dock system. More than 28 million tons of traffic is handled here annually, this being the sixth largest town in France. Draining the Massif Central, the Garonne is a rather hectic navigation, beset with rocks and a swift current. Travel plans should acknowledge the five knot flood tide, which is preceded by a bore, producing a wave up to 1 m/3 ft high. Commercial traffic is busy, which is just as well, for the *péniches* offer best guidance as to where the deep water channel lies. If the tide has ebbed more than halfway, great care should be taken through the two bridges at Langon, 5 km/3 miles downstream of Castets, for there are shallows in the swift current. Several well known wine-producing villages such as Barsac are passed during the agreeable but unspectacular journey, but suitable moorings are few.

Meilhan, charmingly situated beside the Garonne and its lateral Canal. The little hilltop square offers splendid views over wooded countryside.

Above: *little changed since their building in the 17th century, the oval chambers of Canal du Midi locks are a characteristic feature of the navigation. This is the upper chamber of a 2-rise staircase near the village of Homps.*

Left: *deeply shaded by plane trees which line much of the route, a laden péniche makes its leisurely way along the winding summit level. Regular commercial users of the Midi have declined in recent years to fewer than a dozen.*

Above: *cruising through Trèbes, close to the city of Carcassonne.* Below: *an ancient door in the narrow hilly streets of Agde, where a short branch connects the* colourful fishing port on the River Hérault with the canal's main line. Below: *fresh produce for sale in Sète, noted also for its Mediterranean seafood.*

Although much restored in the last century, Carcassonne is easily Europe's finest medieval city and one of the Canal du Midi's leading attractions.

Canal latéral à la Garonne   Although little of this length achieves the mellow and timeless charm of the Canal du Midi beyond Toulouse, it is full of interest for the canal enthusiast and a number of the towns and villages are well worth exploring. The finest time for a journey is in early summer, when the banks are lined with masses of brilliant yellow iris. The Garonne is never very far distant and sometimes sweeps close to the canal banks as at the delightful village of Meilhan (18 km/11 miles from Castets). Here a little village square is perched high above the navigation and the river which has now lost its traffic. From time to time, small laundry bays are passed, where local women scrub the family clothes on worn stone walls at the canal's edge. Creation of a wash through excessive boat speed is not popular. Elsewhere, these structures are in the village centres, roofed and providing multiple washer-woman stations.

Four locks at Agen, 'capital of prunes', where giant-sized examples of these dried plums are a speciality confection, follow a short branch to the Garonne (disused), the river being crossed by a 600 m/656 yd aqueduct. The prettiest reach now follows to Moissac, with an aqueduct over the River Tarn. In 1930, the adjacent railway bridge was washed away in serious floods, and express trains were diverted along the towpath for many months while repairs were in progress. The abbey church of St Peter contains fine cloisters.

Montech (151 km/94 miles from Castets), marks the beginning of a 10 km/6 mile branch to the medieval river port of Montauban on the Tarn, once navigable for 109 km/68 miles upstream; the 31 locks are all ruined. The branch, however, remains open, although little used. In 1973, five of the nine locks were by-passed by construction of a unique water-slope inclined plane (*pente d'eau*) (see page 125). Pleasure craft must use the original locks. The final 42 km/26 miles to Toulouse are rather dominated by road and railway and the attractions of the Midi and the far off Mediterranean are factors that inhibit lingering.

Canal du Midi   Progressive canal development at the Port de l'Embouchure, Toulouse, is evident from the short Canal de Brienne which links with the Garonne. A white marble bas relief between the *Ponts Jumeaux* commemorates Riquet's achievement in linking the two seas. The latéral Canal enters the basin at right angles, with minimum visibility. Toulouse is a busy city of the south, fourth largest in France. Its canals are lined with planes, and compared with life in the neighbouring countryside, there is a bustling feeling of constant activity.

The magic of the waterway is present almost from the beginning: old locks with curved sided chambers, the ranks of shelter-providing plane trees, sleepy keepers' cottages supporting a range of livestock, and (hopefully) a dry heat as the sun beams down to the water. In mid-July fields are ablaze with sunflowers, a constant reminder of Van

Gogh. As dusk arrives thousands of cicadas begin their incessant chatter in the branches; later, a thick blackness engulfs the canal, any light of the moon blotted out by the foliage overhead. Rising fish assume the imagined size of dolphins as they splash in the still water.

A steady climb through locks, including a number of 2-rise pairs ends at the Écluse Océan (51 km/31 miles from Toulouse); this is followed by a 5 km/3 mile summit pound to Écluse Méditerranée. Close to the west end of the summit is an obelisk to Riquet and a large octagonal basin forming part of the vital feeder system. Near E. Méditerranée it is worth halting to visit a wood fired pottery. The next feature is a huge canal basin more than 1·6 km/1 mile in circumference at the fine old town of Castelnaudary, whose houses rise above the water in the manner of a little sea port. Here is the main Blue Line Cruisers base, with all facilities for private craft. Excellent shops will be found in the town close by, and every restaurant will attempt to serve you with the local speciality – cassoulet – a dish largely composed of sausage and white beans, whose origins are believed to date from the town's final meal of available oddments when under siege at the hands of the English! A rapid descent is made via the 4-rise locks of St Roch, electrically worked from a cabin perched high over the structure.

Riquet's line of canal followed the River Fresquel near Carcassonne (105 km/65 miles from Toulouse), but this was unsatisfactory both through avoiding the city and for the silting that occured in time of flood. A 5·6 km/3·5 mile deviation was finally opened in 1810, involving the excavation of a deep stone-banked cutting at the approach to Carcassonne's rather noisy basin between the modern town and the railway station. Once moored here during 14 July, when the locks are closed for a public holiday, the author witnessed scenes of competitive jollity including greasy pole contests and an astonishing game in which all the young bloods leaped into the canal in pursuit of terrified ducks released from wicker baskets. As night approached, the most remarkable and spectacular firework display illuminated the dozens of turrets which surround the totally walled Cité, a 19th-century restoration of the greatest medieval fortification in Europe. Encircled by three walls and much visited by tourists, the town within is still inhabited by those whose chief occupation is supplying the needs of souvenir hunters. For all that, Carcassonne is essential to any cruising itinerary; very small children should not be expected to complete the lengthy circuit of the outer walls.

Beyond Carcassonne, the influence of the south

At Béziers, the canal's Long Pound is terminated by the Fonserannes lock staircase. Small electric motors have *been fitted to gates and paddles, so operation is quick and efficient.*

becomes more pronounced. Avenues of cypress trees, vineyards (whose autumnal colouring is one advantage of a late holiday), lockside gardens with such exotic offerings as aubergines, peppers and peaches, and views of the distant *Pyrénées*, are all to be enjoyed. A chain of locks at regular intervals, including several multiple risers, leads to the Écluse Argens, beginning of the 53 km/33 mile long level (*Grand Bief*). This is lazy cruising at its best, as one winds for hour after hour along the contours, shaded for much of the time by the welcome plane trees. Between Paraza and Ventenac, the Repudre aqueduct of 1676 with its 10 m/33 ft span is the oldest structure of its kind anywhere. Le Somail, a sleepy little village, was the trans-shipment port for Narbonne until opening of the nearby La Nouvelle branch in 1776. This 31 km/19 mile canal offers yachts an alternative exit to the Mediterranean, and its upper part to Narbonne is well worth navigating for its own sake. Umbrella pines mark the lonely beginning of the branch, and in the little town of Sallèles, the lower chamber of a 2-rise lock is ingeniously designed as a barge dry dock: another

example can be seen in Béziers. Soon after, navigation passes into the River Aude, with a crew-operated automatic lock in the splendid city of Narbonne. The Roman bridge carries a double line of buildings and with a headroom of just 3·04 m/10 ft, is lower than any other on the system. The sea lies beyond marshes at La Nouvelle.

Back on the *Grand Bief*, the route is tortuous in the extreme, especially in the winding loops at the approach to Capestang, whose ancient arched bridge bears the scars of many collisions from craft whose dimensions are close to the maximum. As the town's name implies, there was formerly a great lake here, now drained, and the grey stone church with open ironwork bell tower stands high above the fertile fields. A spectacular bank burst caused a three-month stoppage in the winter of 1776.

A pre-Roman village – Oppidum d'Enserune –

The famous white horses of the Camargue graze among the tamarisk trees on the banks of the Canal du Rhône à Sète near Aigues-Mortes.

Above: *sunrise over the Etang de Thau, a huge salt lake at the Mediterranean terminus of the Canal du Midi. Encircled by a series of small fishing harbours, the Etang offers fascinating cruising, the only hazards being occasional rough conditions when the Mistral is blowing and the acres of oyster beds, marked by lines of wooden stakes. Here, a fishing boat glides into Marseillan at the end of a night's work.*

Right: *a jousting contest in progress in the town centre of Sète. This ancient sport enlivens a number of places in Southern France, the Rhône and the Saône, but is seen at its noisy best here, in Riquet's canal town. Combatants, armed with lances and shields, take turns on the platforms to propel their opponents into the water, the oarsmen encouraged by Moorish pipes and drums.*

149

can be visited near the 194 m/212 yd Malpas Tunnel, shortly before Béziers. The first navigation tunnel anywhere, Malpas cuts through friable, sandy rock; the legend that it was dug in a mere six days seems unlikely in the extreme. The long pound terminates at a remarkable staircase of seven locks – les Écluses Fonserannes – electrified and working to a rigid timetable. Downhill craft: 6.30 h–9.00 h and 13.00 h–15.00 h. Uphill craft: 10.00 h–12.00 h and 16.00 h–18.15 h. As built, the Midi was lowered into the River Orb, to make a crossing on the level. But since 1857 traffic has been carried over the river via a seven arch stone aqueduct with series of floodlit arcades. The fortified cathedral of St Nazaire dominates the hilltop city above the river. All 20 000 inhabitants were slaughtered in the Albigensian massacre of 1209.

The character of the canal now changes as the coast draws ever nearer. La Redoute beach – an unsophisticated sandy resort, is within walking or cycling distance of the waterway at Cassafières. Riding is a popular pastime, with mounts available at hourly rates. Reeds fringe the swampland through which the canal passes and vines flourish on the sand dunes – *les vins du sable*. An extraordinary device, an assemblage of gates, iron work and stone arches, marks crossing of the River Libron. When the river is in spate and laden with silt, craft enter the chamber of this lock-like structure; the flood is diverted ahead and then astern of the boat which is thus isolated from the strong flow.

Agde, the Midi's final town, is perhaps its most interesting. A fishing port founded by the Phocaeans, it lies on the banks of the Hérault, 5 km/3 miles inland; sun-baked buildings line the quay in the shadow of a great fortified 12th-century cathedral of black rock. Narrow, hilly streets full of interesting shops lead to a large square at the top of the town. At the mouth of the river, Cap d'Agde is one of the modern seaside towns of the Languedoc-Roussillon development of this, the less fashionable end of the French Mediterranean coast (marina, camping, hotels, naturist quarter etc).

A short branch canal enables fishing boats and other craft to enter the Midi from the river, the junction being made at the Round Lock, which is consequently equipped with three sets of gates. Shortly the Hérault is entered above the town weir, and for several hundred meters navigation is along the river as far as Écluse Prades, a stop lock on the opposite bank. An interesting possibility is to continue upriver, however, for about 5 km/3 miles to the romantic ruins of a fortified mill by a weir near Bessan. There are no facilities of and kind en

Marseillan Harbour, one of several delightful little ports on the Etang de Thau shared equally by pleasure boats and commercial fishing craft.

route, and the journey is distinctly Amazonian.

The Midi comes to an end at Les Onglous, where lighthouses on the edge of a salt marsh mark entry to the Étang de Thau.

Étang de Thau A great sea-water lake, 17·5 km/11 miles long, separated from the sea by a sandbank carrying a railway and the N.108 road. Riquet's canal town of Sète will be seen in the distance, grouped at the foot of Mont St Clair. Several small fishing harbours are well worth a visit. First is Marseillan, home of the Blue Line Cruisers' secondary base with moorings for visiting craft. The Noilly Prat *caves* offer conducted tours, and most boating people take the opportunity of eating ashore at the Château du Port, an imposing 19th-century edifice built for one of the wine merchants. There is a thriving market in the nearby town centre.

Huge beds for the culture of mussels and oysters dominate the west side of the Étang (sea food is one of the delicacies of the area). Navigation can be difficult when the *mistral* is blowing, but otherwise hazards are few. Mèze harbour is filled with commercial fishing boats and pleasure craft, but visiting cruisers can usually find space near the entrance. The town seems little visited by tourists and is all the better for it. A small sandy beach (*plagette*) will keep the children amused. Bouzigues, to the north, is a lost and almost sullen village with moorings on a jetty by the tiny harbour. When the English landed in 1710, the inhabitants fled at the first musket shot! Opposite lies Sète, a substantial port, and entry to the Mediterranean through a canal in the heart of town. It is thronged with fishing vessels and noted for the periodic jousting contests staged aboard specially equipped galleys. A congenial week's holiday could well be spent on the Étang alone, especially if a car is available to make trips into the surrounding countryside and to the excellent beaches.

Canal du Rhône à Sète   Beginning in the industrial zone of Sète, this is a waterway of the salt lakes and strange marshlands to the north of the Camargue. It is a land of black bulls and white horses, tamarisk trees and fish that teem in the

---

A local family fishing party outside the ancient walls of Louis IX's port of Aigues-Mortes, gateway to the Camargue.

warm waters. There are connections with the coast via branches at Palavas-les-Flots, Carnon and Aigues-Mortes, much of the coastline sporting ultra modern holiday architecture. Aigues-Mortes is a completely intact walled city, founded by Louis IX as a port for his Crusade. Excellent moorings are found on the Chenal Maritime by the Tower of Constance. On arriving here by canal, the author hired the town's only taxi (which also served as ambulance) and enjoyed an expert tour of the great Camargue nature reserve, to the east. One of Europe's leading saline wildernesses, it features 9000 nesting flamingoes, real cowboys (whose traditions are older than the North American variety), annual gipsy gatherings at Stes. Maries-de-la-Mer, and vast lagoons, where salt is evaporated for domestic and industrial use. Rice is cultivated in paddy fields.

Between Franguevau and St Gilles is a junction with the Petit Rhône, a slow moving navigation connecting Stes. Maries-de-la-Mer with the Rhône itself near Arles (see page 135.)

Germany

The Rhine Gorge at Die Pfalz, Kaub. This 14th-centu[ry] island fortress was built by King Ludwig the Bavarian a point for exacting tolls from passing vessels.

Routes Through Germany

For reasons that should be fairly obvious, the German Democratic Republic (East Germany) is beyond the scope of this book. Tales that pleasure craft which stray from the West are liable first to be shot at and questions asked later, are in no way exaggerated. While the determined boatman *may*, perhaps, cross the border near Lauenburg or Brunswick, this course of action cannot be recommended. In any event, the 4700 km/2920 miles of waterways within the Federal Republic offer ample scope. In the context of this book, therefore, 'Germany' should be taken as a reference to the West.

The rivers and canals range from outstandingly beautiful navigations to some of the most industrialised waterways in the world. The great majority are modern, equipped with large mechanised locks; and being at least Class IV, they admit craft of 80 m length × 9·50 m beam × 2·50 m draught × 4·40 m headroom/262·5 ft × 31·2 ft × 8·2 ft × 14·4 ft.

Unlike most other European nations, few circular cruises are possible, the three available in the north offering little scenic attraction, compared with rivers elsewhere.

Private craft should be capable of reaching a speed of 10 knots, especially if any of the Rhine is to be negotiated. Speed limits, where imposed, vary between 6 kph/3·7 mph on the Ems and 14 kph/8·7 mph for the River Neckar. On the Dortmund-Ems Canal, a lower limit of 6 kph/3·7 mph is enforced, with yachts restricted to a top speed of 9 kph/5·6 mph. Regulations, although comprehensive, present few problems and for craft of less than 15 tons displacement, the only necessary papers are passports, insurance and registration certificates and preferably a yacht club membership or equivalent, implying a reasonable level of competence. For further information on technical requirements, consult *Through the German Waterways*, by Philip Bristow, one of the few sources of practical advice published in English. Roger Pilkington's *Waterways in Europe* is equally essential, providing much material on suitable moorings and the kind of surroundings that

can be expected along any given navigation. (For details of other publications and charts, consult the Bibliography, page 233.)

Hire cruisers and passenger craft There are very few opportunities for chartering self-drive cruisers on the German waterways, a fact which doubtless has bearing on the frequent encounters with German people boating in Ireland, France, Holland and Sweden. Many German navigations exist primarily for commercial transport and are ill-suited to novices. The German Tourist Offices should be able to give some help. Otherwise try ADAC, Postfach 700080, D 8000 München 70. One firm with craft available on the River Main is G Berghof, Walter vom Rathstrasse 10, 6000 Frankfurt. A further possibility is to advertise in one of the German boating magazines for the hire of a private cruiser; in this case the owner will need to be satisfied that his vessel will be in good hands. A holiday exchange of craft might also be arranged, always an inexpensive solution for the boat owner who has neither the time or ability to take his cruiser abroad.

A number of riverside towns like Heidelberg on the Neckar have small craft for hourly charter. Similarly, in most places on the very attractive tourist routes passenger boats can be located for trips up to a day's duration. These include the Danube (Passau – Regensburg; Kelheim – Weltenburg through the Danube Gorge; and at Ulm), the Elbe (Hamburg – Cuxhaven), the Fulda (Kassel – Hann Münden), the Lahn (Limburg – Niederlahnstein and at Bad Ems), the Main (Mainz

---

Although hire cruisers are extremely rare in Germany, private craft are widespread. This high speed launch is on the Rhine, upstream of Bonn.

– Frankfurt; Frankfurt – Seligenstadt; and Bamberg – Nuremburg), the Moselle (Trier – Koblenz), the Neckar (Heidelberg – Neckarsteinach; and Stuttgart – Heilbronn), throughout the Rhine, the Ruhr (Müllheim – Kettwig), the Weser (various points to Hamelin and to Bremen), and on the waterways of West Berlin.

Hotel boat cruises of between several days and two weeks duration may be taken on the Rhine (see page 165), Moselle, Weser and Fulda and Danube. The German Tourist Office will be able to supply particulars.

The Rhine Tributaries

From a pleasure boating viewpoint, the most rewarding waterways in Germany are a series of rivers flowing into the Rhine, itself described in detail on pages 165–177.

River Neckar From the Rhine at Mannheim to Plochingen; 202 km/126 miles, with 27 locks. Craft pay for the use of locks, the rate being reduced if accompanying a barge. Traffic between Stuttgart and the Rhine is quite heavy, but apart from the rather featureless reaches below Heidelberg, the Neckar is a beautiful and very interesting waterway. A long-term plan to extend the Neckar from Plochingen to the Danube at Ulm and onward to join Lake Constance, all to admit 1350-ton barges, is not expected to see completion until well into the 21st century.

Heidelberg, one of Germany's show towns, is dominated by a huge red sandstone castle, constructed between the 14th and 17th century. The University, Germany's oldest, dates from 1386 and unruly students fill the streets. Until 1914, the most troublesome of them were placed in a special Students' Gaol. Dense woodlands, the southern edge of the Odenwald, accompany the river beyond Heidelberg, followed by a landscape of orchards and vineyards. There are no fewer than four castles at Neckarsteinach, with further fortresses at Hirschhorn, Zwingenberg, Neckarzimmern, Gundelsheim and Bad Wimpen. Beyond Heilbronn, Schiller's birthplace and museum may be visited in Marbach. Stuttgart, a modern industrial town, is the home of the famous Mercedes car factory, with a fascinating motor museum, displaying models from 1883 to the present.

River Main From the Rhine at Mainz to Bamberg, junction with the completed portion of the Rhine–Main–Danube Canal (see page 161), 392 km/243·6 miles, with 37 locks. One of Germany's leading rivers, the Main is destined to form part of a vital link between Rhine and Danube by 1985. In 1976, over 20 million tons of cargo was carried on the Main and length of Rhine–Main–Danube Canal

Modern duplicated locks on the Neckar, above Heidelberg. Rails on the left are for small trolleys used by canoeists, thus avoiding use of the lock.

then linked with it. Boats are charged at locks according to the horse-power of their engines, but pleasure craft pass free if in the company of commercial barges.

Passing largely through splendid Bavarian countryside, with scores of villages, market towns, churches and cathedrals, the Main presents few cruising difficulties. Its lower reaches from Mainz to Frankfurt and Offenbach are rather industrial. Then begin the forests of the Odenwald, followed by extensive vineyards upstream of Gemünden. At one time, tugs hauling on a submerged chain were in service all the way from the Rhine to Bamberg, but these have long since been replaced by self-propelled 1350-ton motor barges. Wertheim's 16th and 17th-century half timbered houses are dominated by a great castle, while Würzburg has two cathedrals and a baroque palace. Bamberg is reached via the short River Regnitz, the only remaining section of the disused and romantic Ludwig's Canal, which provided access to the Danube until the early 1930s (see page 161). The Kleinvenedig (Little Venice) area comprises a series of brightly painted fishermen's houses, together constituting one of the outstanding waterway sights in Europe.

River Lahn From the Rhine near Koblenz to beyond Limburg; 67 km/41·6 miles, 12 locks. Smaller than most German waterways and with little commercial traffic, the very attractive Lahn admits craft up to 34 m length × 5·3m beam × 1·6m draught/111·5 ft × 17·4 ft × 5·25 ft. Care should be exercised in the vicinity of several power station outfalls where the current runs swiftly. Purchase of a comprehensive lock pass is cheaper than paying for them individually. The highlight of the journey is Limburg with its great 13th-century Gothic cathedral. Elsewhere, at Nassau, Laurenburg and Balduinstein, there are castle ruins overlooking the water.

River Moselle With a source in the French Vosges mountains, the Moselle is currently being made navigable for Eurobarges from Neuves Maisons, 24 km/15 miles above Toul, France. When this upper portion is completed, the total length to the Rhine will be 363 km/225·6 miles. In its final form, there will be 21 French locks in addition to two in Luxembourg and ten in Germany. At the majority of German locks, there are crew-operated electric chambers for craft up to 3 m/9·8 ft beam. These are free, as are the normal German and Luxembourg locks if accompanying freight or passenger craft. Otherwise a charge is made (but not on the French section). Parts of the river are fully canalised, notably between Nancy and Metz and from Metz to Thionville. Here, close to the French/German/Luxembourg border, begins the great Moselle International Waterway, opened

---

School children wait to board a passenger vessel on the River Weser upstream of Hamelin, where rats made of bread and sugar are just one manifestation of the Pied Piper legend, a source of considerable tourism for the town.

The well preserved doorway of a bargeman's house in Lauenburg at the junction of the River Elbe and Elbe-Lübeck Canal in Schleswig-Holstein. Until the 16th century there was an important salt trade between here and Lübeck.

as a result of inter-state co-operation in 1964. From this point to the Rhine, the river's sloping banks are frequently devoted to the culture of grapes, with numerous ancient castles and splendid scenery. Following an extremely winding course, the Moselle is one of Europe's most spectacular navigations, the really dramatic reaches being found between Bernkastel and Koblenz.

As bankside mooring is difficult because of the wash of passing barges, pleasure boat harbours have been established at various points. Perhaps the greatest tourist attraction is Cochem, where a 19th-century castle, reconstructed in the 14th-century style with turrets and pinnacles, towers over the river. Trier, capital of Roman Gaul, has witnessed navigation on the Moselle since the 3rd century AD. Its Porta Nigra, or Black Gateway, was restored to its original appearance by Napoleon in 1804 and is the leading Roman relic in Germany. The fortress-like cathedral is based on a 4th-century core, but is mainly 11th and 12th century. Ranging in width between 100 and 250 m/330 ft and 820 ft, the Moselle finally joins the Rhine at Koblenz (derived from the Latin, *confluentia*) (see page 177.)

The Ruhr Basin

Downstream of Cologne, the Rhine becomes progressively more industrialised as it passes through Düsseldorf and Duisburg, eventually to cross the Dutch border and flow into the North Sea via a bewildering range of channels. A pair of parallel waterways, the Rhine–Herne Canal and the Wesel–Datteln Canal, head eastwards from the Rhine, converging at Datteln, near Dortmund. Both contribute greatly to the wealth of this region, which since the 19th-century development of Germany into a world power, has been the most intensively industrialised area in Europe. Coal mining encouraged steel production, in turn bringing about the establishment of chemical works and heavy engineering. While forming an important part of the through route between the North Sea at such ports as Emden and Bremerhaven, these waterways have little to offer the pleasure boatman; of the two, the Wesel–Datteln Canal is the more agreeable. Commercial traffic is very heavy.

The Dortmund–Ems Canal and Associated Routes

The Dortmund–Ems Canal, from Dortmund, in the Ruhr Basin to the North Sea coast at Emden, contributes much to the prosperity of the region. It is 267 km/166 miles long, with 18 locks and a vertical lift and is, for the most part, surprisingly rural and pleasant through the province of

Situated on the River Ilmenau, Lüneburg is a fine old brick-built town, SE of Hamburg. Once busy with salt barges, there remains little traffic. Germany's unconditional surrender was signed on Lüneburg Heath in May 1945.

Typical of Germany's constant waterway modernisation is the vertical boat lift at Henrichenburg, Dortmund-Ems Canal. Able to pass barges of 1500 tons, 90 m/295 ft long, it has a rise and fall of 14 m/46 ft and was opened in 1962.

Westphalia. Leaving the extensive docks of Dortmund (here, the Westphalia Park's magnificent formal gardens are dominated by a 220 m/722 ft television tower with revolving restaurant), the canal negotiates a modern barge lift at Henrichenburg, junction with the Rhine–Herne Canal (see page 157). Münster has risen from the ashes of the Second World War, illustrating the ability of the modern German state to reconstruct medieval buildings indistinguishable from the original. From Rheine, the waterway uses the course of the River Ems, the final 9 km/5·6 miles of the estuary being duplicated by a lateral canal.

Canals on the Left of the Ems Several waterways within this strangely-named classification include the Ems–Vechte Canal, 20 km/12·4 miles, 1 lock; the Süd–Nord Canal between Nordhorn and Rütenbrock, 46 km/28·6 miles, 7 locks; the Haren–Rütenbrock Canal, providing access across the Dutch border, 14 km/8·7 miles, 4 locks; and the Alte Piccardie Canal, from the Süd–Nord to Coevorden, Holland, possibly no longer navigable throughout. Constructed to *péniche* barge size and offering about 1 m/3·3 ft draught, they traverse deserted flat countryside, with occasional local traffic.

Mittelland Canal From the Dortmund–Ems Canal to Rühen (terminus for pleasure craft) and thence into East Germany, 259 km/161 miles, 2 locks and several short branches. A modern waterway, finally completed during the early part of the Second World War, the Mittelland was designed to connect Berlin and the Rhine. It is heavily used by barges, including many from the East Sector. All the way from the Dortmund–Ems to Hanover, 200 km/124 miles, the canal maintains a level, thus producing what is most likely the longest canal pound in Europe. At Minden is a celebrated junction with the River Weser. Craft either keep to their level and cross the river via a ferro-concrete aqueduct 375 m/1230 ft in length, the longest such structure in Europe. Alternatively, they descend to the Weser in the *Schachtschleuse*, a drop of 13·2 m/43·3 ft; a system of economiser basins enables two thirds of the water used in a descent to be reutilised for a succeeding uphill passage. More than 30 000 barges pass the junction each year and more than 150 000 visitors come to watch the locking.

The Weser Valley

Running in a north–south direction through Lower Saxony, the Weser flows from Hanoversch Münden, junction with the River Fulda, to the North Sea at Bremerhaven, 448 km/278 miles, with eight locks through which passage is free. The waterway is tidal from its estuary to Hemelingen Lock, a short distance above Bremen. Second only to Hamburg, the port of Bremen and the 37 km/23 miles downstream through the estuary is an exceptionally busy shipping and ship building area. Already a market town in the 8th century, Bremen is an attractive city, with a Gothic Town Hall and 11th-century cathedral. Canalisation of the Middle Weser, completed in the 1960s, has produced a flourishing navigation with electrically-operated locks. High banks and flat, agricultural countryside with few waterside towns characterise the section up to Minden, junction with the Mittelland Canal. Beyond this point, at Hamelin, there is but one lock in 200 km/124 miles, with the result that in the hilly surroundings of its upper reaches, the Weser has a swift current of about 5 knots in places.

Hamelin is a superb small town of richly decorated 16th and 17th-century Weser Renaissance buildings and a thriving tourist industry with rats in bread and chocolate widely available. The story of the Pied Piper has its origins in the 13th century when over-population forced an exodus of young people to colonise lands to the east. Many of the valley towns have romantic castles such as that at Sababurg (the original of the Grimms' Sleeping Beauty fairy tale) and Krukenburg. Between May and September, a paddle steamer service operates

The monumental portals of a remarkable 'economiser' lock on the Dortmund–Ems Canal at Henrichenburg, now disused.

between Hamelin and Hanoversch Münden, taking two days for the upstream journey, one downstream. Commercial traffic in the Upper Weser is fairly light, with downstream barges sometimes navigating by power of the current alone, upstream craft being hauled by tug. Following periods of reduced rainfall, a *Welle* (wave) produced by releasing water from the Eder Dam, provides increased draught as vessels travel downriver on the tail-end of the flood, rather in the manner of barges riding the Severn bore (see page 42.) Until the partition of Germany, there were plans to improve the navigation of the Upper Weser, with a link via the River Werra to join the Rhine–Main–Danube Canal near Bamberg. For the present, the upper navigation limit of the Weser Valley is Kassel, reached by means of 27 km/16·8 miles of the River Fulda, with 8 locks. The economic capital of Hesse, Kassel has a museum devoted to the Brothers Grimm, and the magnificent Wilhelmshöhe Castle, with 18th-century gardens and fountains.

The Elbe and Navigations in Schleswig-Holstein

The River Elbe From the North Sea at Brunsbüttel (south west end of the Kiel Canal) to Lauenburg, junction with the Elbe–Lübeck Canal and the East German border, 131 km/81·4 miles, with one lock at Geesthacht, between Hamburg and Lauenburg. This great estuary navigation should be attempted only by experienced pleasure boatmen and below Hamburg (customs station) is regarded more as a tidal seaway than an inland waterway. The city itself has numerous small navigations and many sights in addition to its infamous pornographic street, the Reeperbahn. Lauenburg is a charming little town of boatman's houses, best viewed from a great bridge over the broad river.

Lauenburg on the River Elbe is an important barge building and repair centre.

There are barge building yards grouped at the entrance to the Elbe–Lübeck Canal and a small waterways museum (see page 235). Care must be taken to avoid straying upriver into East Germany!

River Ilmenau From the Elbe at Hoopte, between Hamburg and the Geesthacht lock, to Lüneburg, 29 km/18 miles, 3 locks. Tidal for its first 9 km/5·6 miles, the Ilmenau once formed part of an important salt route between Lüneburg and Lübeck. Commercial traffic is infrequent above the first lock, and the rural scenery through farmland is extremely pleasant. Lüneburg's salt deposits encouraged a thriving trade in the Middle Ages, supplies being shipped throughout the Baltic. The old town of brick houses is particularly attractive, especially around the port – *Wesserviertel* – with galleried buildings and an 18th-century crane.

Elbe Lateral Canal From the Elbe near Lauenburg to Fallersleben on the Mittelland Canal near Brunswick, 115 km/71·5 miles, with one lock and one vertical lift. An outstanding example of modern waterway construction in Germany, the *Elbeseitenkanal* was authorised in 1965 and completed in 1976 as a 1350-ton barge route between the north and the industrial Brunswick–Salzgitter–Hanover triangle. A chief reason for its building was to avoid the section of the River Elbe in East Germany, hampered with political difficulties. Soon after the opening, there was a serious breach of the new works at Erbstorf, adding about 82 million DM to the 1300 million DM cost of the project. Three large harbours at Uelzen, Wittingen and Lüneburg have been created to handle traffic. The outstanding feature of the

The twin vertical barge lifts of Lüneburg, Elbe Lateral Canal.

A succession of ocean-going ships approaches Holtenau Locks at the eastern end of the Kiel Canal.

waterway is the twin vertical lift at Scharnebeck, near Lüneburg, providing a change in levels of 38 m/124·7 ft, and already a great tourist attraction (see page 162). Uelzen Lock, rising and falling 23 m/75·5 ft, uses three economiser basins, whereby almost two thirds of the water consumed in a downhill operation is conserved to be employed in the next uphill working.

Elbe–Lübeck Canal   From the Elbe at Lauenburg to the Baltic Estuary of the River Trave at Lübeck, 60 km/37·3 miles, with 6 locks. Never far from the border between East and West, this waterway was built in its present form early in the 20th century and passes through Mölln, a fine old salt town where the 16th-century joker Till Eulenspiegel is buried. Lübeck, a well-preserved medieval city, is ringed by canals and is now a centre of ship building. Travemünde, at the river mouth, is a seaside resort. Following the completion of the Elbe Lateral Canal, there is now considerable support for the reconstruction of the Elbe–Lübeck Canal to 1350-ton standard, thus creating a Eurobarge navigation all the way from the Baltic to the Mittelland Canal.

Kiel Canal (Nord-Ostsee Kanal)   From the North Sea at Brunsbüttelkoog, in the Elbe Estuary, to the Baltic at Kiel, 98 km/61 miles, with entrance locks at each end. This great ship canal was opened in 1895 at a time when Germany was emerging as a powerful maritime nation. The scale of the works and craft encountered are massive and once in the waterway, pleasure boats are forbidden to moor up. (All craft must carry a copy of the regulations, *Betriebsordnung für den Nord-Ostsee Kanal*.) Two

possible stopping places are on the Gieselau Canal which provides access to the River Eider, about half way along the ship canal, or in Rendsburg. The Eider is navigable between the North Sea at Tönning and Rendsburg, where it is now blocked.

Eastwards to the Danube

One of Europe's most far-reaching canal projects is the Rhine–Main–Danube Canal, running from the Main at Bamberg to the Danube at Kelheim, near Regensburg. The expected year of completion has advanced to 1985, when 1350-ton barges will be able to make an inland journey of 3500 km/2174 miles between Rotterdam and the Black Sea. Such a possibility has long been a dream: in the 8th century, Emperor Charlemagne actually began a canal and a short section of water-filled excavation can be seen to this day. The breakthrough eventually came in 1846, when the 172 km/107 mile Ludwig's Canal, with 101 locks admitting 120-ton barges, joined the two great rivers. Almost deserted by the 1920s, it was officially abandoned in 1950. The new waterway comprises 100 km/62 miles of artificial canal between Nuremberg and Kelheim, with 15 locks to overcome a change of levels of 175 m/574 ft while passing through the Franconian Jura Mountains. A further 34 km/21 miles of the Danube between Kelheim and Regensburg has been much enlarged and improved. An estimated 20 million tons of freight will pass through the canal within a year of its opening. Serving Western Europe, Austria, Czechoslovakia, Hungary, Yugoslavia, Romania, Bulgaria and the Soviet Union, it remains to be seen whether use of the Danube route will be a practical proposition for yachtsmen. More certain is the prospect of booking cabins for the journey across Europe in passenger ships.

Canal Engineering

Nowhere in Europe is there quite the urgency associated with new canal construction and modernisation as in West Germany. Two examples of German waterway engineering techniques are shown on these pages: a 1962 barge lift near Dortmund and the very latest vertical lift on the Elbe Lateral Canal at Lüneburg.

Below: *views of the impressive Henrichenburg Vertical Barge Lift on the Dortmund–Ems Canal (see also pages 157 and 158). The top picture shows the beautifully landscaped surroundings for this popular tourist attraction. In the lower pair of photographs, the progress of a barge is followed into the caisson and up to the higher level.*

Three views of the massive pair of Vertical Boat Lifts on the Elbe Lateral Canal, seen during final completion works in the summer of 1977. (See also pages 160 and 161.) Providing the greatest rise and fall of any similar structure in the world, the Lüneburg Lifts are truly an indication of the shape of waterways in the 21st century.

Below: *an interior view of one of the pair of water-filled tanks, with guillotine gate closed at the far end. The Lüneburg Boat Lift, while strictly functional, has a distinct architectural beauty.*

Above: *the channel of the Elbe Lateral Canal immediately south of the Lüneburg lifts, seen during repair works that were necessary shortly after its initial opening. Piers on the left are for barges waiting to enter the Lift.*

Below: *this concrete aqueduct carrying the Elbe Lateral Canal over a main road is so large that the waterway width remains unchanged for the crossing.*

The Rhine

The greatest water highway of Europe, in its passage from Lake Constance (Bodensee) to the North Sea near Rotterdam, the Rhine runs for 1030 km/640 miles. (The upper 145km/90 miles beyond Rheinfelden is not navigable.) In its journey through Switzerland, France, Germany and Holland the interest to pleasure boaters varies considerably, from the world-famous Rhine Gorge of its middle reaches to the frankly industrial or desolate lower sections near the border with Holland. The following detailed description is confined to that part of the waterway of greatest attraction.

From Rheinfelden, Switzerland to Cologne (Köln), Germany.

Distance 555 km/345 miles.

Locks Swiss section, 2. French section (Grand Canal d'Alsace), 8. Strasbourg to Karlsruhe, 3 (1 completed, 1 under construction, 1 planned.)

Maximum craft dimensions As the whole river is exceptionally heavily used by barges loading up to 2000 tons, the main consideration for pleasure craft is sufficient engine power to cope with a current which can exceed 6 knots.

Navigation authorities, fees, opening times Being very much an international highway, the whole of the river is under the control of the Central Commission for the Rhine. For craft less than 15 tons displacement, there are no special permits required, although it is stipulated that a copy of the *Rheinschiffartpolizeiverordnung* (traffic regulations) be carried on board (see Bibliography, page 233). A small charge is levied for use of the Swiss locks while those of the Grand Canal d'Alsace are free. Night navigation is normal for commercial traffic and decidedly ill-advised for pleasure boats.

Time to navigate The large passenger vessels providing cruises between Rotterdam and Basle complete the run in four or five days, depending on direction. Private craft will certainly wish to spend considerably longer, with ample opportunities for sight-seeing ashore.

Maps and charts See the Bibliography, page 233.

Hire craft Not surprisingly, there are no opportunities for self-drive hire cruisers on the Rhine, although sailing craft and motor cruisers are available on Lake Constance, a beautiful stretch of water 63·5 km long × about 14 km wide/39·5 miles × 8·7 miles.

Passenger craft This is Europe's leading waterway for hotel boat cruises: many of the vessels are the size of small ships, with three or four decks, dining accommodation for 1200 people and swimming pool! For most travellers, this is undoubtedly the best method of exploring the Rhine. A leading company, with more than 20 vessels navigating the Rhine, Main and Moselle, is the German Rhine Line (Frankenwerft 15, 5000 Cologne 1. Tel: 02 21-2 08 81,) founded in 1827. The fleet includes three venerable paddle steamers

Travelling up the Rhine Gorge at 40 mph/64 kph by hydrofoil.

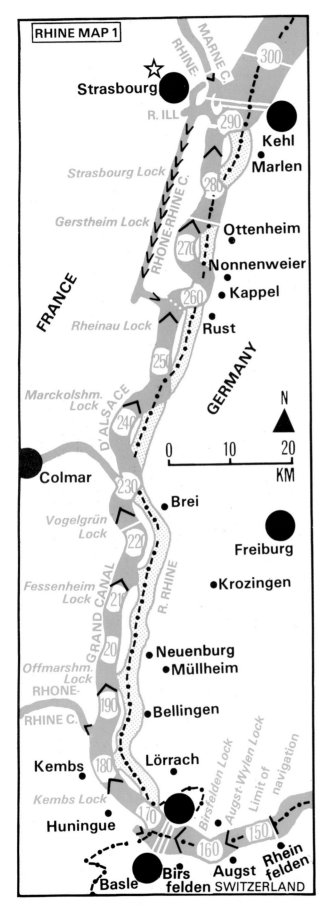

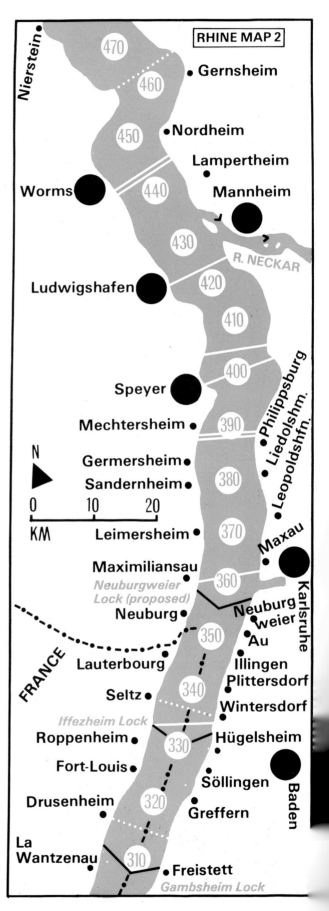

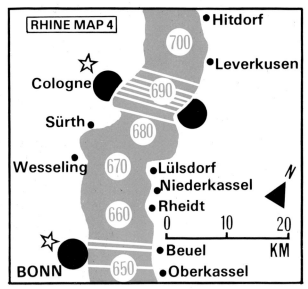

and the 40 mph/64 kph hydrofoil *Rheinfeil*. There are ample opportunities for day trips, especially along the most dramatic Rhine Gorge between Bingen and Koblenz, with convenient return facilities by rail. Timetables, printed in English, are readily available at all landing stages.

Two Thousand Years on the Rhine

It is impossible to consider the history of Europe without repeatedly encountering references to the Rhine. The river has always been of great strategic, political and economic importance; but only in the period since the end of the Second World War has it become a truly international highway, of vital consequence to the countries through which it flows. Widely used by the Romans, who established a toll station at Cologne about AD 70, the Rhine witnessed the departure of Emperor Maximilian's fleet to quell a revolt in Britain, about AD 300. By the Middle Ages, no fewer than 62 toll points had been set up between Basle and Rotterdam, with robber barons stretching chains from their castles in the Gorge, in order to exact dues from the passing traffic. Traction was provided by teams of horses or bow-hauling by gangs of men where a suitable towpath could not be built. This pattern changed after 1817 when the first steamer, the *Caledonia* reached Koblenz from London. She was followed by German steamers arriving in Strasbourg by 1827 and in Basle by 1832.

During the 19th century many improvements were made to the navigation channel by the construction of training walls in the upper reaches and the removal of over 80 reefs in the reach below

Bingen alone. In places the entire course of the river was altered, water levels lowered and traffic consequently increased. As it had done for centuries before, ownership of Alsace (on the west bank) continued to change, being taken by Germany in 1871, restored to France under the Treaty of Versailles in 1919, annexed to Germany by Hitler in 1940 and finally given back to France in 1945. In 1928, powers were granted for the building of the Grand Canal d'Alsace on French territory, mainly for the establishment of hydro-electric stations, but also to benefit shipping. The first four locks were built to accommodate six 1500-ton barges, with architectural help from Le Corbusier. When building began again in 1956, the remaining length to Strasbourg combined four artificial sections of channel with portions of natural river in an attempt to reduce the severe ecological and flooding problems that the earlier canal had caused. When Strasbourg lock was finished, the barrage encouraged terrible erosion below it, so that in 1969 agreement was reached to build further locks at Gambsheim (completed in 1974), Iffezheim (completed in 1977) and Neuburgweier. This procedure is a vicious circle, for although conditions improve above the new works, the combined effects of scouring and removal of washlands have created the possibility of catastrophic floods in the Karlsruhe–Speyer–Mannheim area. As a final solution, thought is now being given to the building of numerous additional barrages in these middle reaches to contain the flooding and return the Rhine to something like its original form.

The Rhine is now the third busiest shipping waterway in the world (second only to the Missouri-Mississippi waterway and Canada's St Lawrence seaway.) It carries one fifth of all German freight and is regularly navigated by no fewer than 14 000 craft. Industrial development has been encouraged by the hydro-electric power, good transport facilities and quantities of water for cooling purposes; ten atomic reactors are now planned for the Basle–Mannheim length alone which will encourage further industry. With massive pollution swimming is dangerous, the fish and plant life poor and the ecology of the natural landscape in jeopardy.

Journey down the Rhine

The Swiss Section It comes as something of a surprise to realise that Switzerland can be reached by inland waterway direct from such places as the Channel Ports or Holland. Admittedly, only about 15 km/9 miles of the Rhine is currently navigable

within the country, between Rheinfelden and Basle, but even this short length past the southern edge of the Black Forest is decidedly Swiss in character, with typical dairy farms scattered through the villages close to the river bank. Kilometre marker posts begin as the Rhine leaves Lake Constance, 145 km/90 miles above the head of navigation. Although the waterway forms the frontier between Germany and Switzerland, the river is Swiss-controlled until Basle, with two huge locks at Augst and Birsfelden. In Augst, the swift current does not deter a local rowing club and numerous small cruisers. The town dates back to Roman times and was founded by Caesar Augustus; there is a large amphitheatre and a museum of Roman relics. In the hinterland forests, there are marked hiking routes, wild boar and deer.

Basle, situated at the borders of Germany, France and Switzerland, is a flourishing commercial city, noted for its chemical industry in which the river transport plays an important part. Much traffic is handled at the Kleinhüningen harbour, a quarter of all Swiss imports and exports travelling via the Rhine. Tripping boats offer an opportunity for getting afloat.

Above: *tanners' houses in the Petite France quarter of Strasbourg, on the River Ill.* Opposite page: *a Rhine steamship poster of 1897, when passenger vessels had already been established for many years.*

Rhein-Dampfschiffahrt
KÖLNISCHE UND DÜSSELDORFER
GESELLSCHAFT.

On the Upper Rhine Navigation. Opposite page, top: *Birsfelden Lock, Basle, is administered by the Swiss. A duplicate chamber was being built 1977–8.* Opposite page, bottom: *Marckolsheim Lock, a modern concrete structure on the Grand Canal d'Alsace, and completed in 1961.* Left: *an antique shop on a quay overlooking the River Ill in the Petite France quarter of Strasbourg.* Below: *one of the most agreeable city centre moorings throughout the entire Rhine lies off the river itself and on the Ill in Strasbourg.*

Grand Canal d'Alsace For 120 km/75 miles between Basle and Strasbourg navigation continues along the French-operated GCA, an enterprise of gargantuan scale with eight duplicated locks and associated hydro-electric stations. The lower portion combines artificial channel with original lengths of the Rhine (see page 167). The Canal du Rhône au Rhin makes a connection below the lock at Kembs, part of its former course towards Strasbourg having been taken out of service. Often carried high above the rather dismal swamps, tree-covered thickets and stagnant pools of the deserted Rhine, the GCA features great shingle banks, few moorings suitable for pleasure craft and a ceaseless wash as commercial vessels surge up and down. Production of gravel is a major industry, with barge loading conveyors and sizeable water-filled pits. Shortly below Vogelgrün lock, a branch canal, part of the Canal du Rhône au Rhin, leads through three locks to the town of Colmar, a centre of Alsatian wine production. In the generally deserted (and desolate) surroundings of the GCA are several nature reserves with plentiful water fowl.

From Basle to Strasbourg the river descends 107 m/351 ft. The eight power stations using this giant force generate an annual output of about 7000 million kw/h, roughly equivalent to the total yearly consumption of Greater Paris. The canal now passes some 25 000 vessels each year, carrying 8 million tons. After the sixth GCA lock, Rheinau, craft up to *Freycinet* dimensions can leave the frankly tedious and occasionally alarming large waterway and follow the course of the Canal du Rhône au Rhin for 34 km/21 miles through 15 locks to the heart of Strasbourg. This course is altogether preferable for pleasure boats, with frequent mooring possibilities. Strasbourg is a great port with docks off the Rhine and although very German in character, it is totally within France. Local enquiry will reveal the route to the little River Ill Navigation which provides one of the most exquisite urban moorings in Europe in an area of ancient half timbered tanners' and fishermen's houses, known as 'La Petite France'. All the city sights are close by, including a fine covered market and the great cathedral with its astronomical clock. Tripping boats and waterborne jousting contests are two attractions of this superb city.

Strasbourg to Mainz For 60 km/37 miles downriver of Strasbourg, the west bank of the Rhine is French, the east being German. But after Lauterbourg the waterway lies wholly within Germany. Commercial traffic apart, there is rather a shortage of interest in these dull reaches, with stone banks, willow trees and much industrial develop-

ment. There are the new locks of Gambsheim and Iffezheim to be negotiated, frequent car ferries plying between customs posts and, a little inland, much leisure activity on the banks of landscaped gravel pits, where dinghy sailing, camping and fishing are popular pastimes. Considerable areas of the French side have been colonised by weekending Germans in this way, a trend that results in frequent resentment from the natives. Lauterbourg, surrounded by vineyards, is a fine old half timbered French frontier town, in contrast to the industrial port of Karlsruhe, downstream on the eastern bank.

Speyer (west bank) has a rebuilt 11th-century cathedral and good pleasure boat moorings in a harbour downstream of the bridge. Mannheim, at the confluence of the Rhine and the Neckar, is the second largest river port in Europe. A considerable centre of culture, its 18th-century castle is the biggest baroque palace in Germany. Although heavily industrial, the city has pleasant wide streets, formal gardens and fountains. Worms, downstream (west bank) is rather dull in spite of its historical associations. Among the sights are St Peter's Cathedral and remaining sections of town wall with moat and gateways. Several small towns now follow, with mooring facilities in protected basins as at Gernsheim. It is fascinating to note that the river's swift current and constant heavy traffic does not deter the use of every category of small pleasure craft from canoes to rowing eights and high speed cruisers.

The Rhine Gorge The world famous and most spectacular length of the river begins soon after Mainz, junction with the River Main, a place destined to become a crossroads of the waterways of Europe with completion of the Rhine–Main–Danube Navigation (see page 161). Best moorings in Mainz are about 1·5 km/0·9 miles downstream of the centre at the *Zollhafen*. In this stylish modern shopping centre, well landscaped, older relics include the great Romanesque cathedral. More remains of previous centuries at the spa town of Wiesbaden, a little east of the Rhine, created by the Romans around the thermal springs. Of the various methods of touring the Rhine Gorge, 60 km/37 miles between Bingen and Koblenz, the most fulfilling is from aboard a private motor cruiser, allowing for halts at the various harbours. Failing that, passenger craft operate a frequent service with regular setting-down points. Another possibility is to drive the *Rheingoldstrasse* (the Golden Road) which maintains fairly regular contact with the river shores along each bank. This route is duplicated by railway tracks, providing a magnificent journey. Finally, for a reasonable outlay, light

Above: *commercial and passenger traffic on the Rhine upstream of Bonn.* Below: *the famous Mouse Tower at Bingen, where the Rhine current runs at its fastest.*

Above, right: *at Andernach, this 16th-century horse-operated crane unloaded barges until 1911.*

On the Middle Rhine. Top: *a courtyard in Stolzenfels Castle, high above the Rhine opposite the mouth of the Lahn. It was built on the site of a medieval ruin by Friedrich Wilhelm IV, King of Prussia, between 1825 and 1842.* Centre: *stemming the swift current at the Loreley Rock, in the Rhine Gorge.* Bottom: *commercial and pleasure traffic at Linz.*

The magnificent paddle steamer Goethe *is one of the last three such craft in the Rhine passenger boat fleet. Here, she passes Andernach. Cruises vary from a few hours to nine days for a return trip, Rotterdam to Basle.*

aircraft can be hired from an airport above Rüdesheim, so giving a bird's eye view of the valley with its crags and castles. If time is limited, thorough exploration of this section of the river is recommended, rather than attempting to do justice to the less interesting lengths above and below.

Three aids to sight-seeing are the *Michelin Green Guide to Germany* (extremely authoritative on the Rhine Valley), *The Finest Legends of the Rhine* and *Castles on the Rhine*, all available in English (see the Bibliography, page 233). There is space here to offer only a briefest outline of the highlights. The narrowness of the valley has precluded building of any large towns, and there is not a single road bridge between Mainz and Koblenz. Tourists at the height of summer can be something of a problem.

There are almost 40 castles on the river, some ruined, others occupied. Many are open to the public and offer splendid views from their hilltop perches. Everywhere, the steep slopes are terraced into vineyards and production of Rhine wines is a major industry. With such a wealth of interest crowning every crag and a new excitement appearing with each bend of the river, it is perhaps best to restrict visits to two castles and a handful of the villages: retain the detailed memories of these, superimposed on the magnificent panorama of the river scenery viewed from the slightly detached situation of a boat.

The Gorge proper begins at the twin towns of Bingen and Rüdesheim, connected by a car ferry. Each is devoted to wine production and consequent tourism, Rüdesheim being the more brash of the two, with a wine museum. High above Rüdesheim, the massive Germania statue of the Niederwald Monument commemorates the foundation of the Empire in 1871. There is a superb view to the river. Moving downstream, the notorious Binger Loch is a narrow and rapidly flowing section of river: many of the barges require tug assistance for the upstream passage. At the head of an island surrounded by evil-looking rocks, the buff and red *Mäuseturm* (Mouse Tower) is now a navigation control point. Legend claims that Archbishop Hatto of Mainz collected a group of starved beggars and imprisoned them in a barn which was then fired. 'Listen to my mice squeaking', he cried joyfully. Whereupon, a swarm of mice chased him to the Tower, where he was eaten alive! Looking down on the scene (east bank) Ehrenfels Castle was built in the 13th century and partly destroyed in 1689.

Passing through the tourist village of Assmannshausen, noted for red wine, Rheinstein Castle, opposite, is a creeper-clad monument of the 13th century; it contains art treasures and a collection of armour, and is open to the public. Other castles follow to the gap in the cliffs occupied by Lorch (east bank). Next comes what is perhaps the most extraordinary Rhine castle of all, the Pfalz, upstream of Kaub. Situated on a rock island at the foot of terraced vineyards, its white-washed walls and slated turrets recall a great battleship. Boat trips offer the possibility of a tour of about 1½ h. High above the charming town of Kaub, another castle, Gutenfels, has the full appearance of a horror film set, complete with massive timber door in the main tower and great iron bell pull; privately owned and open as a hotel at weekends, it was restored during the 19th century.

Oberwesel, known as the 'Tower Town' (west bank) has a very useful harbour and much intact walling. It is surmounted by Schönburg Castle, now a youth hostel. A little downriver, the famous Loreley Rock rises black and forbidding almost from the river bed (east bank). Pierced by a railway tunnel with Gothic portals, the Loreley is one of the best places for viewing barge traffic, controlled by an efficient system of light signals. High above the Rock is a viewpoint from a Nazi-built sports stadium. Katz Castle overlooks the downstream end of the Loreley reach, followed by St Goarshausen, connected via a car ferry to St Goar, on the west bank. Rheinfels Castle, above St Goar, was built for toll protection in the 13th century and for many years was the most powerful fortress on the central river. Now largely ruined, it is amazingly extensive, with vast vaulted cellar, dark passages and spiral stairs up its towers. Perhaps the most romantic of the Rhine ruins, it contains a museum with navigation relics.

A pair of twin ruins (east bank), Sterrenberg and Liebenstein, are known as the 'Enemy Brothers'. At a sharp bend by Boppard, the scenery becomes less rugged, and fruit trees will be seen alongside the vines. Marksburg Castle (east bank) is the only fully preserved medieval fortress on the Rhine, presented to the Association for the Preservation of German Castles by Wilhelm II in 1899. The attractive River Lahn (see page 156) joins the Rhine at Lahneck, facing Stolzenfels Castle, substantially rebuilt by Friedrich Wilhelm IV, later King of Prussia, between 1825–42. One of the public rooms of this amazing 'Victorian' edifice, contains the coats of arms of Queen Victoria and Prince Albert in stained glass, emphasising the then close links between the royal houses of England and Germany. Of all the Rhine castles, Stolzenfels and Rheinfels provide the best – and most contrasting – excursions. By the time Koblenz is reached, at the junction with the River Moselle (see page 156), the glories of the

Rhine Gorge are finished. The thriving, modern city is characterised by flyovers and motorways. One of Europe's largest fortresses, Ehrenbreitstein, was constructed in its present form by Prussia during the early 19th century. It contains, *inter alia* a Rhine Museum. On the second Saturday of August, the spectacular 'Rhine in Flames' event features floodlighting of the river from Braubach to Koblenz, with fireworks and bonfires.

Koblenz to Cologne This central portion of the Rhine has little of the grandeur of the Gorge, but in its considerable widenings it does become a stately river. In spite of large centres of population, heavy industry is sparse and the attractively landscaped banks through the towns combine to create a holiday area with much appeal. Below Neuwied with its great new suspension bridge slung from a single, central inverted V structure, the old town of Andernach (left bank) has remains of ancient walls, with waterside hotels, luxuriant gardens, a floating

---

The Pfalz on its rocky island at Kaub, where vines flourish on the steeply terraced slopes of the Rhine valley.

restaurant and a 16th-century crane which was used for loading millstones on to barges until 1911. Near the 620 km (385 mile) mark is a barge works (right bank) and harbour opposite.

Through Bad Breisig, a beautiful reach extends past Linz-am-Rhein (right bank), with pastel-coloured houses scattered along the waterfront and up the hillside. Suitable pleasure craft harbours are now frequent (Oberwinter, at the Middle Rhine Yacht Club, being one of the most convenient). Roland's Arch (left bank) is all that remains of a castle opposite the tourist town of Königswinter, where one can be photographed at a curiously antiquated studio with plate camera, cut-out backgrounds and a live donkey. On a pudding-shaped rock is Drachenfels Castle, providing one of the most famous Rhine views from a height of 321 m/1053 ft. Nearing the outskirts of Bonn is the last of the Rhine castles, Godesburg (left bank), a site of pre-Christian sacrifice now topped with a massive stone tower.

Since 1949, Bonn has been the seat of the Federal Government, a situation that is curious for such a small city and one which many Germans regard as a temporary measure until Berlin can be restored to its former position. Affluent suburbs with tree-lined streets, the imposing British Ambassador's residence overlooking the river and charming landscaped water parks contrive to make Bonn a delightful city. In front of the extraordinary *Rathaus* (town hall) of pastel colours and rich gilding, is a flourishing pedestrianised precinct with excellent shops. Close by is Beethoven's birthplace, with a façade gleaming in polished brass fittings. Sadly, mooring facilities are virtually non-existent.

Flat, open countryside accompanies the Rhine downstream to Cologne, past the residential suburbs of Sürth and Rodenkirchen. Cologne is the capital of Rhineland and one of Germany's largest cities. After the devastation of the Second World War, Cologne has been rebuilt with flair. It is dominated by the spires of its Gothic cathedral, soaring to 157 m/515 ft, best viewed from the opposite river bank, reached by cable car slung high over the water. Upstream of the first of many bridges in the city centre is a useful pleasure boat harbour. In common with most German towns there are good, lively shops and a street railway system of multiple trams.

Much of the remaining 340 km/211 miles of the Rhine to Rotterdam is heavily industrialised, especially from Düsseldorf through the Ruhr coalfields to the Dutch border. When travelling by water, these lower reaches are best navigated without delay, saving time for the outstanding length of the river described in this Guide.

Belgium

A tripping boat station for tours
the medieval canals of Bruges.

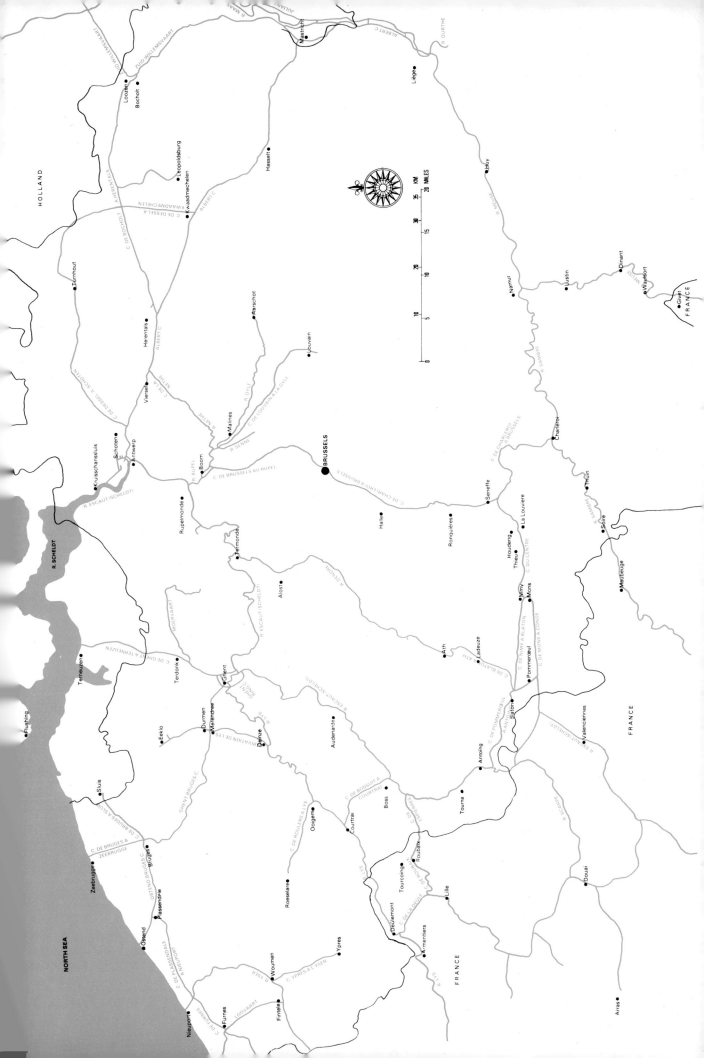

The Waterways of Belgium

Belgium is a small country, bounded by the North Sea, France, Luxembourg, Germany and Holland. Little known among inland cruising enthusiasts, there is nonetheless considerable scope for exploration of the river and canal network, although only the River Meuse (page 184) can boast spectacular scenery and be described as a 'tourist' route in the full sense of the term. Two rivers provide the main trunk routes of the network, the Meuse (Maas) and the Escaut (Schelde), with its tributary the Sambre, all rising in Northern France. Entry to the system is via several North Sea ports or at various border crossings with the neighbouring countries.

Most large towns have grown up with waterway connections – Ghent, Bruges, Antwerp, Mons, Liège and Namur; and since the late 1950s a comprehensive waterway enlargement scheme has been carried out to improve mainly 19th-century 300-ton routes to the 1350-ton European barge standard. These include the Ghent Ostend Canal, the Haut Escaut, the Nimy Peronnes Canal, the Charleroi – Brussels Canal, the Albert Canal, the Ghent Circular Canal and the Rivers Sambre and Meuse. More than 100 million tons of freight travels by water every year and pleasure boating takes a very secondary rôle. While scarcely encouraged, small cruisers are generally made welcome.

The network currently extends to about 1560 km/969 miles, all well maintained and presenting no particular hazards beyond the conditions that are to be expected on routes capable of accommodating craft of 1350 tons or (in the case of 353 km/219 miles) 2000 tons.

A speed limit of 3·5 knots is generally enforced and regulations relating to pleasure craft coming from abroad are few, provided their stay is less than two months' duration. When arriving in Belgium, pleasure boats should report to the first *Bureau de Perception des Droits de Navigation*; likewise on leaving. All enquiries should be addressed to the Ingénieur en Chef-Directeur, Service d'Exploitation des Voies Navigables, Résidence Palace, 155 Rue de la Loi, Brussels. This office will be able to supply details of any *chômages* (stoppages for repairs). The charges for locks are payable as incurred, and are very small. Lock opening times vary considerably

with the time of year, ranging from 6·15 h–16·30 h in the middle of winter to 3·30 h–20·30 h at the height of summer.

Maximum dimensions of craft for the smaller canals are similar to those found throughout France, the most important measurements being 5·15 m beam and 1·80 m draught/16·9 ft × 5·9 ft.

Hire cruisers are at present unknown in Belgium, although enquiry at the Belgian State Tourist Office *might* produce results in the future. There are, however, a number of opportunities for travelling on passenger craft for periods ranging from an hour to a whole day. Such locations include most towns on the Meuse; the Scheldt between Antwerp and Lillo; the Charleroi – Brussels Canal at Ronquières; in the city of Bruges; the Bruges – Sluis Canal; along the Bruges – Zeebrugge Ship Canal; and in Ghent.

Scenery is often similar to that of Holland, except when approaching the French border and the dramatic Ardennes on the Meuse. There are, however, several features which rank with the greatest waterway attractions of Europe, and these have been singled out for special mention.

The Ronquières Inclined Plane 32 km/20 miles south of Brussels, on the Charleroi – Brussels Canal, 40 km/25 miles of 300-ton standard waterway with 27 locks and a 1050 m/1149 yd tunnel was replaced during the 1960s by a completely new 1350-ton canal. At Ronquières, a change in levels of 68

Above: *richly ornamental ironwork on a tripping boat seen on the Belgian River Meuse.* Opposite page: *barges travel in each direction on the Ronquières Inclined Plane, seen from the top of the 125m/410 ft viewing tower.*

One of the gigantic tanks of the Ronquières Inclined Plane. Courtesy, Robert Shopland.

m/223 ft is overcome by the world's largest inclined plane. Twin tracks enable a pair of water-filled tanks, each fitted with 236 wheels, to ascend and descend while laden with a 1350-ton barge or up to four 300-tonners. The weight of each tank varies from 5000 to 5700 tons, depending on water levels at each end of the 1432 m/1566 yd slope. Apart from greatly increasing the capacity of

the canal, travel time over this section has been reduced by 20 hours, 38 former locks being replaced by 10 new ones and the inclined plane. Ronquières has become established as a nationally important tourist attraction and apart from the passenger boat cruises from the lower end of the incline to lock 26 on the old canal, the entire structure is overlooked by a slender concrete viewing tower 125 m/410 ft high. Open to the public and equipped with a high speed lift, this provides a remarkable panorama of the amazing complex. Guided tours and souvenirs are available.

The Vertical Lifts of the Canal du Centre A series of four vertical boat lifts on the 19 km/11·8 mile Canal du Centre between Mons and the Charleroi–Brussels Canal, was built between 1888 and 1917. Located at Thieu, Strepy-Bracquegnies, Houdeng-Aimeries and Houdeng-Goegnies, within a distance of 6·7 km/4·2 miles, the quartet of lifts together overcome a change in levels of more than 66 m/216·5 ft. Modernisation plans will soon replace the lifts by a single 74 m/242·8 ft structure and an action group has been formed to devise means of preserving the historical equipment, with a canal museum at Thieu. Regular boat trips between all four lifts were being run during 1978.

Left: *the vertical lift at Strepy-Bracquegnies.* Photograph, Ministère des Traveaux Publics.

Bruges This Venice of the north is one of the most delightful waterway towns in Europe and should be visited by all canal lovers even if they have time for nothing else in Belgium. Once a leading seaport, in the 15th century Bruges received as many as 150 foreign ships a day, trading from as far away as Poland, Venice and Ireland. Over the years the Zwijn Estuary silted up; trade fell away and Antwerp on the Scheldt was selected by the Flemish merchants for the import of goods from Asia, Africa and the furthest corners of Europe. This was in one sense fortunate, for the red brick merchants' houses of Bruges remained intact, a delight for the 20th-century visitor. Short motor launch excursions can be made along the tiny canals of the city, while a wonderful view over the roof tops is provided from the 83 m/272 ft bell tower, standing on the edge of the main square.

Right: *a tripping boat station overlooked by the bell tower of Bruges.*

Medieval merchants' houses in the centre of Bruges, seen from the top of the great belfry. Incomparable among canal cities of Western Europe, Bruges is perhaps best explored by water, taking one of the small passenger launches that glide quietly under ancient bridges and past moss-covered walls.

The River Meuse

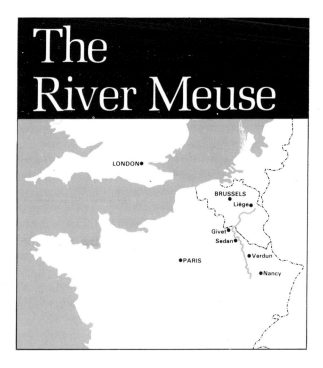

From   Liège, Belgium to Troussey, France.

Distance   Liège to the French frontier at Heer, 114 km/71 miles. Heer to Troussey, commonly known as the Canal de l'Est (Branche Nord), 272 km/169 miles.

Locks   Belgian section, 16. French section, 59.

Maximum craft dimensions   Belgian section, 100 m length × 12 m beam × 2·20 m draught × 3·70 m headroom/328 ft × 39·3 ft × 7·2 ft × 12·1 ft. French section, to the *Freycinet* standard, 38·50 m length × 5·20 m beam × 2·20 m draught × 3·70 m headroom/126·3 ft × 17 ft × 7·2 ft × 12·1 ft.

Navigation authorities, fees, opening times

For Belgium: Ingénieur en Chef-Directeur, Service d'Exploitation de Voies Navigables, Résidence Palace, 155 Rue de la Loi, Bruxelles. (For navigation dues, see page 180). The locks are available, roughly speaking, during daylight hours (details of the times appear on page 180).

For France: Direction Départementale de l'Equipement, 13 place Winston Churchill, 08 – Charleville. There is no navigation charge for pleasure craft. Locks are manned from 6.30 h to 19.30 h, April to September, with slightly reduced hours during the months of winter. They are closed for public holidays on Easter Monday, 1 May, 14 July, 11 November and 25 December.

Time to navigate   The minimum, allowing for exploring a little of the surrounding towns and countryside, would be one week. But the Meuse has so much to offer that two weeks or longer are preferable.

Maps and charts   For the Belgian Meuse, contact

The Editor, Etablissements d'Imprimerie Dantinne, Stree, Hainaut, or, Commisariat Général au Tourisme, Gare Centrale, 1000 Bruxelles. In France, the strip maps contained in Volume II, *Guide de la Navigation Intérieure*, (see Bibliography, page 233), are probably quite sufficient. However, a larger scale map of the French Meuse is published by *Journal de la Navigation* (address, see page 233).

Hire craft   At the time of writing there are no hire cruisers available on the Meuse, and the charter of boats in Holland for this purpose raises difficulties of frontier crossing. But their owners may be able to make the necessary arrangements. Otherwise, exploration must be carried out with private boats. At most of the larger towns on the Belgian section, tripping vessels operate for day cruises.

Through Belgium and France

The Meuse is a multi-national river, being navigable through north east France, Belgium and finally Holland, where as the Maas it eventually reaches its delta and the North Sea. Thus, it defies the country classification used in the rest of this Guide. The lower 214 km/133 miles downstream of Liège are largely unattractive and can in no way be compared with the gloriously lovely reaches around the French border: consequently, the description that follows deals only with the waterway above Liège.

Belgian section   The Meuse is generally a gentle waterway, slow-flowing and well suited to transport of large quantities of freight. For a long distance downstream of Liège, the river course is duplicated by the Albert Canal, an important connection to Antwerp and the North Sea. The

The magnificent valley of the Meuse at Lustin.

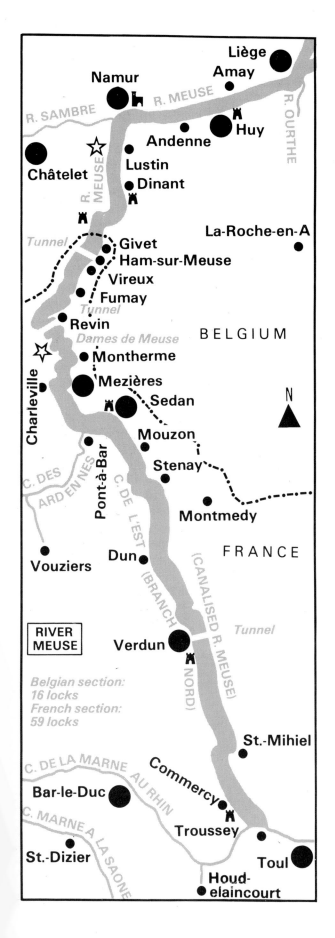

RIVER MEUSE

Belgian section:
16 locks
French section:
59 locks

River Ourthe also flows into the city from the south. The third largest town of Belgium, Liège is industrial especially along its riverfronts, where the scene is greatly enlivened by barge traffic and repair yards. Coal is a major freight. The lower slopes of slag heaps are cultivated as vegetable gardens. A little upstream of the town centre is a yacht harbour (opposite the Holiday Inn Hotel). Liège is obviously flourishing and worth a visit if only for the excellent shops.

Moving upriver, there is little to linger for in the 40 km/25 miles to Huy, although the constant barge traffic maintains its interest. Huy is dominated by a grey fortress – *La Citadelle* – built in 1818 by the Dutch and used as a concentration camp from 1940–44. A cable car may be taken to the summit. Trip boats operate from the quays and the bridge is decorated with flags of many nations. Scenery now begins to improve through the small town of Sclayn, where the lock has duplicated chambers. In spite of cement works, granite quarries and barge building years, the rural character of the best sections of the waterway is already evident: weekend and summer houses are dotted among the trees at the water's edge, for this is the start of one of Belgium's most beautiful areas – the densely wooded hills of the Ardennes. It was on the cliffs at Marche-les-Dames that King Albert suffered a fatal climbing accident in 1934.

At the junction with the River Sambre, Namur, like so many towns of the Meuse, has always been of great strategic importance. Once more, there are tripping boats and a huge fortress approached by a snaking motor road; the view of the river from the top is outstanding. *Fin de siècle* waterside hotels include the extravagant Casino, for this is very much a resort of the fashionable south of Belgium. Boating is catered for by yacht clubs and chandlers.

Perched at a dizzy height above the wooded cliffs of Lustin, the Belvedere restaurant is a fine objective for an uphill walk (about 1·8 km/1·1 miles from the river). The view is superb, especially when the rather frequent rain is absent. Application to the restaurant proprietor will (for a fee) produce a key to an iron gate, providing access to the fascinating network of narrow tunnels and caves carved out of the cliff face. The darkness within is intense.

Several locks with associated broad weirs lead to Dinant, whose main objective is tourism. Again, there is a fortress with cable car access, river excursions and a complex of caves – *La Grotte Merveilleuse* – with stalactites. Sheltered by a cliff rising from the town centre is a bulbous-spired church. Local specialities are gingerbread, copper objects and stuffed animals including wild boar

Scenes on the River Meuse in Belgium and France. Left: heavy traffic on the industrial reaches at Liège. Above: a misty summer morning at Monthermé, a leading centre of tourism for the most spectacular parts of the Meuse Valley. Here, in the Ardennes, the river twists and turns through wooded cliffs. Right: village fountain in Euville, in a style that is unmistakably French. Below: Belgian barge operators have the reputation of being hard-working and conscientious (or expressed otherwise, they are the first to display impatient bad temper if delayed for any reason!). But there was no denying that it was 5.30 h in mid-May when this laden example was photographed chugging through a dawn mist at Dames de Meuse.

from the woods. A short railway trip to Houyet can be made for a descent of the fast-flowing River Lesse by canoe or manned punt.

Beautiful wooded reaches lead past the rock pinnacle of Rocher Bayard and the Château de Freyr (16th–18th centuries), with gardens in the French style by Le Nôtre (open to the public). At the French border Belgian customs must be visited at Heer-Agimont and their French counterpart at Givet. In the absence of proper facilities pleasure craft must moor alongside a barge.

French section Known as the Canal de l'Est (branche Nord), navigation nevertheless continues along the natural course of the Meuse for the best part of 150 km/93 miles; even thereafter the lateral canal frequently enters the original line of the river. The 80 km/50 miles of the French Meuse describe an extremely circuitous route through most dramatic Ardennes forestland. Beyond Charleville, the countryside is flatter, more open and highly productive, with constant reminders of wartime engagements. After the admirable use and popularity of the Belgian river, the contrast with the wild and little visited French Meuse is remarkable. Gone for the greater part are the resort towns, bankside villas and passenger craft: for this is the north of France and those with money tend to gravitate towards the attractions of the southern, Mediterranean coast.

A considerable curiosity is the 565 m/618 yd tunnel at Ham-sur-Meuse, made necessary by a canal section which avoids a great loop of the river. Little patches of industry provide interest to the journey, for abundant wood supplies have long been responsible for iron foundries. But the chief impression here, is that the Meuse is a forest river.

Early morning at Les Dames de Meuse, *in the heart of the Ardennes.*

The waterway makes a wide sweep around Fumay, a brooding little quarry town. Ahead, successive folds of the hills become ever more blue in the distance and regularly spaced *péniches* purposefully plough through the still water. A further tunnel (110 m/120 yd) in Revin marks the by-passing of an almost completely circular bend of the Meuse. We shortly reach the navigation's *pièce de résistance* 4 km/2·5 miles of thickly wooded cliffs, known as *Les Dames de Meuse*, the *dames* in question, according to legend, being three unfaithful wives who were turned to stone by the intervention of divine rage! The hills tower to a height of 402 m/1319 ft, their tops frequently enshrouded in cloud. There can scarcely be a more dramatic reach of river anywhere in Europe.

The unnavigable River Semoy enters the Meuse at Monthermé, tourist centre for exploring the valleys of each watercourse. Several outstanding viewpoints can be reached by climbing into the hills. One is much inclined to linger in these idyllic surroundings, but although they rarely reach grandeur to match *Les Dames de Meuse*, the valley has many further delights in store. Charleville-Mézieres offers an urban interlude, the town having been built in the 17th century by Charles de Gonzague, Duke of Nevers and Rethel. He stands immortalised in statuesque form in the centre of the huge Place Ducal, a magnificent square of pink brick and brown stone arcaded buildings, now somewhat crumbling. A lively market occupies the middle of the square, certain stalls offering irresistible *bric-à-brac* such as antique 'peasant' furniture, agricultural implements and ancient decorative iron stoves. Astride a backwater, the ducal mill, resembling a town gateway, houses a first rate museum devoted to Ardennes slate and iron crafts and the local 19th-century poet Arthur Rimbaud.

Soon the waterway totally changes its character and becomes a place of meadows, willows and peaceful towns and villages, where the main street is frequently composed almost entirely of farmhouses with attendant chickens and barns piled with hay. A junction with the Canal des Ardennes is made at Pont-à-Bar (see page 113), shortly to be followed by Sedan, where Napoleon III surrendered to the Prussian Emperor in 1870. Occupied throughout the 1914–18 war and further damaged in 1940, Sedan is dominated by its fortified *château* and in carrying on its commercial life of the present day, one realises that the horrors of the past are not easily forgotten. Indeed, from here until the far side of Verdun, the sad reminders of war are ever present. Concrete pill boxes are dotted along the river banks and every ridge of the broad cornfields seems to be devoted to a war cemetery.

A little above the river in Mouzon stands an old toll gate, strangely large and defiant for such a small town. Crossing from the Ardennes *département* to Meuse near Pouilly-sur-Meuse, one encounters sleepy backwater villages where the public telephone box may well be sited in a barn and function only at specified times! Beds of reeds, white poplars and fishing punts complete the scene of inactivity. By now, the gradual change from river to canal is complete and locks occur at almost every village. In this little known and very pleasant corner of France, the canal continues to play an important part in the largely agricultural economy. Typical sights are an encampment of travelling people in a field with skinned rabbits hanging at the window of a van and landscaped gravel pits with well planned camping sites for the ubiquitous anglers. One decided asset of this route for the pleasure boatman is an almost total lack of others of the same kind: such a balance of commercial and cruising craft was to be found in England during the 1940s and early 1950s.

For all its beauty, this is a sad valley: in Dun, bridge railings with a stars and stripes motif commemorate establishment of an American bridgehead; there is a German cemetery of the 1914–18 war at a suitable distance from the centre of Liny-devant-Dun, with ranks of headstones and well maintained monument. Sixty years on, there must be few survivors to remember the dead and visits must annually become progressively less frequent. Man-sized shell cases decorate cottage doorway and village memorial alike, and in the rough copses rusting tin helmets lie mossed. It is a sobering thought that in many places few trees are older than the First World War.

And so to Verdun, a centre of battlefields whose

Poignant reminder of the Great War: a battle cemetery near Verdun.

current rôle in the tourist trade strikes a discordant note. For those who so wish, there are preserved forts and cemeteries to visit – there are more than 160 000 war graves in this valley of death. A great citadel, open to the public, is preserved as an underground centre of operations, with offices, kitchens and sleeping areas. There are good boat moorings in the city centre.

In the village of Lacroix – a small place of no apparent importance – is an astonishing classical fountain built in 1836: its Latin inscriptions, flamboyant stone fish and references to Meuse and Moselle suggest that arrival of a piped water supply was an event to remember. Predictably, more recent wording enables the structure to double as a very French war memorial. The writer once encountered a rather badly organised rowing regatta on the river in St Mihiel, a variation of the French provincial celebration which might equally well have been a fête or commemoration of Bastille Day. No one takes these occasions too seriously and enjoyment appears to be a prime concern.

The last town of note is Commercy, an iron-working district and well known as a source of *madeleines* (cakes). There is a substantial 18th-century *château*. Villages such as Euville are enduringly rural with great stacks of cut timber piled in readiness for the winter fires.

At Sorcy, the lock is mechanised and it appears that all locks along the canal are gradually being converted from hand-winders. Beyond, Troussey lies some distance from the junction with the Canal de la Marne au Rhin (see page 113), with a cement works dominating the otherwise pleasant setting of water meadows.

Holland

An old waterfront in the city of Zwolle, close to the Riv Ijssel.

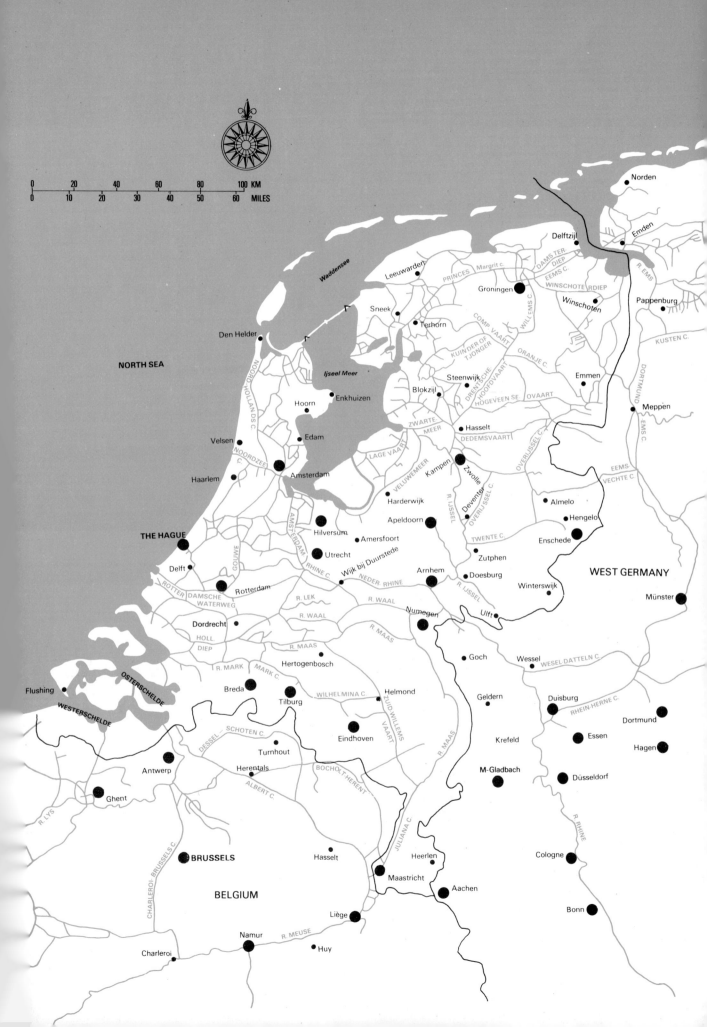

NORTH SEA

Waddensee

Norden

Delftzijl

Emden

R. EMS

Pappenburg

Den Helder

Leeuwarden

PRINCES   Margrit c.

DAMS TER. DIEP

EEMS C.

WINSCHOTE RDIEP

Groningen

Winschoten

WILLEMS C.

KUSTEN C.

Sneek

Terhorn

COMP VAART

KUINDER OF TJONGER

ORANJE C.

DORTMUND EMS C.

Ijseel Meer

Hoorn

Enkhuizen

Steenwijk

DRENTSCHE HOOFDVAART

HOGEVEEN SE. OVAART

Emmen

Meppen

NOORD HOLLANDS C.

Blokzijl

ZWARTE MEER

Edam

Hasselt

DEDEMSVAART

OVERIJSSEL C.

EEMS VECHTE C.

Velsen

NOORDZEE C.

LAGE VAART

VELUWEMEER

Kampen

Zwolle

Almelo

Haarlem

Amsterdam

Harderwijk

Deventer

OVERLIJSSEL C.

Hengelo

R. IJSSEL

TWENTE C.

Enschede

AMSTERDAM RHINE C.

Hilversum

Apeldoorn

THE HAGUE

Utrecht

Amersfoort

Zutphen

Wijk bij Duurstede

WEST GERMANY

GOUWE

Delft

NEDER. RHINE

Arnhem

Doesburg

R. IJSSEL

Winterswijk

ROTTERDAMSCHE WATERWEG

Rotterdam

R. LEK

R. WAAL

Numegen

Ulft

Münster

R. WAAL

Dordrecht

HOLL. DIEP

R. MAAS

R. MAAS

Goch

Wessel

WESEL-DATTELN C.

R. MARK

MARK C.

Hertogenbosch

Flushing

OSTERSCHELDE

Breda

WILHELMINA C.

Helmond

Geldern

Duisburg

RHEIN-HERNE C.

WESTERSCHELDE

Tilburg

ZUID WILLEMS VAART

Dortmund

DESSEL- SCHOTEN C.

Eindhoven

Krefeld

Essen

Hagen

Turnhout

R. MAAS

Antwerp

Herentals

BOCHOLT-HERENT

M-Gladbach

Düsseldorf

ALBERT C.

JULIANA C.

Ghent

R. LYS

BRUSSELS

Hasselt

Heerlen

Cologne

BELGIUM

Maastricht

Aachen

CHARLEROI: BRUSSELS C.

Liège

Bonn

R. RHINE

Namur

R. MEUSE

Charleroi

Huy

NORTH SEA

0   20   40   60   80   100 KM
0   10   20   30   40   50   60   MILES

The Waterways of Holland

Holland and canals are synonymous. In a country measuring about 193 km/120 miles east to west, and about 305 km/190 miles north to south, there are around 7400 km/4600 miles of navigable river and canal. It would seem to be a waterways enthusiast's paradise! Certainly, for inland cruising under sail there is probably nowhere to beat the Frisian Lakes. But among long distance motor boating devotees, Holland does not rate very high. For most of us, the interest in inland waterways derives from a range of factors: varied scenery including hills and tunnels, locks, aqueducts, and wooded river valleys. In Holland the countryside is, of course, flat in the extreme. Locks are few in number and the scenery of huge skies and endless open landscapes is not to everyone's taste.

This rather bland quality is, in part, compensated for by the beauty of many of the old brick-built towns, where brightly painted gabled houses line canals alive with houseboats and trading craft.

Holland is the only country in Western Europe with a specific Water Tourism Authority, and boating facilities are second to none. One in every 200 of the Dutch owns a boat, and well-equipped yacht harbours are established throughout the country. The people are particularly friendly, especially to British visitors, and English, although by no means universal, is widely encountered, especially among the younger city dwellers.

Hire craft, motor cruisers and sailing boats, can be chartered almost everywhere: a list of addresses can be obtained from the Dutch National Tourist Office. It is also possible to book a cabin on one of a number of passenger vessels, cruises through the bulb fields in late spring being most popular.

Statistically, Holland is among the most thickly populated nations in the world, a fact that is sometimes difficult to believe when black and white cows, windmills and red tiled farmhouses are the only features in a landscape that extends to a distant horizon. But it will be noticed that every portion of land is put to productive use. Since the 11th century, a constant battle has been waged to win land from the sea, first by building protective dykes and, after the 15th century, by using drainage mills to pump water from the areas so enclosed. Reclamation of the Ijsselmeer (formerly the Zuiderzee) has now added 218 530 hectares/540 000 acres of fertile farmland.

Infrequent locks mean that very considerable daily cruising distances can be achieved – an important consideration if the Dutch waterways are being used as a route between the coast and Belgium, France or Germany.

It is not practicable to describe the numerous cruising routes of Holland here. Study of the excellent tourist charts (see Bibliography, page 233) will help in planning a tour. Two standard reference books that provide useful information on places of interest and the kind of scenery to be expected are Philip Bristow's *Through the Dutch Canals* and *Holiday Cruising in the Netherlands*, by John Oliver.

Below: *on the Eemskanaal, near Groningen.* Opposite page: *barge enthusiasts sailing at Sneek, Friesland.*

Cars are halted on the canalside road as a coaster is launched sideways into the Winschoterdiep, near Groningen. Photograph, courtesy, Aerophoto Eelde.

A variety of Dutch barge bow shapes on a canal in Groningen. Here, as in most Netherlands' towns, houseboats are a popular and attractive addition to the scene.

A Cruise in the Netherlands

There must be few villages in Holland that are not served by the waterways network. Therefore it is possible to cruise from virtually any part of the country to anywhere else. Rather than follow the form established in other sections of this book, it has been decided to present an account of a two week journey made by the author. In this way, some of the flavour of the Dutch rivers and canals should become evident.

Books and charts *The Inland Waterways of the Netherlands*, by E Benest, in three volumes, and a series of 16 Dutch charts published by ANWB, the national waterway authority (see Bibliography, page 233), provided material for advance planning and for navigation purposes while cruising.

There were twelve of us in all: John Humphries, then Chairman of the Inland Waterways Association and his family and John Heap, present Chairman, with his wife, son and nephew. Although between us we possessed considerable expertise in inland boating, Holland was totally new territory apart from two short visits I had made while advising Government officials on how they might best exploit the cruising potential of their country.

Our plan was to fly from London to Amsterdam and take a minibus to Terhorne, a small town on the shores of the Sneekermeer in Friesland, one of the most popular boating regions. From here, we intended to head south, into the Ijsselmeer and so reach Amsterdam. The return route would depend on progress made during the outward journey. It was April, and arriving at the boatyard we were somewhat dismayed by the force of the wind, whipping up sizeable waves on the lake beyond. One of our two British-built Caribbean hire cruisers was missing, having been abandoned by the panic-stricken previous occupants. Holland in the spring sunshine, fields of brilliant tulips and blue skies had been our expectation. We had miscalculated!

The second cruiser eventually materialised, received a quick exterior polish, for it was drenched with spray, and we settled aboard. With some difficulty we located our position on the great lake and spent a blustery Saturday cruising along deep and wide canals where farm buildings with steep red tiled roofs presumably sheltered the legendary Friesland cattle, for the bright green fields were largely deserted. In early summer, this area must be quite delightful, a mass of wild flowers among the dozens of water-pumping windmills. We were glad that the boats had an interior helmsman's position in addition to the exposed wheel on the roof. In Holland, locks are few and frequently rise and fall only slight distances. We negotiated one, the Dreiwegsluis, appropriately with three entrances, and accepted from the keeper a useful present of plastic refuse sacks. Down the Heloma Vaart, we moored for the night in the peaceful village of Ossenzijl. Next day, being Sunday, brought enforced inactivity, for in these country districts at least, bridge keepers are not on duty and we had not yet realised that opening spans can frequently be raised by offering a packet of choice cigars.

The delay provided an opportunity for watching Dutch village life at close quarters. Local people cycled down the towpath in their best clothes to attend church services. From time to time the Ossenzijl milkman buzzed past our mooring in an ancient spoon-shaped wooden punt, stacked with churns and powered by a small outboard. Little thatched weekend retreats and farmhouses lined the banks and when we cast off in the late afternoon to cruise a short distance to Kalenburg for dinner ashore, a severe bearded individual, noting our red ensigns, hoisted a Union Jack on the flag staff at his front door.

Next day, anxious to make up for lost time, a 6.30 a.m. blow on our horn brought the bridge

Friesland is interlaced with tiny canals used by reed cutters, farmers and even local tradesmen making deliveries to outlying buildings.

Above: *Commercial traffic in full cry on the constantly busy waters of the River Ijssel near Doesburg.*

Below: *Blokzijl's town crier, complete with brass gong, pauses to exchange gossip with the local lock keeper.*

keeper from his cottage in pyjamas, a service which earned him a substantial tip. Breakfasting as we cruised, we soon came to a lock in Blokzijl with a remarkable circular brick-lined basin, surrounded by 17th-century gabled houses. By no means for the last time, we decided that the interest of Dutch canal cruising lies chiefly in the beauty of the towns that can be reached by water. It was here that I encountered a charming anachronism in the form of a somewhat scruffy, cigar-smoking, clog-wearing town crier in conversation with the lock keeper. From time to time he would recall his employment and give several hearty bangs on a brass gong, shout a few items of local news and then lapse into gossip once more. Enquiry revealed that his was a daily task.

We had now passed from Friesland into the Noordoost Polder, a reminder that towns like Blokzijl had once been coastal ports. This was a strange country of reedy lakes, forests of navigation markers and the first real sign of commercial barge traffic. A bouncy crossing of the Zwartemeer brought us to our first major town, Kampen, on the lower reaches of the great River Ijssel. Traffic on the water was never-ending, barges laden and unladen constantly passing in coupled groups of two or even three. The force of the stream was considerable, but with care, we discovered, it was possible to make reasonable headway upstream. Pausing for lunch in Kampen, we next moved downriver into the mêlée of commercial traffic and beyond some flashing beacons found ourselves in an angry expanse of open water – the Ketelmeer. Seemingly tiny lakes (when examined on the chart) were in reality very

Opposite page : *heavy traffic works through a lock on the Lower Rhine (Neder Rijn). As 24-hour operating is normal, craft are directed by means of traffic lights and amplified spoken instructions.*

large. In summer, the willow-covered islands and distant horizons would make this a delightful sailing area. But under leaden April skies we were pleased to reach the safety of a shallow lock – Roggebotsluis – for a brief respite from the wave-tossed water. The necessity of keeping strictly to the narrow buoyed channel was dramatically emphasised when our 8 knot speed was instantly reduced to nil on impact with a sandbar less than 3 m/10 ft from a marker post!

Beyond Elburg we were in a long inlet of the Ijsselmeer – the Veluwemeer – stretching far into the distance and with absolutely no shelter available. Some confidence was supplied by being able to follow in the wake of a small barge, but over 3 hours of constant crashing through waves of more than a metre/4 ft, shipping water over the bows and having the contents of the galley crashing about us, was a trying experience. Broads-built Caribbeans, we realised, were suprisingly seaworthy but such flat-bottomed craft are designed for inland use only. By evening, tired and not a little worried, we made for the fishing harbour of Harderwijk and dined off local smoked mackerel and eel. By a majority vote it was agreed that Amsterdam, on the far side of the Ijsselmeer, was beyond our scope: in these boats and weather conditions at least. Therefore, the next day we retraced our way, without incident, back to Kampen and the River Ijssel. By taking the river southwards, we still hoped to reach Amsterdam on enclosed waters.

Ahead of us now lay 122 km/76 miles of untamed lock-free river navigation, careering along at great speed and beset with motor barges for 24 hours a day. Bank protection takes the form of training walls built of loose boulders; avoidance of these and the working boats removed any possibility of boredom which might otherwise have been present, for the river banks are generally without much interest. It was necessary to consult our text books to interpret barge signals: those displaying a blue flag (blinking lights by night) indicated that they were abandoning the correct side of the fairway to benefit from reduced current or deeper water. In this way, we struggled upstream to Zwolle, a fortified city established in the 13th century, encircled by a wide canal. It was good to be off the river, safe for the night, and able to explore shops among which were several excellent ship's chandlers.

The following day's travel featured another ancient Hanseatic town, Deventer, but little else until our chosen night's mooring in a pleasure boat marina at Zutphen. Here, we enjoyed a cheese market, strolled around three large squares and

admired the formal displays of tulips, soon to reach a colourful climax. The obvious regard of the Dutch for indoor plants is prompted, it seemed to us, by the inhospitable winds that rage in the open air!

Ijsselkop marked a junction with the Neder Rijn, another huge river, but lacking the ferocity of the Ijssel. A series of vast and modern locks controls its flow and in any event our shaken confidence was rapidly returning! Packed like a pair of sardines at the back of the lock chambers, astern of many thousands of tons of ceaseless shipping, we were treated with utmost courtesy by the keepers and were privileged to be able to make conversation with some of the barge families whose immaculate floating homes give them a social standing that was never approached by their English counterparts.

Downstream of Arnhem, remembered for its great battle in September 1944, traffic appears to increase. A frantically busy water crossroads is reached at Wijk bij Duurstede, a small town dominated by a windmill so large that cars may drive through an archway in the base. This is the junction of the Neder Rijn, River Lek and the modern Amsterdam-Rijn Canal which has locks on each side of the crossing. A water policeman with binoculars permanently raised, controls signals from a sort of lighthouse. We learned that one flashing yellow light indicates vessels approaching from the west; two, that they are coming from the Prinses Marijkesluis to the east; three, that craft are

Below: *Dominated by the brick-built tower of its church: the town of Hasselt on the Zwarte Water.*
Opposite page: *cruising into the old city of Utrecht.*

Above: *Holland is justly proud of her watery history and boat relics are carefully preserved in many of the leading museums. This charming lady originally adorned a small wooden canal barge, but now lives in the Zuiderzee Museum at Enkhuizen.* Right: *sharply pitched roofs, a bascule bridge and a windmill: these are the ubiquitous ingredients of the rural Dutch waterway. This scene is near Groningen.*

converging from both directions! We turned hard to starboard and found ourselves in a queue for the Prinses Irenesluis, a pair of really huge duplicated chambers with guillotine gates and reputedly the largest locks in Europe. We were *lowered* from river level at the tail of a fleet of barges and found ourselves on the equivalent of a canal motorway, constantly buffeted by a violent wash.

Now within easy reach of both Amsterdam and Rotterdam, we calculated that we had time to visit neither if we were to be back at the Friesland base on schedule. Therefore, we set our sights on the old university city of Utrecht, which lies off this major navigation. Its system of old waterways, considerably less extensive than that of Amsterdam, is quite as charming and picturesque. Twin pairs of low brick arched bridges, each bearing a carved stone name plaque, carry streets over the water. Broad tree-lined quays once provided barge unloading facilities to the cellars of old buildings, many of them now converted into night clubs and boutiques.

We were able to linger here for the best part of a day, mooring in the heart of the city. Disappointed at our failure to achieve our original objective, Utrecht was nonetheless an agreeable substitute. All too soon it was time to begin our homeward journey, so we retraced our way back along the Amsterdam-Rijn Canal.

The wind continued to blow with unabated strength and it was only with difficulty that we were able to manoeuvre into a congested little commercial harbour in the shadow of Wijk bij Duurstede's great windmill for a safe night's mooring. Instead of being a tiny riverbank village (as it had seemed from the water) it turned out to have an extensive shopping centre. It was like arriving in a Cotswold hamlet, only to discover Oxford Street hidden round the back. In the gusty showers of twilight, I came upon a huge ruined castle set in a gloomy tree-covered park: a perfect setting for a film with vampires and grave robbers.

Next day, Sunday, witnessed a decrease in Rijn

traffic to a mere one barge every five minutes. For several hours we happily made our way upriver until suddenly the engine of my Caribbean coughed and stopped dead. Our sister ship took us in tow and we swung into a small marina on the outskirts of Arnhem. A telephone call to the owners resulted in the eventual discovery that a vital section of the drive assembly was smashed beyond repair. For 48 hours we endured a display of total inefficiency while Northern Europe was scoured for a replacement. Eventually, it was suggested that the operational cruiser should tow her lame sister back to Terhorn, a distance of perhaps 320 km/200 miles. With no great enthusiasm, but clinging tenaciously to what remained of our holiday, we set off, festooned with towlines and flying the regulation signal flags to indicate our predicament.

There were problems encountered in the tide race that marks the junction of Rijn and Ijssel, but by now we had the current in our favour. Within five minutes it was obvious that this fact made the

operation suicidal. The towed cruiser crashed about uncontrollably in the frequent wash of passing barges; nylon ropes snapped and one of the steel cleats was even torn out of the deck. Only by a miracle did we avoid collision with the piers of a railway bridge. Time and again, in trying to keep clear of breasted barges we grated on the rocks at the side of the river. I glanced at John Humphries whose anguished face agreed with my declaration that 'I have done some pretty foolhardy things with boats in my time, but never anything as lunatic as this!' With a sickening crunch we were thrown on to the bank.

By a fortunate combination of circumstances, the services of a river police tug were obtained, the crippled boat taken to the safety of a harbour in Doesburg and the Humphries family departed for London, relieved to have got away with nothing worse than an amputated holiday! I now transferred to the Heap's boat, to help them cruise back to Terhorn.

Above: *an unladen barge hurries down the Neder Rijn near Arnhem.*

Below: *the great Rijn-Lek windmill of Wijk bij Duurstede.*

In the interest of variety, we decided to take a new route home after leaving the Ijssel at Zwolle. Once on the Zwarte Water, never ending big barges and rocky shores became a bad memory and the few days that remained provided us with generally carefree boating. True, we were almost written off outside Baarlo Lock when an approaching barge somehow failed to notice us. But the weather had turned almost summer-like and the prospect of revisiting the magnificent circular basin of Blokzijl encouraged us to press on into the evening. In this way, we found ourselves on a totally deserted and very muddy little country canal – the Steenwijker Diep. Hitherto, all navigations, large and small, had been admirably maintained, but this deserted by-way resembled the most unkempt parts of the Staffordshire & Worcestershire Canal. Full throttle

produced a bare 3 kph/2 mph and a trail of gas bubbles in our wake. That night, moored in Blokzijl, a family of duck plodded endlessly over our coachroof, doing their utmost to keep us awake with a peculiarly penetrating 'kwaakjing'!

Our last major waterway was the busy Princes Margriet Canal, with the bustling yachting town of Sneek beyond. Here were dozens of beautifully preserved old sailing barges, used as houseboats or holiday craft and we were able to appreciate that Friesland is a summer boating paradise.

A lesson learned from our extended journey was that the smaller, rural waterways of Holland are more suited to cruising than the great trade routes. And nowhere are they more inviting than in the lovely province of Friesland.

Sweden

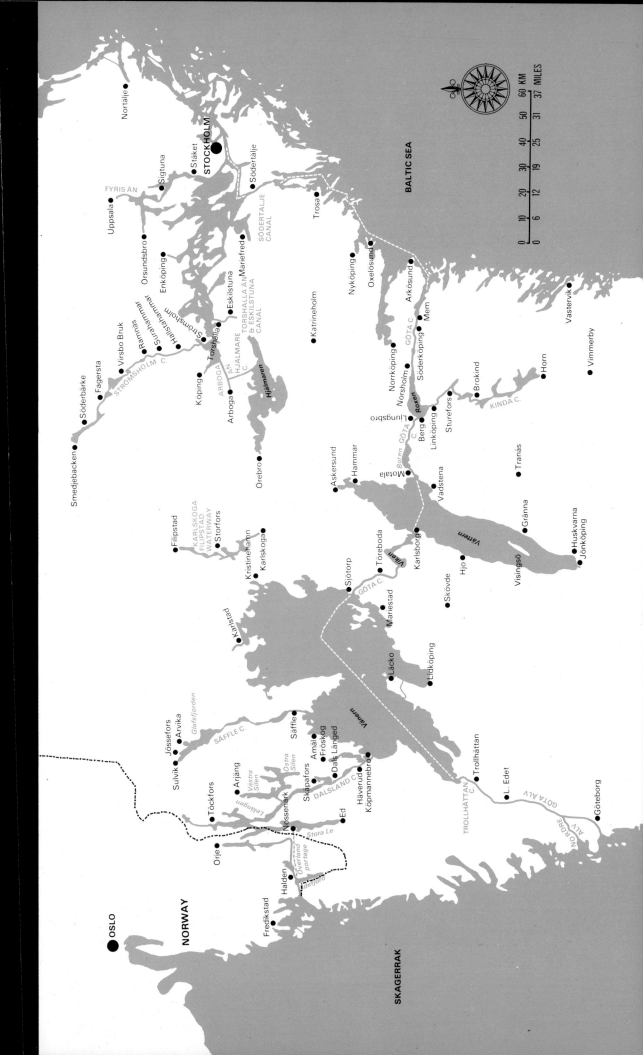

The Waterways of Sweden

The fame of the Göta Canal is international, but less well known are many other navigations scattered throughout Central Sweden which were created as extensions to the main coast to coast line, opened in 1832. Most of these are in good navigational condition, having suffered a period of decline from the reduction of commercial traffic to the present boom in pleasure boating.

In a northern land like Sweden, where long, cold and dark winters give way to warm summers and short nights, boating is perhaps the leading outdoor activity. Hardly a village is without its cluster of small boats for use on lake, river and canal. The fishing is of a legendary quality and the deserted countryside itself is wild, unpolluted and extremely beautiful.

Although foreign visitors by boat are still something of a rarity, the Swedes will offer an outstanding welcome. Their language is a difficult one for the British to master, but English is commonly spoken, especially by the younger people.

Of all the countries covered in this Guide, Sweden is perhaps the least like Britain. This is a land of lake and forest with a population of only 8 million, spread at the rate of 18 people per km²/46 per mile² (the United Kingdom has 250 and Holland about 380).

Notable features of Central Sweden, which contains most of the few large towns, are the wooden buildings constructed from the forests which cover more than half the country's surface area. These range from little waterside cottages, painted in pastel shades or the distinctive Falu red, obtained from iron ore, to substantial wooden churches, sometimes with separate timber bell towers. The Swedes are great lovers of the countryside and many city dwellers have second homes in the rural areas. Often the national flag flies on a gilt-topped pole in the unfenced garden surrounded by rocks and pine trees. Another standard feature of front gardens is the painted or copper spherical sundial, almost a national emblem.

Wild elk roam the forests; in a country that was the birthplace of the great 18th-century botanist Carl Linnaeus, it is fitting that wild flowers of many varieties will be found in profusion in spring and summer. Equally, town squares and waterside gardens are generally attractively planted and landscaped, with emphasis on huge, natural rockeries of granite. In late May and early June tulips flourish everywhere, from the formal lakeside beds at Vadstena to the clusters grouped around town square statues, executed with a grace that typifies modern Swedish design and architecture.

One could spend many happy summers cruising the connected lakes and waterways alone; a lifetime exploring thousands of miles of canoeable but otherwise unclassified small rivers. Passenger craft ply over most routes during the summer months, offering day trips or, in the case of the Göta Canal route an extended hotel boat voyage. Some details are given on page 214. Small self-drive cruisers and cabin sailing craft are widely available for hire (page 216).

Short of bringing ones own sea-going cruiser to Sweden by water, possibly the best way of getting afloat is to bring a trailed cruiser from Britain on the North Sea car ferry. In this way, several distinct areas could be visited during a three or four-week holiday. The range of itineraries available is extensive, but might well include the major part of the Göta Canal (one way); the glorious Dalsland Canal (believed by many to be the most beautiful lakeland waterway in Europe); and one of the other navigations such as the Kinda Canal.

Even if one normally recoils from the notion of canoeing on the grounds of its being too energetic for a holiday, Sweden could make you change your

Sweden's endless forests ensure that plastic has not ousted timber for boat building.

mind. Party holidays by Canadian canoe on the lakes and rivers of Värmland are arranged by the Nordmarken Canoe Centre at Arjäng (connected to the Dalsland Canal system). Rather more 'easy going' and suitable for families, is the all-inclusive holiday offered by the Fryksdalens Canoe Centre, 68500, Torsby, Värmland. Costs for one week's hire of a two-seater canoe, life jackets, maps, itineraries, food parcels and overnight stops at chalet-type shelters are about 400 Sw.Cr.

Dalsland Canal

From the west shore of Vänern at Köpmannehamn to Lake Stora Le, with connections to a series of other lakes.

Distance   254 km/158 miles.

Locks   29, 22·7 m length × 4·2 m beam × 1·8 m draught/74·4 ft × 13·7 ft × 5·9 ft draught. Headroom is 11·5 m/37·7 ft south of Töcksfors and 5 m/16·4 ft beyond.

Navigation authority   Dalsland Canal AB, Box 89 S–662 00 Åmål. Tel: 0532–143 66.

Utter peace, as evening falls on the superb Dalsland Canal.

Pleasure craft fees   For each lock, dues are payable at the rate of 3 Sw.Cr. – 6 Sw.Cr., depending on size of craft. An additional 'personal' fee of 1.50 Sw.Cr. is paid to the keeper of each lock and bridge.

Opening times   From 1 June to 31 August only. Locks are closed on Sundays, except in July when an additional fee of 50 per cent is payable.

Regulations   These are in no way unreasonable and are listed in the official guide. Two points worth repeating are that passenger vessels on regular schedules have priority at locks; and the speed limit on all artificial canal sections is 2½ knots.

Map   Chart 136, Dalsland Canal, published by Sjöfartsverket, Stockholm, at about 36 Sw.Cr.

Books and guides   A brief guide with regulations, costs etc is published by the navigation authority (see also the Bibliography, page 233).

Passenger craft   Three vessels operate between June and August (check times in advance.) *Dalsland* provides a return cruise of 3 hours 30 minutes from Håverud, including the locks and aqueduct, lakes Åklången and Råvarpen and a half hour pause to inspect Bronze Age rock carvings in Tisselskog Forest. All-day cruises are available on board *Dalslandia* and *Storholmen* between Köpmannebro and Bengtsfors or vice versa. Rail and bus

connections are made in order to return passengers to the starting point. Tickets may be ordered in advance through local tourist offices.

Cruiser hire Addresses of firms with craft convenient for the Dalsland Canal may be obtained from offices of the Swedish Tourist Board.

The Dalsland Canal system is easily one of the most attractive inland cruising areas in Europe. Comprising a number of lakes in the provinces of Dalsland, Värmland and a small portion of Norway, a mere 10 km/6 miles is made up of artificial canal. The rest is spectacularly unspoiled lakeland. Although now well frequented by pleasure-craft, more than 2000 passages being made each summer, it is literally possible to moor for the night out of sight of any building or indeed sign of man's activity. For half an hour absolutely nothing will disturb the intense stillness: then the spell is broken by a fish rising or a pair of duck flying overhead! For the most part, the lake water is so pure that one drinks it without a second thought.

Two factors prompted building of the navigation: to carry ironworks and timber products to Lake Väner and hence the rest of Central Sweden and to create a link between Sweden and Norway, then united under one crown. Working from 1864 until 1896, the engineer Nils Ericson created canals to join the lakes. Commercial traffic had declined by the mid-20th century to the extent that abandonment was considered. Fortunately, the very high touristic value of the navigation was appreciated; since 1971 about £125 000 has been spent on improvements, including some lock mechanisation, provision of markers and other facilities.

The most outstanding feature is the canal at Håverud, where a 15 m/50 ft waterfall barred the way between one lake and another. Four locks were carved from the granite of the ravine, and where it was necessary to cross from one bank to the other a 33 m/108 ft span iron aqueduct was constructed. The works are bridged by a railway and, at an extreme height, a road. The white wooden railings

---

One of the most remarkable canal complexes anywhere is this short link between two lakes at Håverud on the Dalsland Canal. The change in levels of about 15 m/50 ft is overcome by a series of four locks fitted into a ravine complete with waterfall. Where the cliff becomes too steep to accommodate the canal, it elegantly leaps from one side to the other by means of a cast iron trough aqueduct. A railway bridge also spans the gap, and high above that is a single arched road bridge. Work began on this outstanding navigation in 1864.

A Swedish Albin cruiser works through a staircase lock at Dals Långed. Electric gear is fitted to gates and paddles.

---

of a footpath zig-zag up the cliff face, while a charming timber gazebo surveys the entire wonderful complex.

One can moor to a jetty at Högsbyn to inspect Bronze Age palaeoglyphs – more than 300 designs carved in rock, depicting hands, footprints and ships. Dals Långed, with its four locks and paper works, is a centre for Dalsland arts and crafts. One friendly shop specialises in everything necessary for hunting, shooting and fishing in this land of lake and forest. Here also you can buy such unusual (but typically Swedish) souvenirs as spherical copper sundials and gilded knobs for flagpoles. At the mid-18th-century industrial (but not in the least unpleasant) town of Billingsfors is a 500-seat open air theatre, originally built for the mill workers.

At Nössemark, half way down Lake Stora Le, there are facilities for lifting craft of up to 9 m length × 3·5 m beam/29·5 ft × 11·4 ft with a weight under 3 tons, out of the water and via a 30 km/18·5 mile overland portage to Halden and the extensive Haldenvassdraget system of Norwegian waterways. A week's notice for this service, which costs around 300 Sw.Cr., depending on craft size, should be given to AB Norman & Söner, Nössemark, S-660 01 Ed, Sweden. They may also be able to cope with larger craft. This exercise, in addition to its considerable novelty, would make possible a round trip to the Norway coast and via Göteborg and the Trollhätte Canal back to Dalsland.

Säffle Canal

From the north west shore of Vänern, via the papermills of Säffle and the River By to Arvika.
Distance About 90 km/56 miles.
Locks 1, in Säffle, 42 m length × 7·5 m beam × 3 m draught/137 ft × 24·6 ft × 9·8 ft.
Navigation authority Information from the office at Säffle Lock, where a small charge is levied.
Map Chart 134, published by Sjöfartsverket, Stockholm at about 36 Sw.Cr.

More of a lake navigation than an artificial waterway, the Säffle Canal largely comprises the Glafsfjord lake. Small commercial ships remain regular users. Säffle Lock is an admirable structure built of rough granite sides, overlooked by a substantial timber keeper's house, richly carved. The author's own chief interest in the region was to visit the quayside engineering works of A B Seffle Motorverkstad, from which the hot bulb semi-diesel engine of his converted ice breaker *Parry II* was despatched to England in 1961. Machinery of this type is legendary in Scandinavia and became synonymous with early powered narrow boats of the British canals.

Above: *a small coaster on the Säffle Canal, near its junction with Vänern. Although timber processing works are widespread, they are rarely unsightly and it is obvious that the Swedes are concerned to protect the visual amenities of their country.*

Karlskoga – Filipstad Navigation

From Karlskoga to Filipstad, beginning close to the north east shore of Lake Väner, but totally isolated from all other waterways.
Distance 70 km/43 miles.
Locks 5, 21 m length × 3·6 m beam × 1·2 m draught/69 ft × 11·8 ft × 3·9 ft.
Navigation authority Information from the Storfors Båtklubb or the Bofors Motorbåtsklubb, Riksbyggevägen 2B, 691 00 Karlskoga.
Map Available from the Bofors Motorbåtsklubb.

Passing through the River Tims and the Bjurbackens Canal, this chain of lakes is of use to the visitor with a trailed boat. A railway bridge at Nässund, near the half way mark, limits headroom to a mere 1·9 m/6·2 ft. A reasonable charge is levied at the first lock.

Kinda Canal

From Linköping, on the southern side of Lake Roxen (Göta Canal) to Horn.
Distance 80 km/50 miles.
Locks 15, 24·5 m length × 4·5 m beam × 1·3 m draught × 3·09 m headroom/80·3 ft × 14·7 ft × 4·2 ft × 10·1 ft.
Navigation authority Information from Östergötlands Turisttrafikforbund, Stora Torget 1, Box 202, 581 02 Linköping.
Map *Kinda Kanal och Dess Sjösystem*, published by the Kinda Kanals Vänner and available in Linköping.
Passenger craft A tripping vessel runs the length of the navigation during the summer season.

This especially lovely waterway was opened in 1872, but fairly soon commercial traffic deserted it. In 1971, as the result of a campaign by local restorationists, it was reopened throughout on account of its great beauty and attraction to tourists. At Hackefors is Sweden's deepest lock with a rise and fall of 6 m/19·6 ft. A visit to the harbour office in Linköping is advised to obtain details of the opening times for certain of the lift and swing bridges together with prevailing water levels in the lakes. The journey is mainly along the River Stångå and a series of narrow lakes. At Hovetorp, before arriving at Lake Stora Rängen, there is a 4-rise lock,

followed by 2·5 km/1·5 miles of idyllic canal with overhanging trees. The 10 km/6 mile long Lake Ämmern, reached by means of the short Skedevi Canal, boasts heron colonies around its shores. The line eventually ends near the Småland border at Horn, notable for the baroque spire of its church. The Kinda Canal provides a thoroughly enjoyable excursion off the main line of the Göta Canal, and if at all possible several days should be allocated for its exploration.

Lake Mälar

This huge expanse of water, constituting Sweden's third largest lake, is said to contain around 10 000 islands. Stretching from Stockholm, on the Baltic Coast, almost to Strömsholm, the lake is about 117 km/73 miles long. Perfectly suited to pleasure boating under power or sail, Mälaren is also served by passenger craft connecting Stockholm with various destinations around its shores. Navigation is covered by three charts, numbers 111, 112 and 113, published by Sjöfartsverket, Stockholm, at about 36 Sw.Cr. each. Parts of the lake are used by sea-going ships.

In addition to connections with the Baltic via Stockholm and the Södertälje Canal (page 226), various other waterways may be reached from Mälaren as follows:

Below: *The Göta Canal in Motala, designed as a waterway 'new town'. Here, the Canal Company established its headquarters and today many industries have been added to the original plan to build lock gates, bridges and canal boats. The warehouses in timber cladding are protected with* Falu rödfärg *or red paint manufactured from iron oxides, and widely used on wooden structures throughout Sweden.*

Strömsholms Canal

From Lake Mälar near Strömsholm to Smedjebacken.

Distance 100 km/62 miles.

Locks 26, 20·1 m length × 5 m beam × 1·35 m draught × 2·5 m headroom/65·9 ft × 16·4 ft × 4·4 ft × 8·2 ft.

Navigation authority Strömsholms Kanal AB, 73400, Hallstahammar, Sweden.

Map Strömsholms Kanal, chart 115, published by Sjöfartsverket, Stockholm at about 36 Sw.Cr.

All but 11 km/6·8 miles of the route consists of natural lakes. These were joined by canals in the middle of the 19th century for the carriage of coal and iron ore. When commercial traffic came to an end in 1945, the works were abandoned, being completely rebuilt between 1962 and 1970, at a cost of about £240 000, contributed in part by the region with 50 per cent aid from central government.

The area of the canal is fairly heavily populated by Swedish standards, with steelworks at regular intervals. This should not be taken to imply objectionable industrialisation, for this is a clean and pleasing part of the country. A steelworks museum may be visited in Surahammar, while Ångelsberg has a very early blast furnace in a complex in use from 1590.

The marinas and other pleasure boating facilities have been admirably planned, and much information will be found in a booklet *Strömsholms*

Kanal Informerar, available free from the proprietors. At the top of the Hallstahammar Locks, one of the original canal company buildings now houses a first rate canal museum.

Lake Hjälmar and associated Waterways

This 75 km/46 mile wide lake lies south west of Mälaren. Dotted with innumerable islands and inclined to produce sizeable seas in a south west wind, it is covered by chart 114 from Sjöfartsverket, Stockholm. It is reached via the Arboga River and the Hjälmare Canal, opened in 1639 but totally rebuilt in the last century. The canal is 13 km/8 miles long, with 9 locks. Maximum dimensions are 32·1 m length × 7·1 m beam × 2·1 m draught/105·3 ft × 23·2 ft × 6·8 ft. After a period of dereliction, it was reopened for pleasure craft in 1965, and features a totally deserted course, partly through birch woods. There is a canal museum at Hällby Docka.

Fyris River

A chain of lakes to the north east of Mälaren leads via the towns of Stäket and Sigtuna to the Fyris River; thence to the historical university town of Uppsala. Here is the largest cathedral in Sweden, dating in its present form from 1893, and the much restored 16th-century castle of Gustavus Vasa. The Linnaean Gardens, established in 1655, and associated museum commemmorate the world famous botanist who died here in 1778.

A sight-seeing tour of the canals of Göteborg.

The Göta Canal

From   Göteborg to Stockholm.

Distance   630 km/391 miles. Comprising a number of individual waterways, much of the route is via river, lake and even sea:

Göteborg to (Lake) Vänern is via the River Göta (Göta Älv) and the Trollhätte Canal, 82 km/51 miles. After crossing Vänern, the Göta Canal proper is entered at Sjötorp; this passes through artifical channels and lakes to Mem, on the east coast of Sweden, 190 km/118 miles.

One final section of canal remains, the 3 km/2 mile Södertälje Canal, linking the coastal part with Mälaren, the lake system on which Stockholm is situated.

Locks   Göteborg to Vänern, 6, including the famous series of 4 at Trollhättan.

On the Göta Canal itself, there are 58.

Södertälje Canal, one.

Maximum craft dimensions   Göteborg to Vänern 88 m length × 13·1 m beam × 5·3m draught/288 ft × 43 ft × 17·3 ft. Draught on the Nordre Älv (North River), an alternative route from the River Göta which by-passes Göteborg, is reduced to 3 m/9·8 ft.

Göta Canal, Sjötorp to Mem, 32 m length × 7 m beam × 2·82 m draught/105 ft × 23 ft × 9·25 ft. Södertälje Canal, 120·7 m length × 18·28 m beam × 5·48 m draught/396 ft × 60 ft × 18 ft. Headroom is unrestricted throughout the whole voyage.

Navigation authority   Göta Kanalbolag, 591 01 Motala, Sweden. Tel: 0141–101 45.

Pleasure craft fees

Overall length	Göteborg – Vänern	Vänern – Vättern	Vättern – the Baltic	Vänern – the Baltic
up to 6 m/19·6 ft	40 Sw.Cr.	77 Sw.Cr.	99 Sw.Cr.	165 Sw.Cr.
6–9 m/19·6 ft – 29·5 ft	40 Sw.Cr.	116 Sw.Cr.	149 Sw.Cr.	250 Sw.Cr.
9–12 m/29·5 ft – 39·3 ft	80 Sw. Cr.	161 Sw.Cr.	207 Sw.Cr.	350 Sw.Cr.
12 m/39·3 ft or over	120 Sw.Cr.	231 Sw.Cr.	297 Sw.Cr.	480 Sw.Cr.

Boats making a return passage through the whole waterway during the same year qualify for a 25 per cent reduction in fees for the second journey. The fees quoted are those in force during 1977. Payment may be arranged in advance or at various toll points *en route*.

Opening times   Unless closed by ice, locks between Göteborg and Vänern are open throughout the year. The west line of the canal (Vänern – Vättern) is normally operational between mid-April and early December, ice permitting. Locks are closed on Sundays before 15 May and after 15 September. The east line (Motala – the Baltic) operates from 15 May, 8.00 h until 15 September, 20.00 h. With the exception of the passenger craft which navigate day and night, canal locks are available between 8.00 h and 20.00 h, with a lunch break from noon to 12.30 h. However, once negotiation of a lock or bridge has been commenced, it is allowed to be completed.

Time to navigate   At one extreme, the passenger craft working between Göteborg and Stockholm complete the journey in 57 hours, but this is achieved by day and night working. Depending on the number of detours to be made along connecting waterways, a minimum cruising time of two weeks for the one way journey is advisable for pleasure boats. Equally, the connected waterways network of this part of Sweden provides scope for cruising throughout the summer opening season.

Regulations   Full details of conditions applying to pleasure craft are contained in *Guide for Tourists Göta Canal – Trollhätte Canal*, published by Göta Kanalbolag, 591 01 Motala.

Maps and charts   Basic cruising maps, with details of locks, beacons, lighthouses etc for the entire Göta Canal route, together with most connected navigations, are contained in *Svensk Lots Del IV, 1972*, published by Sjöfartsverket, Stockholm, at about 36 Sw.Cr. (in Swedish). The same firm produces a series of large-scale charts which are essential for safe navigation of all but the canal sections; these are listed in a catalogue and cost about 23·50 Sw.Cr. each.

A good tourist map of the route is available in a

folder providing brief topographical information in Swedish and English. Bookshops in most towns in the area have copies.

Books and guides   See the Bibliography.

Passenger craft   The Göta Canal offers Europe's classic passenger boat journey. Indeed, there is nothing quite like it to be found anywhere in the world. Consider the attractions: one passes from coast to coast across a beautiful country of lakes, green farmland and majestic pine forests. From time to time during the voyage there is the interest of the early 19th-century canal structures: the locks, bridges, warehouses and keepers' cottages. At the height of summer the days are exceptionally long and when darkness does fall, it is but a brief interlude before dawn brings with it another extended day. Almost unique to Sweden, the canal voyage is accepted as the leading method of getting to know a country intimately and as such it is perhaps the first choice of all tourist excursions. Since the middle of the last century, passenger voyages along the Göta Canal have been popular with travellers from many countries.

The Göta Canal Steamship Co Ltd (Rederiaktiebolaget Göta Canal), S–401 24 Göteborg, PO Box 272, Hotellplatsen 2. Tel: 031–17 76 15; and S–111 30 Stockholm, Branch Office, Skeppsbron 16. Tel: 08–10 04 57 or 10 77 52, operates a fleet of three magnificent vessels whose distinctively lofty superstructures contrive to fit maximum accommodation into the restricted hull size dictated by the confines of the locks. All built as steamers, they are now converted to diesel propulsion. *Juno* was launched in 1874, *Wilhelm Tham* in 1912 and *Diana* in 1931. The *Wilhelm* has the distinction of having run aground in fog in the Trosa archipelago and sinking in 1933. Respectively, they carry 74 cabin and 76 deck passengers, 70 and 80 and 73 and 77. Operating between Göteborg and Stockholm (or vice versa), they run for three full days, travelling by day and night. It is easy to appreciate the economic reasons for this seemingly hurried progress, but one cannot escape the impression that this system is for the tourist rather than the true traveller. Inevitably you miss a proportion of the glorious scenery, either through darkness or the sheer necessity of catching a little sleep. Conversely, there is a very special luxury in being able to lie in bed and watch the

Commanding a splendid position at the head of a peninsula at the southern end of Lake Väner is Läckö Castle, converted in the 17th century into a baroque palace. With 248 rooms, it is open to the public and served by a well-designed guest harbour.

watery world pass by outside; and the sounds and sensations of working through locks in the hours of darkness are treats that you will always remember.

In addition to 'full board' passengers, 'short stage' travellers may join the boats at various points throughout the route. Both accommodation and catering are to a high standard. There are several opportunities for sight seeing, and passengers can also disembark as the little ships negotiate flights of locks.

English speaking people will experience few language difficulties (much the same applies throughout the more accessible parts of the country), and although the majority of fellow passengers will be natives, perhaps twenty per cent come from North America with smaller groups of Germans, Danes, Dutchmen and English people.

There are about 70 sailings during the season, from mid-May until mid-September. At 1977 rates, the all-inclusive fare is from 550 Sw.Cr. to 975 Sw.Cr., depending on the accommodation selected. If required, cars can be transported by trailer from one end of the route to the other.

Cruiser hire   Sweden is a nation of inland boaters, and there is scarcely a village that does not have its cluster of motor cruisers or small cabin sailing craft. Self-drive cruisers are widely available at various places, although there may be some difficulty in locating a yard convenient for exploration of the whole route. One of the most popular types is the range of home-produced Albin craft, power and auxiliary/sail. Well equipped for their purpose, they tend to offer slightly more spartan domestic facilities than their counterparts in England. Full details may be obtained from offices of the Swedish Tourist Board. One further way of enjoying a holiday is to stray off the beaten track by hiring ones own Canadian canoe. This form of camping holiday offers the possibility of discovering smaller rivers and lakes. The Tourist Board recommends some 50 routes of varying length and difficulty.

The Building of the Göta Canal

Nearly nine per cent of the area of Sweden is made up of lakes – some 96 000 of them all told. The four largest are all situated in the central part of the country – Vänern, Vättern, Hjälmaren and Mälaren. Vänern, at 5550 km²/2140 mile², is the third largest in Europe. In such broken terrain, it was long a dream to create a navigation for the carriage of goods and passengers between the North Sea and the Baltic, but the link was not finally achieved until canal building techniques had been fully perfected in the early 19th century. The Göta

Canal route was not brought to realisation until 1832.

First attempts were carried out in the early 16th century by Bishop Hans Brask. The Reformation put paid to the Bishop's scheme, although John, son of King Gustavus Vasa, subsequently made excavations in an attempt to link Lake Roxen with the Baltic via the port of Söderköping. Some remains of the work can be seen near the line of the successful navigation at Norsholm.

At the western end a lock was constructed on the Göta River at Lilla Edet in 1607. The stone chamber is preserved near the site of the present ship lock. Simultaneously, the Karls Grav Canal was dug to by-pass the Rånnum waterfalls and thus enable craft to proceed a short distance from Vänern towards the river.

One huge and daunting obstacle lay between Vänern and its river outlet to the North Sea: the famous Trollhättan falls. Tumbling 32·4 m/106 ft down a rock-strewn ravine, all goods had to be loaded onto waggons before their journey could be resumed by water. During the 18th century success was virtually achieved when a series of locks was engineered by Christopher Polhem; at a critical moment a vital dam burst and most of the structures blasted out of granite were rendered useless. There

The Trollhätte Canal during construction, from a drawing made while work was in progress.

was suspicion that local people who derived an income from the trans-shipment of freight had resorted to sabotage! Finally, in 1800 the Trollhättan locks were opened to traffic. They consisted of a 3-chamber staircase at the lower end with further locks at the top. Now the great lake and a sizeable part of the Swedish interior were directly connected with Göteborg and the sea.

Among the directors of the Trollhätte Canal was Admiral Count Baltzar Bogislaus von Platen. Inspired by what had already been achieved, he conducted research into creating a waterway onwards to link with the east coast – the Göta Canal. It became his all-consuming obsession and although he did not quite live to see its completion, it is certain that but for Count von Platen the navigation would not have been built. In his own land the Count is accorded virtually total credit for the enterprise, and it is almost possible to remain unaware that Britain's genius canal builder Thomas Telford was responsible for much of the engineering expertise. Certainly, the partnership of the Swede and the Scot was a remarkable one.

There were a number of similar features between the Göta and Telford's other great coast to coast navigation, the Caledonian Canal. Each relied on a series of lakes linked by artificial cuts; both waterways utilised lock staircases where practicable. Not surprisingly, there are common design elements in lock gates, swing bridges and paddle gear. The Caledonian was begun in 1803 in an era when Britain led the world in canal building. Platen asked Telford to inspect the line of the Göta in 1808, and with the help of two assistants he did so within a 20-day period for which he was paid £5·25 a day, a princely salary. Various changes were made to the route and the number and size of locks was increased.

A public company was formed in 1810 to carry out the work, the shares being oversubscribed by 100 per cent. Headquarters were established at one of four planned canal 'new towns' – Motala, and the work of construction commenced, labour being supplied by the Östgöta Grenadiers.

In complete accordance with normal practice of the day, estimates of cost and completion time were wildly wrong. Telford considered that £400 000 and ten years would see the project finished. In fact some 22 years and more than £2 million were required. As many as 5000 soldiers and sailors were employed on the works at one time, 60 000 being involved in all.

Telford and Platen conducted a long and detailed correspondence as the building progressed, although the British engineer's involvement in

home projects allowed him to make only one more visit to Sweden, in 1813. Swedish engineers were despatched to Britain to gain practical experience in the art of canal construction, but heavy reliance was also placed on a team of British experts resident in Sweden. Quantities of equipment ranging from dredgers to lock gates, paddle gear and steam engines were sent across the North Sea, and as skills were acquired the necessary imitations were produced in the company's Motala workshops.

All manner of hardships were endured: severe ice in winter frequently brought progress to a complete halt. The engineer Samuel Bagge, who had supervised completion of the Trollhätte Canal, was drowned with his companions when a storm on Lake Vätter swamped their boat.

Statistically, the canal was a huge undertaking: 85 km/53 miles of artificial cut added to 214 km/133 miles of lake navigation required excavation of 280 million ft³/8 million m³ of earth; 7 million ft³/198 170 m³ of granite had to be blasted away and almost 9 million ft³/254 790 m³ of masonry laid; 58 locks and 35 bridges were produced along with a comprehensive range of temporary buildings needed to serve the great work force. In all, about 80 million man hours were logged.

By 1822, the western line (Vänern – Vättern) was ready to carry traffic and earn revenue for the company. Platen died in 1829, aged 64, and thus was denied the pleasure of accompanying the King, Queen and Crown Prince of Sweden when the royal yacht *Esplendian* sailed into the eastern line of the canal at Mem in September 1832. The great work was finished and ships could now cross Sweden from coast to coast.

Freight and passenger craft quickly became established, the paddle steamer *Admiral von Platen* starting a regular run between Stockholm and Göteborg in 1834 with ten passengers; the journey was then accomplished in nine days. By 1890, between 4000 and 5000 vessels were passing through each year, the majority of the commercial boats being sailing schooners loading about 220 tons. Horses or oxen were used to haul them through the canal sections. At the time of the First World War, most craft were fitted with auxiliary engines such as the monumental single cylinder semi-diesels that are so much a part of Scandinavian marine engineering. By 1939, commercial transits of the waterway numbered 5273, but thereafter trade on the canal proper has declined almost to the point of extinction. With a maximum payload of about 250 tons craft are no longer considered competitive with other transport forms. There are

Traditional Swedish fishing boats, owned and maintained by enthusiasts, at a small shipyard on the canal at Klevbrinken near Söderköping.

Below: *rocky shores fringed with pine woods where the Göta Canal crosses Lake Viken.*

Centre picture: *Timber rafts at Olshammar, Lake Vättern.* Above: *A BP fuel tanker on the Södertälje Canal, south of Stockholm.*

current demands to enlarge locks and other structures at least on the Vänern – Vättern section, thus enabling 3500-ton ships to reach towns like Motala and Vadstena from the North Sea.

Locks on the Trollhätte Canal, enlarged in 1844 by the engineer Nils Ericson, were again rebuilt between 1909 and 1916. All three systems can be seen to this day. Further improvements were made to the channel of the canal between 1972 and 1975. Each year about 7000 cargo ships up to 3500 tons navigate the waterway from Göteborg to Vänern. Oil and products associated with forestry account for about half the 4 million annual tonnage of goods. Thus, the Trollhätte Canal continues to play an important rôle in the economy of Central Sweden.

At the eastern end of the route, the short Södertälje Canal between the Baltic and Lake Mälar, was enlarged in 1819 and again in 1924.

Journey Across Sweden

Göteborg (Gothenburg)   For many visitors the first sight of Sweden is from the deck of a North Sea ferry as it negotiates an archipelago of tiny rocky islands, in the mouth of the Göta River estuary. The second largest city and the chief seaport of the country, Göteborg boasts 10 miles/16 km of quays. It is a modern, well-planned city provided with green parks and avenues of trees. Founded only in 1619, it was built on the model of a Dutch town, with canals laid out as moats as a contribution to the system of fortifications. Some of these remain with landscaped banks. Small craft can be hired and there is a regular tripping boat service lasting 55 minutes. The city has excellent shops; two of the

many attractions are the Shipping Museum (*Sjöfartsmuseum*) and the Museum of Industrial History (*Industrihistoriska Samlingarna*).

The wide Göta River leaves the city in somewhat industrial surroundings, but these soon give way to rocky, wooded banks and agricultural scenery that is typical of this central part of Sweden. Navigational aids include lights and marker posts, and although frequented by sea-going ships, the waterway is in no sense a difficult one for small pleasure craft.

Kungälv   Situated at the confluence of the Göta River and the Nordre Älv (North River), this is a pretty little town, dominated by the ruins of medieval Bohus Castle. In the early 14th century, this was a leading stronghold: its twin round towers are known as 'Father's Hat' and 'Mother's Bonnet'.

Lilla Edet   A patch of industrial works at Älvängen and an evil-smelling sulphite plant at Göta punctuate a largely rural landscape of small villages set in rich pastures with the majority of buildings constructed in timber with red tiled roofs. Lilla Edet is a little town with hydro-electric works and a paper mill. It was here that Sweden's first pound lock was opened in 1607. Its stone-faced remains are preserved in a small landscaped garden. A subsequent lock, built in the 1830s was replaced by the present large Ströms Lock in 1916. As usual at such sites of industrial archaeological interest, there is a sign board illustrating development of

One of the fleet of substantial motor ships that regularly travel up the Göta River to Lake Väner.

water transport over the centuries. A devastating fire destroyed much of the wooden town in 1888.

Trollhättan Well wooded cliffs herald the approach of this famous canal town where a series of nine waterfalls proved an insuperable barrier to further navigation for almost two centuries. Modern entry to the canal bypass of the Göta River is up a remarkable staircase of three ship-sized lock chambers on the right bank of the river. These are fully manned and mechanised, and although somewhat daunting to small craft are operated with full consideration by the keepers. A splendidly spiky wooden watch tower crowns the summit of this ravine, torn out of the solid granite. One further single lock lifts craft to the uppermost level. The area is justly popular with tourists and is well served by an anticipated collection of refreshment kiosks and souvenir sellers. Nearby the 1844-built locks (arranged in staircases of 4, 4 and 3 chambers) although disused, are substantially intact. To complete the picture of progressive improvement, the 3- and 5-chambered staircases of 1800 are preserved gateless but extremely impressive, especially when one realises that the labouring was contrived with nothing more sophisticated than gun powder and wheelbarrows. The disused cuts provide a haven for several lovingly preserved former trading craft – bluff-bowed motorised sailing barges, massively built in varnished or white-painted timber.

The lower approach to Trollhättan Locks, blasted from solid granite.

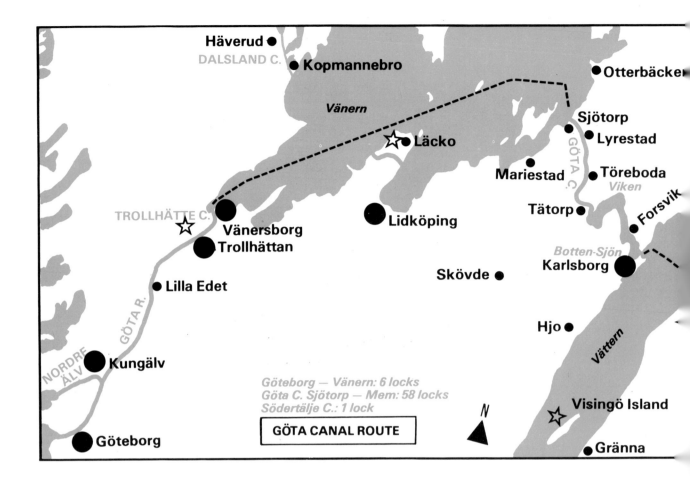

Häverud ●
DALSLAND C.
● Kopmannebro
● Otterbäcke

Vänern

☆ Läcko

Sjötorp
● Lyrestad

Mariestad ●
Töreboda ●
Viken

Tätorp ●
Forsvik

TROLLHÄTTE C.
☆ Vänersborg
● Trollhättan

Botten-Sjön
Karlsborg ●

● Lilla Edet

GÖTA R.

Skövde ●

Hjo ●

NORDRE ÄLV

● Kungälv

Göteborg — Vänern: 6 locks
Göta C. Sjötorp — Mem: 58 locks
Södertälje C.: 1 lock

GÖTA CANAL ROUTE

N

Vättern

☆ Visingö Island

● Göteborg

● Gränna

Since 1906 no fewer than 13 electrical generating sets have been installed to capitalise on the ideal location of Trollhättan for creation of power supplies. About one sixth of Sweden's electrical consumption is produced by the Trollhätte Power Works, which has stations in the north of the country as well.

Now that the falls have been tamed, the 32 m/105 ft descent has resulted in a mere trickle of water flowing between the giant boulders. So that the remarkable visual spectacle of the waterfalls is not totally lost, they are allowed to perform in their natural state during specified 'Fall Days', beginning on the third Thursday of July. Flood lighting at night further enhances the attraction.

Since 1754, Swedish monarchs have written their names in rock at the Kings' Cave (Kungsgrottan). When King Karl XVI Gustav contributed to this unique 'visitors' book in 1975, he was the eleventh sovereign to do so.

Vänersborg After the Trollhättan Locks, the navigation rejoins the Göta River, passing the twin hills Halleberg and Hunneberg, an area with signs of pre-historic man and Viking burial mounds. Now follows the Karls Grav (Charles' Cut), the early 17th-century canal which by-passed the Rånnum Falls and since enlarged to accommodate seagoing ships. Craft pass through a lock at Brinkerbergskullen and soon arrive at Vänersborg on the shores of the southern part of the great Lake Väner. This small town of 19 000 people was almost totally destroyed by fire in 1834.

Lake Väner This huge lake – third largest sheet of inland water in Europe – is about 140 km/87 miles across at its widest point and covers some 5550 km²/2140 mile². Most is fairly shallow and there are plenty of safe commercial harbours and navigation lights around the shores. Reasonable precautions should be taken for the crossing, for sizeable seas can develop. The chart course for the beginning of the Göta Canal lies close to the southern side of the lake, but there is scope for extended cruising elsewhere. Connections are made with two other waterways: the exquisite Dalsland Canal system, entered at Kopmannehamn (see page 207) and the Säffle Canal, reached via Säffle (see page 210), both on the west shore.

If remaining on the normal route for the Göta Canal one port of call that should on no account be missed is Läckö Castle, situated near the top of the

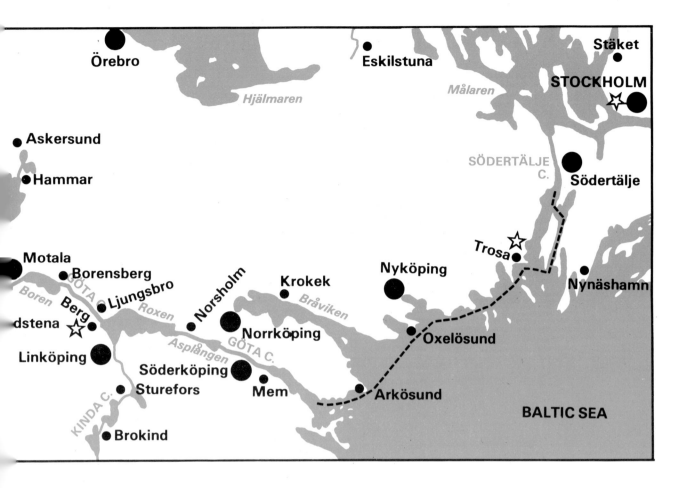

Källand peninsula on the southern shore. There is an excellent pleasure craft harbour and camping site of the wholly uncommercialised kind that is common in Sweden. The castle is a square white-washed structure built on rocks above the water, with slated towers at each corner. Founded in the Middle Ages, it was converted in the 17th century into a sumptuous baroque palace by Count Magnus Gabriel de la Gardie. Confiscated in 1681 by Charles XI, it is now administered by the State and open to the public. The locality is pervaded by the pure air and utter stillness which one soon comes to associate with Sweden. In the quiet of the evening, the distant throb of cargo vessels' engines can be heard far away across the lake. A magnificent waterside path opposite the castle leads over smooth rocks and between pine trees.

Vänern's surroundings, while deserted and seen from the water apparently consisting largely of pine forest, are in fact partly composed of prosperous farmland. Ploughed fields are of a sandy, almost blonde soil in spring; by harvest time they have become a golden sea of corn. There are windmills of thatch and timber on rocky knolls, red-painted farm houses, weekend cottages and wicker duck nests among the reeds around the lake fringe. Beaches of fine sand alternate with rocky shores.

Sjötorp A group of several large islands in the lake north of Mariestad are clustered near the canal entrance at Sjötorp. We are now in authentic Baron von Platen country and the Göta Canal remains much as it did when first opened to traffic. A small wooden pyramid-shaped lighthouse marks the way into a little harbour and the beginning of a series of eight locks. Paddle gear is mounted on the gates and worked either by wheels or a portable windlass with four spokes. The gates themselves are opened and closed by pushing on a wooden bar projecting from a wheel on the ground; by walking a number of revolutions (rather in the manner of a horse gin) the operation is completed. Above a swing bridge with intricately carved wooden keeper's house, is a sizeable basin and boat yard. Fuel supplies can be obtained from the nearby garage.

Lyrestad This is a small town with a church near the canal bank. Surroundings are peaceful meadows as the waterway climbs, lock by lock.

Töreboda Eleven locks at Norrkvarn, Godhögen, Riksberg and Hajstorp, include several short staircases. To speed passage of craft, electrical gear has been added to some of the paddles. The architecture of the keepers' houses is particularly pleasing, with fretted timber barge boarding. Situated on the main railway between Göteborg and Stockholm, Töreboda provides a brief urban intrusion. We have now reached the canal's summit level, 91·4 m/300 ft above sea level.

Tåtorp A lock with elegant iron bascule bridge marks the end of this part of the canal before entering Lake Viken. Here, as at other points, an illuminated signal with moving arm (like the older variety of railway signal) informs craft whether the way ahead is clear or if another boat is approaching the lock. Little boathouses, fishermen and small cruisers indicate that this is a popular weekend resort on the lakeside.

Lake Viken An island-filled stretch of water in the shape of an inverted V. The nature of the shore is graphically described by a prohibition sign erected on the end of a jetty at one point: a diver is shown about to strike the water where a large rock lurks beneath the surface! A ferry transports up to eight cars across a narrows of the lake at Brosunden (free of charge). This, and a series of marker posts warning of rocks necessitates a degree of navigational care.

Forsvik A short canal section links Viken with Bottensjön Lake. There is a lock with double bascule road bridge and a navigation channel so narrow that the somewhat stout passenger boats, with fenders trailing, virtually touch each rocky bank as they work round the sharp bends. Forsvik is an old established industrial centre with Sweden's first ever sawmill.

Karlsborg Situated on the Vanäs peninsula, projecting into Lake Vätter, this is a fortress town founded in 1820. There are impressive earthworks and stone towers, with roadways passing through the walls via narrow gateways. As usual in such a fine waterside setting, there is a good camping site and the Canal Hotel.

Lake Vätter Fourth largest lake in Europe, it is long and narrow, almost 130 km/80 miles from top to bottom and about 30 km/19 miles wide between the canal's entry points. Extending to a depth of 23 m/75 ft below sea level, and with exceptionally clear water, Vättern has a formidable reputation and navigation should only be attempted by small craft in settled weather. Conversely, in the calm of warm summer evenings it is said that strange mirages appear on the surface: dreamlike cities and fleets of ships! There are numerous attractions in the towns scattered about Vättern's shores. From Gränna a 20-minute boat trip may be taken to the 14 km/8·5 mile long island of Visingsö. Horse-

drawn charabancs carry tourists on a sight-seeing tour. Inhabited in Stone Age times, 12th and 13th-century kings lived in Näs Castle, now a ruin at the southern end.

Jönköping is a large town at the bottom tip of the lake and now known for its safety match industry. It boasts an outstanding late 17th-century town hall. By following the Taberg River about 13 km/8 miles (not navigable) the village of Taberg is reached with its impressive 343 m/1124 ft iron ore mountain. A museum of mining illustrates extraction techniques of iron ore, vanadium and titanium.

One of Sweden's most historic towns is Vadstena on the lake's east shore and well worth making a short detour by water before entering the canal again at Motala. The most impressive feature is a massive castle built as a fortress by Gustavus Vasa in the mid-16th century. Encircled by a navigable moat, this is a mooring of true grandeur. The country's patron saint, Bridget, founded a nunnery here in the 14th century. A considerable force in the political and moral affairs of the Kingdom, she was also a woman whose displeasure was best avoided. There are several recorded instances of sudden death following seemingly harmless actions like pouring water on the saint from a window!

Motala It is the Göta Canal's own town, founded by Platen as the nerve centre for his great engineering plan. Today, the original workshops where lock gates, dredgers and tugs were constructed still serve the waterway and the canal company has its headquarters here. These traditions are continued by an independent enterprise specialising in the building of many varieties of heavy machinery. Near the entrance to a large harbour is a pleasure boat yard, and beyond it the canal disappears, via a lock, into a tree-lined cutting. Some distance outside the town Platen lies buried in a truly monumental canalside grave, surmounted by a granite monolith.

Lake Boren Five locks at Borenshult lower the canal into Lake Boren, a beautiful region of Östergötland, where a fertile agricultural plain extends southwards, with dense forest to the north. Several castles and manor houses can be seen from the water.

Borensberg to Berg Locks Several locks and swing bridges punctuate the journey through a tree-shaded length of canal, with Lake Norrbysj providing glimpses of sparkling water to the north. In early summer the brilliant yellow fields of rape seed – a widespread Swedish crop – contrast with the Falu red of farm buildings. This section comes to a spectacular and abrupt end as a series of 15 locks at Berg plunge 40 m/132 ft to Lake Roxen. At the lower end, these are in the form of a most impressive 7-chamber staircase, constituting the greatest engineering work of the route. Each bears the name of a member of the Swedish royal family. The towpath can become quite crowded as sightseers congregate to watch boats pass through, with the wide, blue waters of Lake Roxen as a backdrop at the lower end of the vista. Mechanisation reduces the labour of lock keepers.

Lake Roxen   Almost 27 km/17 miles of open water must now be crossed before embarking on the next canal section. Among places of particular interest are the ruins of mid-17th-century Stänorp Castle (north west shore), destroyed by fire in 1789. A whole range of ancillary buildings including

chapel and farmhouse survive. Open to the public, the castle tower provides a panorama over the lake.

Linköping (south west shore) boasts one of the country's finest cathedrals, mainly 13th to 16th centuries. The other outstanding attraction is the Östergötland Museum, where exhibits range from local handicrafts to masterpieces of European painting. The city is one boarding point for the passenger craft which make day-long trips along the Kinda Canal, connecting Lake Roxen with Horn (see page 210).

Norsholm   A tiny railway village with boatyard and a lock and delightful moorings at the edge of Roxen. A fascinating indication of the low volume of car traffic, compared with most other parts of

---

Below: *Swedish craftsmanship in timber is evident in this bridge keeper's house at Sjötorp.* Bottom: *the first lock of the Göta Canal proper, at Sjötorp, where craft are*

guided in from Vänern by the elegant wooden lighthouse. Below: *the fortress castle of Vadstena, where pleasure cruisers have moorings in the moat.*

Europe, is that the E4 motorway crosses the canal via a swing bridge which must be opened to enable boats to pass through! Several locks through meadowland and woods bring the canal to another lake, the long and narrow Asplången.

Almost for the first time, sizeable embankments characterise the very pleasant course of the waterway.

Klevbrinken   Some of the former swing bridges have been replaced by rolling structures that retreat into the banks to allow craft to pass. A rustic dockyard at Klevbrinken, whose facilities include a commodious dry dock, specialises in maintenance of traditional wooden craft – former commercial fishing boats now owned by enthusiasts. Nine locks after Asplången bring us to the small medieval town of Söderköping.

Söderköping   A charming little place, with shops arranged around a large square complete with modern sculpture and fountain, a seemingly essential ingredient of the Swedish urban landscape. There are boat yards with numerous private craft, ranging from fibreglass dinghies and cruisers to venerable old working boats, whose exhaust chimneys announce the presence of the ubiquitous Scandinavian semi-diesel engines, with their characteristic irregular beat. A market town as long ago as the 10th century, Söderköping has a pair of 13th-century churches. At Mem, the Göta Canal's final lock (and the last to be built) lowers craft into the Slätbaken, a long inlet of the Baltic. As the channel narrows, the ruined tower of mid-15th-century Stegeborg Castle will be seen on a small island. During the 17th century this was one of Sweden's most impressive fortified castles.

Passenger boat Diana *passes beneath a double-leaf bascule bridge spanning the lock at Forsvik.*

The Baltic Passage   For inland craft the prospect of an open sea passage is rather daunting. But here, in the Östergötland archipelago and through the thousands of skerries of Sweden's east coast there is always adequate shelter. From Mem to the final short canal section at Södertälje it is about 175 km/109 miles, but much of this distance is between the islands which contribute greatly to the interest of the voyage.

Oxelösund is an industrial port, one of Sweden's leading export centres from which iron ore is shipped. Further on, Trosa lies near the mouth of the Trosa River which winds through the town centre, lined with small boats moored outside appealing timber houses on each bank. A popular resort area, there are comprehensive boating facilities and camping sites among pine trees overlooking the island-filled sea. Everywhere here is a boating paradise which would take years to know at all well. A long steam up the Himmerfiord eventually brings us to Södertälje.

Södertälje   This ancient town began to expand with the opening of the 3 km/1·8 mile Södertälje Canal in 1819. Creating a shipping link between the Baltic and Mälaren – the huge lake system on which Stockholm is situated – the canal has a single large lock near the town centre, constructed to its present dimensions in 1924. Even in the heart of town, where moorings are within a stone's throw of splendid shops, there is little impression of urbanisation. A notable feature of the waterway is a high level road bridge with double bascule opening span.

Stockholm   The country's capital is reached by navigating through the east end of Lake Mälar, the third largest stretch of water in Sweden. About 3 hours are necessary to complete the journey from Södertälje. Stockholm is rather like a microcosm of the country as a whole. Formed on a series of bridged islands, this beautiful Venice of the north is dominated by its brick and copper roofed City Hall of 1923 which seems to float on water. Its numerous historical and modern buildings, royal palace and castles lie outside the descriptive scope of this book. Certainly, there is sufficient interest in the area to merit a holiday here alone. Boat excursions to various parts of Lake Mälar are available throughout the summer.

Lake Mälar   Something of the order of 10 000 islands are dotted across this magnificent cruising ground, about 117 km/73 miles long and up to 45 km/28 miles wide. The map on page 205 indicates a whole range of further navigations connected with the lake. These are briefly described at the beginning of the section on Sweden.

Glossary

The world of inland waterways has produced a vocabulary of its own. These are words still in everyday use on the canals that will rarely be found in the most comprehensive dictionary. The list that follows also includes a selection of historical terms. Emphasis has, not unnaturally, been placed on English words; many of these are, however, applicable to all countries of Western Europe.

A

Aegre The term in use on the River Trent to describe the tidal wave that affects the lower reaches of that waterway. Known on the Severn and elsewhere as a 'bore'.

Animals A canal boatman's name for donkeys and mules, which were widely used for towing craft on the Worcester & Birmingham Canal and associated waterways. They normally worked in pairs.

Boat boy and animal on the Droitwich Canal, circa 1910.

B

Bad road The effect of locks being set against a boat (chambers empty if a boat is descending a flight). Otherwise a difficult canal journey in general. Opposite expression is 'a good road'.

Balance beam The arms of timber or metal that extend from a lock gate and act as a lever to open the gate.

Bank ranger A lengthsman or maintenance man whose duties include regular inspection of canal banks to check for erosion and for possible sites of trouble such as where a breach could occur.

Bank side The side of a waterway opposite the towpath.

Barge Correctly describes only those craft that are roughly twice as wide as the beam of a 7 ft/2·13 m narrow boat. There are many types of barge: unpowered, motorised and sailing.

Barrow boys The boatmen who negotiated the more difficult waters of the Barrow Navigation in Ireland. They acquired greater skills than boaters who remained on the Grand Canal and Shannon.

Beam A timber plank, fitting across the hold of a narrow boat, into which a stand or mast is slotted.

Billy boy A sailing barge similar to a Humber keel and navigating the same waters of the north east of England, but designed more specifically for sea work.

Blades A boat's propeller.

Blow A collapse of a section of canal bank. Alternatively (as a verb) it can be applied to lock gates bursting under the weight of water.

Blow to To provide a warning to possible approaching craft at bridges or bends in the navigation where the view is restricted. Today a horn is used, but formerly, on horse boats, a whip was cracked.

Bobbins Large smooth wooden beads (often decorated) threaded on to the traces of a boat horse to prevent the harness chafing.

A Seffle hot bulb semi diesel engine.

Bolinder A widely used early semi-diesel engine introduced to British canal boats from Sweden about 1910. Generally preheated with a blowlamp before starting, and usually with a single cylinder, it gave a characteristic uneven exhaust beat, especially when idling. Still to be seen in preserved or converted narrow boats, and 16-hp versions are retained in maintenance barges on Ireland's Grand Canal. Similar units include Seffles and Gardiners.

Bollard A mooring post on a lock, wharf or quayside.

Bore A tidal wave affecting the lower reaches of the Rivers Severn and Parrett and Solway Firth. Known as an 'aegre' on the Trent and *mascaret* on the Seine.

Bostocks Blocks of wood, stone or concrete on which a boat is supported in a drydock, leaving working space under the hull.

Bow-haul To haul a boat by hand, for example, where a motor and a butty are working through a flight of narrow locks. Originally craft were bow-hauled by teams of men on certain river navigations.

Breast The vertical post of a lock gate furthest from its hanging. Also (as a verb) to force a lock gate against a head of water by using the boat's engine.

Breast up To work a pair of narrow boats or barges (usually through flights of wide locks) tied side by side. Continental *péniches* sometimes travel lashed in groups of two or three on rivers including the Seine and Saône.

Bridge hole The channel where a canal passes under a bridge; on some canals a likely place in which to get stemmed up.

Buckby can A sought-after pattern of decorated narrow boat water can (generally with a wooden handle) formerly available from a shop at Buckby, Northants.

Bulk The decorative curved canvas device, padded with straw, sometimes used as an alternative to a cratch at the front of a narrow boat.

Bull's eye A thick pebble-like circular pane of glass inserted in the cabin roof of a narrow boat.

Butty The unpowered boat in a pair, towed by the 'motor'. Normally applied to narrow boats, though short boats also worked the

motor/butty system. As a verb, to work in company with another boat or boats, when shorthanded, in bad wintry conditions, or to share locks.

Bye-trader Anyone or any firm carrying freight on a waterway other than the navigation authority.

C

Campshedding Bank protection in steel, timber, concrete or asbestos.

Chalico A composition prepared from cow hair, horse dung and tar and applied hot to the seams of wooden boats and barges to render them watertight.

Cill A stone bar against which the underwater part of a lock gate closes. Its height determines the maximum draught of a boat that can pass through the waterway.

Cloth up To cover the hold of a freight boat with waterproof sheets. A narrow boat is equipped with side cloths and top cloths.

Clough North of England expression for lock paddle. On the Leeds & Liverpool Canal, ground paddles are known as 'Jack cloughs'. Also once used in the Fens, where it applied to the navigation opening in a staunch or flash lock.

Cock boat A small dinghy or similar craft used as a tender to a larger vessel such as a motor barge or sailing barge.

Compartment boat A rectangular tank-like boat used in trains for carrying coal on the Aire & Calder Navigation and other Yorkshire waterways. Otherwise known as a Tom Pudding or pan. A modern form is the BACAT (barge aboard catamaran container).

Coracle An ancient and rudimentary portable craft used for fishing in rivers and made from plaited laths covered with a tarred fabric.

Cot A swim-ended wooden punt used for fishing in Ulster's Lough Erne and capable of being dragged sledge-like overland. Still built in traditional form.

Cotting A Fen term for removing the roots of rushes and weeds growing in a waterway.

Counter The small deck at the stern of a motor narrow boat. A counter stern is an overhanging deck at the stern of certain sailing cruisers.

Crank A windlass or handle, for working lock paddles.

Cratch Normally a wooden triangular construction at the forward end of a narrow boat hold supporting the top planks.

Culvert A small watercourse that might take a steam under a canal, or carry surplus water round a lock from the higher to the lower level.

Curragh Similar in construction to a coracle, but elongated and rowed by two, three or four men. They survive as seagoing boats off the west coast of Ireland, but were once employed on

Braunston-painted Buckby can.

inland waters also. Nearly circular curraghs were used on the River Boyne.

Cut The commonly used term for a canal or an artificial channel on a river navigation, eg, lock cut.

Cutter A hooped band (usually brass) over the cabin-top exhaust pipe of a narrow boat to deflect the exhaust from tunnel roofs and the undersides of bridges.

D

Day boats Canal boats used to carry freight over short distances and without cabins or any more than the simplest of accommodation. Called 'Joey boats' on the Birmingham Canal Navigations.

Dipper A general purpose domestic metal bowl with handle on one side used on narrow boats. Often decorated with flowers and other painted designs.

Narrow boat dipper.

Dollies Towing studs on the counter of a motor narrow boat. More common are 'bollards', especially on larger craft.

Doors A Fens term for lock gates.

Double lock A Southern Ireland term for a 2-rise lock staircase, where one chamber leads directly to the next via a common pair of gates. (Grand Canal or Barrow Navigation.) Elsewhere refers to lock chambers duplicated side by side.

Draw To open a paddle at a lock.

Dumb boat An unmotorised boat or barge, horsedrawn, towed as a butty, or hauled by a towpath tractor or tug.

Dummy bows A short wedge-shaped boat attached to the head of a train of Tom Puddings and able to cleave the water better than the square end of the leading compartment.

Dydle A Norfolk term, meaning to dredge out.

E

Ebb The tidal flow in a river as it runs to the sea. The opposite is to 'flow' or 'make'.

Eye Fenland term for lock paddle aperture through which the water flows.

F

Fan Barge propeller.

Fair lead A metal guide for mooring ropes on the bows or stern quarters of a boat. Also to be seen on lock gates (Sheffield & South Yorkshire Navigation) to prevent tow ropes being snagged on the handrails.

Feeder A watercourse bringing supplies to a canal from a reservoir or similar source.

Fender (or 'fendoff') Traditionally of plaited rope and now commonly an inflated plastic tube or ball, for protecting parts of a boat hull from

Rope fender on the stern of a motor narrow boat.

damage when in contact with lock sides, walls and other boats. On working boats car tyres or baulks of timber are utilised.

Fest ropes A pair of ropes attached one to each side of a Fen lighter, the loose ends being passed round the steering pole to steady it when in use.

Flash An accumulated body of water that is suddenly released to increase draught in a section of river. Alternatively, a lake caused by mining subsidence as in the salt producing areas of the Trent & Mersey Canal near Middlewich or the upper reaches of the River Weaver. Known in the Black country as a 'swag'.

Flash lock A navigation staunch or weir, consisting of a lock fitted with only one set of movable gates, instead of the two sets at each end of a conventional pound lock. Also known as a 'half lock'.

Flasher Another name for a lock ground paddle.

Flat A sailing barge from the Mersey or Weaver. Alternatively, a small workboat used by maintenance gangs, either open or fitted with an upright cabin.

Fleet Norfolk term for a shallow in a navigation.

Flight A series of canal locks located in close succession, but with short intervening pounds.

Flood lock A lock designed to control flood levels and during summer conditions of normal flow left open at each end. Examples occur on the River Soar and the Sheffield & South Yorkshire Navigation.

Flood paddles Sluices on long canal levels enabling surplus water to be drawn off into a convenient stream or watercourse should there be any danger of the banks bursting or being inundated.

Flow See Ebb.

Fly-boat A working boat running at maximum speed, usually 24 hours a day, to deliver urgent cargoes. To 'run fly' is to navigate nonstop.

Fly paddles An alternative name for ground paddles.

Fresh (or 'freshet') An increase in the flow of a river navigation following heavy rain.

G

Galley beam (or 'lintel') A stout cross-member above each end of a lock, keeping the gateposts in place and preventing them falling in towards each other. Wooden galley beams can be seen on the Essex and Suffolk River Stour, and in steel over the 1971-built Stratford Lock, Warwickshire River Avon.

Gang A train of Fen (formerly also Suffolk River Stour) lighters.

Gang planks The movable walkway, supported by upright stands, which connects the

bows and stern cabin of a narrow boat.

Gas boat A boat or small barge where the hold is decked to provide tanks for carriage of oil, tar and similar liquids.

Gauge The width of a waterway in relation to the maximum beam of craft that can pass through.

Gauging Measuring the weight of cargo on a boat so that appropriate tolls could be charged. Initially each boat was gauged at a weigh-dock, a note being made of the number of 'dry inches' that remained on the hull above water as tons of cargo were progressively added to a hold until it was full. These figures were recorded at each toll point through which the boat would pass. Here the amount of freeboard would be measured with a graduated float in a brass tube known as a gauging rod, and the total tonnage of freight could then be quickly ascertained. Alternatively, a tonnage scale was painted or carved on the hull of a barge, enabling the appropriate weight of cargo to be read from the waterline.

Give way To allow another boat (usually one that can travel more quickly) to overtake on a canal.

Gongoozler A word that seems to originate in *Bradshaw's Canals and Navigable Rivers (1904)* but widely used on the waterways ever since. De Salis describes it as: '*An idle and inquisitive person who stands staring for prolonged periods at anything out of the common. This word is believed to have its origin in the Lake District of England*'. Bridges and locksides are favourite haunts of the gongoozler.

Gravity feed A means of canal water supply relying on natural flow from a spring or reservoir, as opposed to a supply that requires pumping.

Ground paddles The sluices of a lock set in the walls of the chamber, as opposed to paddles that are fixed over apertures in the lock gates.

Ground paddle at Hillmorton, Oxford Canal.

GRP Glass-reinforced plastic, a widely used material for the hulls and superstructures of pleasure craft. 'Fibreglass' is a registered trade name.

Guillotine gates Lock gates or sections of a weir that rise and fall vertically, as opposed to more common mitre gates.

Gunwales The upper edges of a boat's hull.

H

Hack boats Private operators' boats on the Irish canal system. Known as 'Number Ones' on the English canals.

Haling way A towing path (Fens).

Handspike A short wooden pole used as a lever to open certain lock paddles (Calder & Hebble Navigation) instead of a windlass. The winding gear for lock gates on the Caledonian Canal required the use of handspikes before mechanisation. Some sets are preserved. The system survives at several Sheffield & South Yorkshire Navigation locks.

Heel post The vertical post of a lock gate nearest to its hanging, and the axis on which the gate turns. It is rounded at the back to fit the hollow quoin, in which it partly revolves.

(H)'elum The rudder of a butty narrow boat.

Henhouse rangers Men in the Hull area who go fishing in small decked boats.

Hold in, hold out To steer with reference to the towpath side. To 'hold in' is to take the side of the navigation by the path.

Hollow quoin The recess into which the heel post of a lock gate is fitted.

Horse-gin A kind of treadmill, where a horse walked in a circular path, so operating winding gear. Used in coalmines and during the construction of canal tunnels to bring spoil to the surface.

Horse marines Yorkshire men who contracted for the haulage of canal vessels by horses.

House lighter A Fenlands barge fitted with a cabin.

Huffler A freelance casual worker, generally one who assists a boat through a flight of locks, eg, Wigan.

I

Iceboat A horsedrawn or motorised round-bilged boat, pulled and rocked through ice so as to break a passage for traffic.

Ice boat on the Birmingham Canal Navigations, 1954.

Invert The bottom of a tunnel or lock floor, in the shape of an inverted arch, to resist lateral or upward pressure.

J

Jack clough Leeds & Liverpool Canal term for ground paddles.

Jambing pole The pole projecting from the bows of a Fen lighter, except on the first and second in a gang. Leading lighters had no pole, while those that came second were equipped with a longer steering pole.

Josher A boat from the former narrow boat fleet of Fellows, Morton & Clayton, (1837–1948) having a particularly well shaped bow. Derives from Joshua Fellows, a 19th-century director.

K

Keb A rake with half the length of the teeth bent in a right-angle, attached to a long pole, for removing objects dropped in a lock or waterway. It was useful for fishing up coal spilt in the water at a boat wharf.

Keel The main structural member at the centre of a boat's hull. Otherwise a barge used in the Humber area, originally fitted with a square sail and later motorised.

Knobstick A style of narrow boat painting associated with the Potteries area.

L

Land water Water coming down a river from its upper reaches as opposed to tidal flows arriving from the estuary.

Landing A Yorkshire term for a wharf.

Lateral canal A navigation fed by and closely following the course of a river, eg, parts of the Wey Navigation, Canal de l'Est (Meuse), Garonne latéral, Loire latéral, etc.

Leat A water supply line connecting, for example, a pumping station and the navigation it feeds.

Leeboards Movable boards on each side of a flat-bottomed sailing vessel such as a Thames barge or Dutchman, which take the place of a conventional deep keel in preventing the vessel making 'leeway', or progressing sideways.

Legger at work, circa 1900.

Leggers Men employed to work unpowered craft through canal tunnels lacking towpaths or tugs, by lying on their backs on the decking of the boat and 'walking' with their feet on the tunnel walls. 'Wings' or planks were fixed to the bows of a boat passing through a wide-beam tunnel to enable the leggers to reach the sides.

Lengthsman See Bank ranger.

Level When tidal water below a weir reaches the same height as impounded water above, a 'level' is made.

Lighter A type of barge, including Fen and Bridgewater Canal lighters and the swim-headed dumb lighters used in the London Docks trade.

Lock wheel To go ahead of a boat down the towpath, preparing locks in advance. Derived from the use of a bicycle for this purpose.

Loodle A vertical tiller extension used to provide a steerer with vision over the top of a high cargo, such as hay or straw.

M

Mersey flat A sailing barge trading on waterways in the north west of England.

Mitre gates The conventional lock gate, hung at its sides and most commonly one of a pair forming a shallow V when seen in plan.

Monkey boat A London name for a narrow boat.

Mud box A filter fitted to certain types of water-cooled diesel engines to prevent mud and other solids entering the cooling system.

Mud hopper A dumb barge into which dredgings are placed. It is frequently fitted with air tanks inside the hull and drain holes at the top of the hold to prevent overloading and consequent sinking even if it is filled to the brim.

Mud weight A pear-shaped metal weight used as an anchor on the Broads.

N

Narrow boat The normal cargo-carrying craft of the English canal system, radiating from the Midlands.

Navigation weir A flash lock or staunch.

Navvy Derived from 'navigator'. The workman who originally built the canals. Today the term is applied to volunteer workers engaged on restoration projects.

Nip A narrow place in the channel of the River Trent.

Number one A self-employed working boatman.

P

Packet boat A passenger and goods canal vessel working to a fixed timetable.

Paddle The mechanism or sluice valve allowing water to enter or leave a lock chamber.

Pawl A metal wedge on a chain, or hinged metal flap, which engages in the teeth of paddle gear to hold the paddle in the open position.

Pen A Fenlands expression for a lock chamber. As a verb, to pass through a Fen lock.

Peter boat A small open fishing boat used until about 1900 in the lower Thames and estuary. Pointed at each end, it could be propelled equally well in either direction.

Pintles The spiked metal fittings on a boat rudder by which it is hung on the stern, as in a butty narrow boat.

Poling A method of propelling an unpowered boat through a tunnel as an alternative to legging. A long shaft was engaged in slots on the tunnel walls.

Pound Any level stretch on a waterway uninterrupted by locks. A pound varies from a few yards, to many miles.

Puddle A mixture of clay and loam worked with water to make a seal to the bed of a canal or reservoir.

Puffer A small steam powered cargo vessel associated with the Scottish canals and the Western Isles.

Steam puffer on the Forth & Clyde Canal, Kirkintilloch. Photograph, Barnaby's.

Punt A Thames lighter. Alternatively, a long and narrow open pleasure boat propelled by pole or paddles.

Q

Quant A shaft pole, normally terminating in a flat wooden disc to prevent it sinking in to the mud, used to propel or manoeuvre Norfolk sailing wherries. As a verb, to pole a wherry.

Quarter bits A pair of ropes attached from the fore end of the jambing pole of a Fen lighter, one to each quarter of the lighter immediately in front.

R

Rack An Irish term for a lock paddle.

Ram's head   The wooden post to which is attached the rudder blade of a butty or horsedrawn narrow boat.

Butty boat Ram's Head.

Ranter   An alternative name for a ground paddle.

Reach   A pound between locks on a river, or a stretch of tidal water between particular landmarks.

Rimers   The posts in the removable parts of Upper Thames weirs against which the weir paddles are placed. Most structures of this kind have been replaced in recent years.

Riser   A series of locks arranged in a 'staircase', where the upper gates of one chamber form the lower gates of the chamber above. Two-rise locks occur frequently on Southern Irish canals, and at various places on the British network, including west of Leeds on the Leeds & Liverpool Canal. Notable staircases of locks can be seen at Bingley, Yorkshire (five), at Foxton, Leicestershire (two sets of five each), and on the Caledonian Canal, where there are eight locks constructed as risers at Banavie, near Fort William. In France at Béziers and Castelnaudary (Canal du Midi); Sweden (Göta and Dalsland Canals).

Road   The route of a canal, lock by lock (see Bad road).

Rodney boatmen   A mainly Victorian term for the lowest class of boatmen, recruited 'off the land' rather than born to the life.

Roving bridge   A bridge taking the towpath from one side of a canal to the other, otherwise known as a turnover or snake bridge. In this last case the bridge is built with curving approaches, both of which are situated on the same elevation, so that the horse's towrope need not be detached from the boat as it passes through the bridge hole.

S

Scoop wheel   A water wheel used for pumping and normally associated with windmills.

Screw   A boat's propeller.

Seizing chains   Chains by which two Fen lighters are attached to each other when forming part of a gang.

Set   To set a navigation weir or staunch is to close the gate, thus allowing the water level above to build up. Otherwise, a reference to preparing a conventional lock in readiness for a boat to pass through.

Shaft   A wooden pole used to push a barge

or boat away from the navigation bank, or sometimes to propel a dumb vessel through a tunnel, or a sailing vessel along a cut where sailing was impracticable. Also used as a verb. (See Quant.)

Sheerlegs   A stout tripod, erected over a lock, from which gates can be swung when removing old ones or fitting replacements.

Short boat   A wide beam barge about 62 ft/18·90 m long, carrying up to about 45 tons and designed for use on the Leeds & Liverpool Canal. Also a now extinct type of narrow boat whose length was reduced from the normal 70 ft/21·30 m to 58 ft/17·70 m thus enabling it to navigate the Calder & Hebble Navigation and Huddersfield Broad Canal (both with short broad locks) after passing through the Huddersfield Narrow Canal from the Manchester area.

Side pond   A small reservoir connected with a lock chamber via a culvert and paddle. About half the water capacity of the lock can be saved each time a boat passes through by filling or emptying the pond. Where locks are duplicated side by side, one can serve as a side pond to the other.

Side weir   An open cascade or enclosed culvert along which surplus water by-passes a lock from the upper level to the lower.

Slacker   A lock paddle.

Slat   A Fenlands term for a lock paddle.

Slide   A movable section of cabin roof, or hatch facilitating access through the doorway of a narrow boat cabin.

Sluice   A Fen term for a lock, eg, Stanground sluice.

Snake bridge   See Roving bridge.

Snake bridge on the Peak Forest Canal.

Snatcher   A short towing-rope from a narrow boat 'motor' to its butty, normally used when the craft are unladen.

Snubber   A long towing-rope between a pair of narrow boats travelling loaded.

Soap hole   A small recess in the bulkhead of a narrow boat, alongside the cabin stove, for keeping a cake of soap.

Spoil   Earth or rubble excavated from any canal works while under construction.

Spoon dredger   A boat equipped with a scoop suspended on a small crane and used manually or mechanically for removing silt from a navigation.

Staircase   See Riser.

Staith   A point on the bank, usually equipped with chutes, where coal is tipped into boats (Midlands and north of England). On the Norfolk Broads, staith is the normal word for a wharf, where goods were loaded or unloaded.

Stands   Vertical supports along a narrow boat hold that support the gang planks and the cloths.

Stank   A dam normally built of interlocking steel piling to isolate a section of waterway such as the supports of a bridge or where maintenance works are in progress.

Starvationer   An early type of English canal boat of rather crude timber construction with

prominent ribs, such as was used at the Worsley mines on the Bridgewater Canal.

Staunch   See Flash lock.

Steerer   The helmsman of a working boat.

Stemmed up   A boat that is stemmed up is one that has run aground on mud or other obstructions in the navigation channel and especially in bridge holes.

Stop gate   A single gate or guillotine that can quickly be closed to isolate a section of waterway in case of a bank burst.

Stop lock   A lock with little rise or fall at the junction between two canals, installed to prevent water escaping from one concern to the other.

Stop planks   Wooden beams that may be inserted in grooves above or below a lock, forming a dam, so that all water can be drained or pumped from the lock for repair purposes.

Stoppage   Closure of a lock, bridge or section of a canal to traffic while constructional work is carried out.

Strap   Rope used for checking the progress of a boat as it enters a lock. Several turns may be taken round a bollard or round the 'strapping post'.

Strapping post   Virtually a bollard mounted on the free end of a canal lock gate. As a boat enters the lock, travelling downhill, the steerer can take several turns with a strap round the post, slowing his boat and pulling the gate closed behind him.

Strapping post, Camp Hill Locks, Birmingham.

Stretchers   Planks or chains across the hold of a narrow boat to give rigidity to the hull and prevent the sides from 'spreading' when loaded.

Stud   A loose iron pin with a T head, fitting into a socket on a narrow boat, to which towing and mooring ropes are tied. There are fore and stern studs and sometimes a towing stud is mounted on the cabin top of a butty, with the towline passing through a series of 'running blocks' fixed down the length of the hold on the top planks. The length of towline can thus be easily adjusted by the butty steerer.

Summit level   The highest point on a canal approached by rising locks at each end of the summit pound. Long waterways may have more than one summit.

Swan's neck   Plaited decorative ropework between the rudder post and rudder blade on a butty narrow boat.

Sweep   A large oar, used to control boats relying mainly on tidal flow.

Swim   A boat that steers and handles easily is said to 'swim well'.
Swim-ended lighter   A dumb barge used extensively on the lower Thames whose bow and stern are undercut at about 45 degrees. This design makes them more seaworthy than a conventionally bluff-bowed barge and reduces the possibility of suction preventing the lighter from floating freely when the tide rises after it has taken to the ground.

T
Tackle   Boatman's term for horse harness.
Tail   The lower end of a lock. The upper end is known as the 'head'.
Ticket drawer   A small drawer just inside a narrow boat cabin and often decorated. Inside were kept loading tickets and lock passes.
Tow   A number of barges pushed or pulled as a single close-coupled unit.
Trow   A Severn sailing barge.

Model of a Severn Trow. Courtesy, Bristol Museum.

Tub-boats   Small box-like craft loading 3–5 tons, once used on various Shropshire and West Country canals. Alternatively, heavily built skiffs, usually fitted with outriggers and sliding seats, used for training oarsmen instead of racing fours or eights. A 'tub pair' is such a skiff, to be rowed by two men.
Tumblehome   The curvature of a boat's superstructure which falls inward above the maximum beam. Of special relevance to cabin tops being able to pass beneath low, curved bridge arches.
Turk's head   A decorative plaited ropework design, seen encircling narrow boat rudder posts and tillers.
Turns   Waiting or working turns is a system for economising on use of water at a flight of locks in dry weather. An uphill boat must wait for a downhill one to arrive before using the locks, so that maximum benefit is derived from the water consumed.
Tying point   The shallowest part of a navigation, which might be either a lock cill or a shoal. If a boat can pass the point, it will have sufficient draught throughout the rest of the waterway. The tying point of the River Trent is the bridge hole upstream of Newark Nether Lock, deepened in 1972 to provide 7 ft/2·13 m draught.

W
Water gate   A navigation weir on the Warwickshire Avon. None now survive (see Flash lock).
Water point   A place, normally at a lock, wharf or pleasure boat mooring, where fresh piped water is available.
Walkway   A passage for pedestrians over a bridge or lock gate.
Washlands (or Washes)   Embanked areas alongside rivers, designed to accept flood water that can then be directed to the sea. Normally found in the Eastern counties of England.

Weigh-dock   See Gauging.
Weir   A fixed or adjustable barrier across a navigation over which surplus water can pass to the lower level. On navigable rivers, a lock is to be found nearby, enabling boats to overcome the change in levels.
Wherry   Either a sailing barge associated with the Norfolk Broads or a strongly built waterman's open rowing-boat.
Wind   To turn a boat round (rhymes with sinned).
Winding hole   A broad section of canal where long boats can be turned round.
Windlass   A crank handle carried by a member of a boat crew (England and Wales) to operate the paddles of locks. Elsewhere, at manual locks they are normally kept on site.

A Victorian engraving of a boat girl with windlass.

Woolly backed 'uns   Term used by horse-boaters to describe the crews of early steam-driven narrow boats working between London and the woollen trade area of Leicester.

Y
Yacht   Term used by locals when speaking of any kind of pleasure craft using the waterways of Southern Ireland.

Bibliography

During the 1960s and 70s a very large number of books dealing with British waterways were published; consequently those listed here must be a personal selection of the best and most useful. The same situation does not yet apply to countries of mainland Europe where the choice of works in English is considerably more restricted.

As few bookshops are likely to stock more than a handful of recent titles, it is recommended that one of two mail order systems is used. Both organisations keep a comprehensive range of British books and maps as well as some of the more important foreign works. (Lists are available on request.) These are the Inland Waterways Association, 114 Regent's Park Road, London, NW1 8UQ. Tel: 01-586 2510; and *Waterways World* Book Service, Kottingham House, Dale Street, Burton-on-Trent, Staffs DE14 3TD. Tel: Burton (0283) 64290.

In addition to titles mentioned here, references to other useful guides will be found in the main text.

General
Waterways in Europe, by Roger Pilkington, John Murray, 1972 and Universal-Tandem, 1974 (paperback). Excellent cruising information on West Europe, excluding Britain, Brittany, and Holland.
Inland Waterways of Europe, by Roger Calvert,

Allen & Unwin, 1963. Slightly dated but good historical and touring manual.
Inland Cruising Companion, by John Liley, Stanford Maritime, 1977. Full of practical information. **Holiday Cruising on Inland Waterways**, by Charles Hadfield and Michael Streat, David & Charles, 1968. Mainly concerned with Britain, but practical details are relevant for other waters also.
Small Boat Through Belgium; Through Holland; To the Skagerrak; Through Sweden; To Alsace; Through Germany; Through France; Through Southern France; On the Meuse; On the Thames; To Luxembourg; On the Moselle; To Elsinore; To Northern Germany; On the Lower Rhine, by Roger Pilkington, Macmillan, various dates, 1958–71. Invaluable series combining cruise accounts with waterways history. National frontiers are sometimes crossed in one volume, hence the listing here rather than under each country.
Report on Continental Waterways, Inland Waterways Association Inland Shipping Group, 1975. Study of commercial use and development.
The Decorative Arts of the Mariner, edited by Gervis Frere-Cook, Cassell, 1966. Includes section by Hugh McKnight on Vessels of English and Dutch Inland Waterways, with many colour pictures.
A Cruise Across Europe, by Donald Maxwell, The Bodley Head, 1907. Holland to the Black Sea.

Sailing Across Europe, by Negley Farson, Hutchinson, 1927. Holland to the Black Sea.
Canoe Touring Abroad, by Gabriel Seal, Robert Hale, 1969. Includes parts of France, Belgium and Germany.
Map of the Canals of France, Belgium, Holland and Germany, four sheets, *Journal de la Navigation*, 29 Boulevard Henri IV, 75 Paris 4.

United Kingdom
The Shell Book of Inland Waterways, by Hugh McKnight, David & Charles, 1977. Covers entire British Isles and Ireland and includes a detailed gazetteer.
Inland Waterways of Great Britain, by L A Edwards, Imray, Laurie, Norie & Wilson, 1972. Distances, locks, regulations, maps, etc for England, Wales and Scotland.
Source Book of Canals, Locks and Canal Boats, by Hugh McKnight, Ward Lock, 1974. Fully illustrated.
Holiday Cruising on the Thames, by E and P W Ball, David & Charles, 1970.
Holiday Cruising on the Broads and Fens, by L A Edwards, David & Charles, 1972.
Nicholson's Guides to the Waterways: 1 South East; 2 North West; 3 South West; 4 North East, Robert Nicholson, British Waterways Board, 1970s. Invaluable maps and commentary on BWB routes of England and Wales. Now

replaced by similar series with much smaller and less useful maps.

Inland Waterways Cruising Guide to England & Wales, by Hugh McKnight, IWA/Haymarket Publishing, 1978 and annually.

Ladyline Cruising Guides; Llangollen Canal; Oxford Canal; Shropshire Union Canal; Grand Union (North); Grand Union (South); Grand Union by Hugh McKnight, Ladyline Ltd, 1972–4. Acknowledged to contain the best detailed facility maps.

London's Waterway Guide, by Chris Cove-Smith, Imray, 1978. Copious information on the Capital's navigations.

The Canal Book; The Thames Book; The Broads Book, Link House, annually.

Cruising Guides: Birmingham Canal Navigations; Brecon & Abergavenny Canal; Bridgewater Canal; Calder & Hebble Navigation; Coventry Canal; Driffield Navigation; Erewash Canal; Lower Avon; Upper Avon; Lee & Stort; Medway; Great Ouse and Nene; Suffolk Stour; Wey, various publishers, all available from IWA.

Narrow Boat, by L T C Rolt, Eyre & Spottiswoode, 1944 and reprints. Classic travelogue of the late 1930s.

Landscape with Canals, by L T C Rolt, Allen Lane, 1977. Evocative autobiography of leading canal pioneer and writer.

Sailing Through England, by John Seymour, Eyre & Spottiswoode, 1956. Cruise by Dutch barge through East and Northern England.

Voyage into England, by John Seymour, David & Charles, 1966. Travels by hired narrow boat.

Journeys of the Swan, by John Liley, Allen & Unwin, 1971. Narrow boat cruising during the 1960s.

Bradshaw's Canals and Navigable Rivers of England and Wales (1904), by H R de Salis, David & Charles reprint, 1969. Essential guide to England and Wales of great historical interest, comprising distance tables and much else.

The Canal Age, by Charles Hadfield, David & Charles, 1969. Good British historical survey with Continental chapter.

The Inland Waterways of England, by L T C Rolt, Allen & Unwin, 1950 and reprints. Excellent general history.

The Canals of England, by Eric de Maré, Architectural Press, 1950 and reprints. Noted for its superb photography.

Canal and River Craft in Pictures, by Hugh McKnight, David & Charles, 1969. Comprehensive survey of British inland working boats.

Sweet Thames Run Softly, by Robert Gibbings, J M Dent, 1940 and reprints. Gentle book with beautiful engravings.

Time on the Thames, by Eric de Maré, Architectural Press, 1952 and reprints. Thoughtfully written with splendid photographs.

The Thames, by A P Herbert, Weidenfeld & Nicholson, 1966. Collected thoughts of a great Thames enthusiast.

The Water Gipsies, by A P Herbert, Methuen, 1930 and reprints. A classic novel of canal life.

Thomas Telford, by L T C Rolt, Longmans, Green, 1958. Biography of the canal engineer.

British Canals; Canals of the East Midlands; Canals of North West England; Canals of South and South East England; Canals of the West Midlands; Canals of South Wales and the Border; Canals of South West England; Canals of Yorkshire and North East England; Waterways to Stratford, by Charles Hadfield.

Canals of Eastern England, by John Boyes and Ronald Russell, David & Charles, various dates to 1977. Most useful histories from original research.

Series of Inland Waterways Histories, various authors, David & Charles, 1960s and 70s. Studies of many British navigations.

The Flower of Gloster, by E Temple Thurston,

David & Charles, 1968. Reprint of a 1911 narrow boat travel classic.

Idle Women, by Susan Woolfitt, Ernest Benn, 1947. Women volunteers on wartime canal boats.

Maiden's Trip, by Emma Smith, Putnam, 1948. Superbly written account of girls on narrow boats in the war.

Hold on a Minute, by Tim Wilkinson, Waterway Productions, 1977. Working on narrow boats in the 1940s.

The Narrow Boat Book, by Tom Chaplin, Whittet Books, Weybridge, Surrey, 1978. The lore of the working boat.

A Short History of the Narrow Boat, by Tom Chaplin, Hugh McKnight Publications, 1974. Fully illustrated.

Narrow Boat Painting, by A Lewery, David & Charles, 1974. A unique study.

Wherries and Waterways, by Robert Malster, Terence Dalton, Lavenham, Suffolk, 1971. Working boats of the Norfolk Broads.

Boatyards and Boatbuilding; Claytons of Oldbury; Epilogue; Fellows Morton & Clayton; The George & the Mary; Life Afloat; The Number Ones; Roses & Castles; Tankers Knottingley; Fenland Barge Traffic; Mersey & Weaver Flats; Knobsticks, various authors, Robert Wilson Publications, 1970s. Endearing series on various aspects of working boats.

A Life on the Humber, by Harry Fletcher, Faber & Faber, 1975. An autobiography from sailing keels to shipbuilding.

A Canalside Camera 1845–1930, by Michael E Ware, David & Charles, 1975. Fine collection of historical pictures.

Inland Cruising Map of England and Wales, Stanford, regularly revised.

River Thames Map, Stanford.

Norfolk Broads Map, Stanford.

Maps of England & Wales; Kennet & Avon (east and west sections); Middle Level; River Cam and Lower Great Ouse; River Nene; River Wey; River Medway; Upper Great Ouse, Imray, regularly updated.

Scotland

The Caledonian Canal, by A D Cameron, Terence Dalton, Lavenham, Suffolk, 1972.

The Canals of Scotland, by Jean Lindsay, David & Charles, 1968. Historical account.

Map of the Caledonian Canal, British Waterways Board, Clachnaharry, Inverness.

Ireland

Holiday Cruising in Ireland, by P J G Ransom, David & Charles, 1971. Deals with the Republic and Ulster.

The Shannon Guide, Irish Shell Ltd, 20 Lower Hatch Street, Dublin 2. Charts and description.

Guide to the Grand Canal; Guide to the Barrow Navigation, Irish IWA, 2 Clonskeagh Road, Dublin, 6.

Canals of the North of Ireland, by W A McCutcheon, David & Charles, 1965. Historical survey.

Canals of the South of Ireland, by V T H & D R Delany, David & Charles, 1966. Historical survey.

Green and Silver, by L T C Rolt, Allen & Unwin, 1949 and reprints. A voyage through Irish waterways in the late 1940s; still the best book on the subject.

Thanks for the Memory, by H J Rice, 1952, reprinted by the Athlone Branch, Irish IWA, Sean's Bar, Athlone, Co Westmeath. Cruising on the Shannon.

Voyage in a Bowler Hat, by Hugh Malet, Hutchinson, 1960. A cruise across England and Ireland.

In the Wake of the Gods, by Hugh Malet, Chatto & Windus, 1970. More Irish cruising including Ulster.

Land of Time Enough, by Raymond Gardner, Hodder & Stoughton, 1977. Travelogue of southern Irish waterways.

France

Guide de la Navigation Intérieure, 2 vols, Editions Berger-Levrault, 5 rue Auguste-Comte, Paris 6, 1965. Vital strip maps of all French waterways in the second volume (in French).

Inland Waterways of France, by E Benest, Imray, 1978. Includes regulations, distance tables, maps, etc.

France – The Quiet Way, by John Liley, Stanford Maritime, 1975. Excellent practical guide, travelogue and source of inspiration; well illustrated.

Through the French Canals, by Philip Bristow, Nautical Publishing Ltd, 1970. General boating guide.

Holiday Cruising in France, by Gerard Morgan-Grenville, David & Charles, 1972.

Through France to the Med, by Mike Harper, Gentry Books, 1974. Useful record of one yachtsman's voyage.

Barging into France, 1972; **Barging into Southern France**, 1973; **Barging into Burgundy**, 1975, by Gerard Morgan-Grenville, David & Charles. The first volume includes parts of Holland and Belgium. Instructive, entertaining and sometimes alarming accounts of cruising in a converted barge.

An Inland Voyage, by Robert Louis Stevenson, 1878 and reprints. Through Belgium and Northern France by canoe.

The Saône, by Philip Hamerton, Seeley & Co, 1887. Victorian travelogue with many fine drawings.

Our Autumn Holiday on French Rivers, by J L Molloy, Bradbury, Agnew & Co, 1874. Vintage exploration of great charm.

Voies Navigables de France, Service de Propagande Edition Information, 14 rue Druot, Paris 9, 1967. Fully illustrated and useful commercial guide with history and development plans (in French).

Isabel and the Sea, by George Millar, William Heinemann, 1949. Very readable account including a journey from the Seine to the Mediterranean in an auxiliary ketch.

Coming Down the Seine, by Robert Gibbings, J M Dent, 1953. Evocative description of rowing boat voyage with exquisite woodcuts.

Canoeing Down the Rhône, by John Wilson, Chapman & Hall, 1957. A dangerous undertaking, successfully completed!

From Sea to Sea, the Canal du Midi, by L T C Rolt, Allen Lane, 1973. One of the few French waterway histories and a very good one. Includes a description of the navigation today.

The Loire, by Vivian Rowe, Eyre & Spottiswoode, 1969. Excellent illustrated account of the *châteaux* country.

Lord of the River, by Bernard Clavel, Collins, 1972. A novel about 19th-century Rhône barge life, translated from the French.

Blue Line Guide Practique des Canaux du Midi, Blue Line Cruisers (France) Ltd, Le Grand Bassin, BP 67, 11400 Castelnaudary, France. With diagramatic strip maps and comments in French, English and German.

Guides to the Lower Seine; Upper Seine; Oise & Aisne; Marne; Brittany; Paris – Amsterdam; Paris – Mediterranean, Touring Club de France, 65 Avenue de la Grande-Armee, Paris.

Liaison Manche-Océan; Canal de Nantes à Brest et Le Blavet, Le Comité de Promotion Touristique des Canaux Bretons et des Voies Navigables de l'Ouest, Chambre de Commerce, 35 000 Rennes, 1975. Maps and guides for Brittany canals.

Michelin Green Guides, 18 in all, in French. Some also available in English and German editions. Excellent background material for a cruise, with features on the chief river valleys.

Map of the French Waterways, Imray.

Carte de France de Voies Navigables, (large scale map of the whole country); **Guide de Rhône de Lyon à la Mer**, 68 sheets; **Guide de Doubs**, J Vagnon, BP 27 – 69641 Calure, France.

Maps of the French Meuse; Marne; Midi; Canal du Nord; Brittany; Rhine-Saône via Doubs; Rhône; Saône; Lower Seine; Upper Seine; Yonne, Journal de la Navigation, 29 Boulevard Henri IV, 75 Paris 4.

Maps and Guides of the Canal du Nivernais; Lower Seine and Canal de Tancarville; Upper Seine; Marne; Saône (Lyon – St Jean-de-Losne); Saône (St Jean-de-Losne – Corre); Yonne; Canal de Deux-Mers (Bordeaux – Etang de Thau); Canal de Bourgogne, by M Sandrin, Editions Maritimes et d'Outre-Mer, 17 rue Jacob, Paris 6.

Michelin maps, scale 1/200 000. Useful for the country surrounding the waterways.

Germany

Through the German Waterways, by Philip Bristow, Nautical Publishing Co, 1975. A useful guide.

Das Westdeutsche Kanalnetz, Wasser und Schiffartsdirektion West, Münster, 1975. Guide to waterways north of Dusseldorf (in German).

Regulations Relating to Various Navigations and charts of individual waterways, Inland Shipping Publishers, 41 Duisburg, 13 Haus Rhein, Dammstrasse 15–17.

Le Rhin. Guide pour la Navigation, Éditions de la Navigation du Rhin, 3 Route du Rhin, Strasbourg-Neudorf, France. 101-sheet volume in French/German/Dutch.

The Rhineland, by Walter Marsden, B T Batsford, 1973. Well illustrated general (not navigational) guide.

All About the Rhine, by Hans Prager, Frank'sche Verlags-Handlung Stuttgart, 1972. A very useful history and description of current Rhine traffic. Translated into English.

Castles on the Rhine, by Walther Offendorf-Simrock, Wilhelm Stollfuss, Bonn, undated but available in 1978. Well illustrated description in English.

The Finest Legends of the Rhine, by Wilhelm Ruland, Verlag Hoursch & Bechstedt, Bonn, undated but available in 1978. In German or English. Amusing folk lore.

Michelin Green Guide to Germany. (In German

or English.) Includes good articles on various river valleys, eg Rhine, Lahn, Mosel.

Map, Mitteleuropäische Wasserstrassen, Binnenschiffahrts-Verlag GmbH, Duisburg-Ruhrort. Large scale map of waterways of Middle Europe, centred on West Germany.

Rheinkarte, Bodensee – Nordsee, Binnenschiffahrts-Verlag GmbH, Duisburg-Ruhrort. Single sheet map of the Rhine from Switzerland to the North Sea.

Wassersport in Deutschland, Reise und Verkehrsverlag/Kümmerly und Frey. Rivers, canals and lakes with boating facilities marked.

Belgium

Inland Waterways of Belgium, by E Benest, Imray, 1960. Distance tables and regulations. Outdated and out-of-print but still useful.

Through the Belgian Canals, by Philip Bristow, Nautical Publishing Co, 1972. Much useful material on routes, etc.

Dispositions Réglementant la Police et la Navigation, Établissements d'Imprimerie Dantinne, Stree, Hainaut, Belgium. Regulations, distances, opening times, etc.

Holland

The Inland Waterways of the Netherlands, 3 vols, by E Benest, Imray, 1966–71. Very useful maps, distance tables, etc, but slightly outdated.

Holiday Cruising in the Netherlands, by John Oliver, David & Charles, 1974. Practical guide.

Through the Dutch Canals, by Philip Bristow, Nautical Publishing Co, 1974. Practical guide.

On Dutch Waterways, by G Christopher Davies, Jarrold & Sons, late 19th century. Pleasant period piece.

Three Vagabonds in Friesland, by H F Tomalin, Simpkin, Marshall, Hamilton, Kent & Co, 1908. Evocative holiday cruising with beautiful photographs.

Charts of Dutch Waterways, 16 titles, ANWB, Hoofdkantoor, Wassenaarseweg 220, 's-Gravenhage. Also various publications relating to regulations, opening times of locks and bridges, etc.

Sweden

Swedish Cross Cut: The Göta Canal, by Eric de Maré, Allhems Förlag, Malmö, Sweden, 1965, (in English). Includes history and beautiful photographs.

Göta Canal, by Jan Gabrielsson, Generalstabens Litografiska Anstalts Förlag, 1973. Guide (in Swedish or English).

Vi tar Kanalvägen, by Stig Sandelin, Svenska Kryssarklubbens Båtbibliotek, 1971. Guide to inland waterways (in Swedish).

Svensk Lots Del IV, Segelbara Inlandsfarvatten, Sjöfartsverket, Stockholm, 1972. Maps

and cruising guide to Swedish waterways (in Swedish).

Encyclopaedia Guide to Sweden, Nagel, 1973. Includes section on Göta Canal (in English).

Göta Kanal – Sveriges blå band, by Roland Romell, 1967. Photographic study with commentary in Swedish and English.

Göta Canal, Trollhätte Canal, Göta Kanalbolag, 591 01 Motala, Sweden, 1971. The canal company's official illustrated guide, including regulations.

Södertälje Kanal, by Göran Gelotte, Ostra Södermanlands Kulturhistoriska Förening, 1976. A brief history (in Swedish).

Gästhamnar (Guestharbours), STF's Gästhamnsintendent, Stureplan 2, Fack, 103 80 Stockholm, revised regularly. Facilities throughout Swedish waterways, with notes in English.

Dalsland Canal in Sweden, Dalsland Kanal AB, Box 89 S – 662 00 Åmål, Sweden. Official brief guide and regulations (in English).

Karlskoga-Filipstad Waterway Guide, Karlskoga-Bofors Motorbåtklubb.

Strömsholms Kanal Informerar, Strömsholms Kanal AB, 73400 Hallstahammar, Sweden. Official guide, free.

Göta Canal Tourist Map, Generalstabens. Combines historical and modern maps with commentary in Swedish and English.

Charts of Mälaren; Vättern and Göta Canal; Vänern; Hjälmaren; Strömsholms Canal; Dalsland Canal; Göta River and Trollhätte Canal; Säffle Canal, Sjöfartsverket, Stockholm.

Map, Kinda Canal, Kinda Kanals Vänner, Linköping.

Periodicals

Waterways World, monthly, Waterway Productions Ltd, Kottingham House, Dale Street, Burton-on-Trent, Staffs. DE14 3TD. News and features of UK and foreign waterways.

Waterways News, ten times a year, British Waterways Board, Melbury House, Melbury Terrace, London, NW1 6JX. News of British waterways with occasional foreign features.

Canal and River Boat Monthly, Lockgates Publishing Ltd, 15 Newstead Grove, Nottingham, NG1 4GZ.

Water Space, quarterly, Hugh McKnight, Editor, Water Space Amenity Commission, The Clock House, Upper Halliford, Shepperton, Middx TW17 8RU. Features and news on all aspects of water recreation and amenity, with occasional articles on foreign boating.

Motor Boat & Yachting, monthly, IPC Transport Press Ltd, Dorset House, Stamford Street, London, SE1 9LU. Regularly includes UK and foreign waterways features.

Journal de la Navigation, weekly, 29 Boulevard Henri IV, Paris 4. The boat people's own newspaper (in French).

Revue de la Navigation Fluviale Européenne, twice monthly, Éditions de la Navigation du Rhin, 3 Route du Rhin, Strasbourg-Neudorf, France. News of trade and technical developments.

Museums

As soon as the commonplace becomes a rarity, interest in it blossoms. Thus, in Britain the post war demise of most types of smaller waterway freight craft has resulted in a nationwide preservation movement. Some excellent museums or collections of old boats have been established and these add greatly to our understanding of the fascinating social and economic life of rivers and canals in years gone by.

A highlight of a cruise can be a visit to one of these establishments; equally, they make an agreeable objective for a day's excursion by car. The list that follows does not claim to be totally comprehensive: but it does include all museums known to the author, and visitors will not be disappointed by what they find there.

England and Wales

The Waterways Museum, Stoke Bruerne, near Towcester, Northamptonshire. Established by the British Waterways Board in a former corn mill by Stoke Bruerne top lock on the Grand Union Canal in 1963, this is a rich collection of mainly smaller relics of 200 years of inland navigation in Britain. Especially good is the comprehensive collection of narrow boat decorative ware, with a mock-up boat cabin. Nearby, a horse-drawn narrow boat is preserved in a weighing machine. The archives and old photographs are much in demand by students and authors.
Opening times: open throughout the year; for details, telephone Northampton 862229. Souvenir and bookshop. Refreshments obtainable in the village.
North Western Museum of Inland Navigation, Ellesmere Port, Merseyside. Part of the extensive system of basins and warehouses at the junction of the Shropshire Union and Manchester Ship Canals, has been restored by volunteers for the display of a remarkable collection of some 20 working boats. These include Mersey Flat *Mossdale*, Manchester, Bolton & Bury Canal icebreaker *Sarah Lansdale*, Thomas Clayton tar boat *Gifford*, a Birmingham day boat, Leeds & Liverpool Canal short boat *George* and long boat *Scorpio*, and the Oxford Canal horsedrawn narrow boat *Friendship* of former 'Number One' boatman Joe Skinner. A reconstructed boat builder's workshop and steam plant which originally powered machinery in the adjacent docks can be seen.
Opening times: Easter to September, full details from the Honorary Secretary, telephone 061-980 6223. Light refreshments and souvenirs available.
The Black Country Museum, Tipton Road, Dudley, West Midlands. The history of industrial activities throughout the Black Country is represented by a reconstructed village currently in course of erection. In addition to an iron works, rolling mill, forge and chainshops, lock works and associated buildings on a 26 acre/10.5 ha site with 300 yd/274 m canal arm off the Dudley Canal close to Dudley Tunnel, there is a traditional boat dock of the type associated with the Birmingham Canal Navigations. Craft owned by the Museum at present include *North Star*, a horse drawn icebreaker of 1868, *Admiral Beatty*, a 1917 wooden boat used for carriage of steel tubes, *Bessie*, a rivetted iron boat built in 1895, and *Birchills*, a wooden 'Joey' boat of 1953.
Opening times: late May until early September; other times by appointment; telephone 021-557 9643. Refreshments and souvenirs are available.

Windermere Steamboat Museum, Rayrigg Road, Windermere, Cumbria. A fascinating collection of small steam launches and other historical vessels, some of which were recovered from the bed of Lake Windermere after being sunk for many decades. *Dolly*, built in 1850, is thought to be the oldest mechanically propelled boat in existence. More than a dozen equally elegant exhibits can be seen.
Opening times: Low season, weekdays, 10.00 h – 17.00 h; High season, Sundays also, 14.00 h – 18.00 h. Light refreshments available.
The Canal Exhibition Centre, The Wharf, Llangollen, Clwyd. This is an extremely well arranged museum of canal life and artifacts alongside the popular Llangollen Canal in north Wales. A carefully planned sequence of 'panoramas' with working models and recorded sound effects gives a vivid impression of waterway history. Horsedrawn passenger craft operate cruises including one to the remarkable Pontcysyllte Aqueduct.
Opening times: for details, telephone Llangollen 860702. Book and souvenir shop; refreshments available in the nearby town.
Ironbridge Gorge Museum Trust, Ironbridge, Telford, Shropshire. More than £1 million is being spent on creation of this open air industrial museum on a site which extends for almost 1 mile²/2.5 km². Exhibits tell the story of the great iron forges established here in the 18th century of which the dominant reminder is the world's first large iron bridge over the River Severn. An iron tub boat is preserved on a restored section of the Shropshire Canal at Blists Hill, while the spectacular inclined plane boat lift is being partially reconstructed.
Opening times: for details, telephone Ironbridge 3522. Some refreshments available.
Manchester Ship Canal Company Museum, Ship Canal House, King Street, Manchester 2. Relics of the building of this late 19th-century enterprise are available for inspection by appointment only. Contact the Public Relations Officer, telephone: 061-832 2244.
Maritime Museum for East Anglia, Marine Parade, Great Yarmouth, Norfolk. Among the exhibits are items relating to the trading craft of the Norfolk Broads, the black sailed wherries. The only surviving example, *Albion*, is preserved by the Norfolk Wherry Trust and may be hired for cruises under sail: details from D E Anderson, telephone Norwich 714553.
Opening times: (for the Museum), for details, telephone Great Yarmouth 2267.
Merseyside County Museums, William Brown Street, Liverpool, L3 8EN. A huge collection of maritime interest, now currently mostly in store, includes models of local inland craft such as Mersey Flats.

Preserved lift bridge, and joey boat, Black Country Museum. Photograph, Black Country Museum.

Opening times: for details, telephone 051-207 0001.
Crofton Steam Pumping Engine, Crofton, Near Great Bedwyn, Wiltshire. Here, a pair of ancient steam pumping engines situated by the Kennet & Avon Canal in beautiful countryside, have been restored by members of the K & A Canal Trust.
Opening times: Sundays, 10.00 h – 18.00 h; and in steam during certain weekends in the summer; for details, telephone 01-948 1577.
Gloucester Folk Museum, Bishop Hooper's Lodging, 99–103 Westgate Street, Gloucester. Several 16th-century timber-framed buildings are used for a varied collection which includes items on Severn fishing and local canals.
Opening times: for details, telephone Gloucester 24131.

Traditional narrow boat ware at The Canal Exhibition Centre, Llangollen.

Goole Museum, Carlisle Street, Goole, Yorkshire. One display is devoted to Goole canal docks and associated waterways.
Opening times: for details, telephone Goole 3784.
Corinium Museum, Park Street, Cirencester, Gloucestershire. Mainly devoted to Roman remains, although there is a section on the Thames & Severn Canal.
Opening times: for details, telephone Cirencester 2248.
Cheddleton Flint Mill, Cheddleton, Staffordshire. A water-powered mill by the Caldon Canal near the Potteries. Water transport is represented by the restored Fellows, Morton & Clayton narrow boat *Vienna*, built in 1911.
Opening times: Saturday and Sunday afternoons throughout the year, or by arrangement, Mr F Underwood, 4 Cherry Hill Avenue, Meir, Stoke-on-Trent (three weeks' notice required).
Welsh Industrial and Maritime Museum, Bute Street, Cardiff. A general transport museum containing a canal boat.
Opening times: throughout the year; for details telephone Cardiff 371805.
Cusworth Hall Museum, Cusworth Lane, Doncaster, South Yorkshire. Smaller relics are contained in a canal room.
Opening times: for details, telephone 0302 61842.
Exeter Maritime Museum, The Quay, Exeter, Devon. More than 80 working boats from all parts of the world are preserved afloat or ashore in warehouses at the head of the Exeter Ship Canal, built in 1566. Canal craft include Brunel's steam-driven dredger from Bridgwater Dock, launched in 1844, a selection of coracles, estuary fishing boats and a Bude Canal tub boat equipped with wheels for use on that waterway's inclined planes.
Opening times: open throughout the year; for details, telephone 0392 58075. Refreshments available during the summer season.
National Maritime Museum, Romney Road, Greenwich, London, SE10 9NF. Among the inland waterways items in this huge collection is

the Thames Conservancy's steam driven inspection launch *Donola* of 1893, a Manchester Ship Canal steam tug and a reconstructed Upper Thames boat builder's workshop.
Opening times: open throughout the year; for details, telephone 01-858 4422.
Manchester Museum, Oxford Road, Manchester 13. Items of waterways interest include a good range of boat models and decorated ware.
Opening times: open throughout the year; for details, telephone 061-273 3333.
Morwellham Quay Centre, Morwellham, Tavistock, Devon. A fascinating 19th-century copper port with many kinds of transport relics. There are canal inclined planes and the portal of a 2540 yd/2323 m tunnel of the disused Tavistock Canal.
Opening times: every day including Bank Holidays; for details, telephone Gunnislake 832766.

Ireland

Waterways Museum, Robertstown, Co Kildare. One of the series of Georgian canal hotels of the Grand Canal houses various relics relating to water transport, with boat models, printed material etc.
Opening times: local application will secure the key to the building.

The former canal hotel at Robertstown, now used in part as a museum.

France

Museum of Inland Navigation, Conflans Ste Honorine. Located in a *château* by the church of St Maclou, at the junction of the Seine and Oise, this is an excellent institution. Exhibits include items on chain-towage, experimental mechanical propulsion and the lives of the boat families. Also in the town is a floating boatmen's church and social centre. It is within easy travel distance of Paris.
Opening times: 15·00 h – 18·00 h, Wednesdays, Saturdays and Sundays.
Town Museum, Chalon-sur-Saône, Saône-et-Loire. Among items of local interest are relics relating to river transport.
Town Museum, Serrières, Ardeche. This town on the banks of the Rhône, 56 km/35 miles downstream of Lyon, includes river transport among items of local interest in the museum.
St Louis/Arzviller Inclined Plane, near Lutzelbourg, Moselle (see page 124). Although this excitingly modern boat lift is about as far removed as possible from the museum category, the guided tour does include exhibition material.

A passenger vessel is available for rides on the plane and souvenirs and refreshments may be purchased.
Opening times: every day from March to November. Details from Syndicats d'Initiative de St-Louis-Lutzelbourg, France, telephone (87) 07 30 69.

Germany

Rheinfels Castle, St Goar, in the Rhine Gorge (see page 176). The local history museum contains a number of Rhine exhibits, portraits of river worthies, boat models and a miniature replica of a 'floating bridge'.
Opening times: every day during the summer season.
The Rhine Museum, Rizzastrasse 12, Koblenz. A wide range of exhibits is on view.
Ehrenbreitstein Castle, Koblenz. One of the largest fortresses in Europe, last rebuilt 1815–32, the castle contains a Rhine Museum, said to be the oldest river museum anywhere.
Opening times: daily, 10·00 h – 18·00 h, except Fridays. There are two restaurants.
Rhineland Museum, (Rheinisches Landesmuseum), Bonn. An annexe to this large, general collection contains 19th-century engravings and paintings of the Rhine Valley landscape.
Opening times: daily, 10·00 h – 17·00 h (21·00 h, Wednesdays); closed, Mondays and over Christmas.
Henrichenburg Boat Lift, Henrichenburg in Waltrop, near Dortmund (see page 162). An interpretation centre alongside this spectacular vertical boat lift illustrates working of the lift with a model and outlines the importance of the Dortmund-Ems Canal and associated waterways in the economy of West Germany. Refreshments available.
Lüneburg Boat Lift, Lüneburg (south of Hamburg) (see page 163). The pair of huge vertical lifts on the Elbe Lateral Canal have an exhibition room and interpretation centre with an elaborate working model. Refreshments available.
Lauenburg Shipping Museum, Lauenburg (east of Hamburg). In this charming little town of boatmen's houses on the banks of the River Elbe, the museum displays canal and river craft from the 14th century onwards.
Opening times: somewhat limited: local enquiry advised.

Belgium

Ronquières Inclined Plane, Ronquières, Hainaut, 42 km/26 miles south of Brussels by road (see page 180). The great inclined plane of the Brussels-Charleroi Canal is now one of Belgium's leading tourist attractions; indeed, one of the reasons for building a 125 m/410 ft tower at the upper end was to provide a viewing platform. Exhibitions explain the working of this remarkable device and souvenirs can be purchased. Tripping boats (journey about one hour) are available at the lower end.

Holland

Scheepvaart Museum, Amsterdam. A huge collection, begun in 1655, it contains, among other items of waterways interest, some highly decorated 18th-century canal passenger barges.
Opening times: 10·00 h – 17·00 h; 13·00 h – 17·00 h, Sundays and public holidays. Closed 1 January.

Maritime Museum, Rochussen Straat, Rotterdam (a short walk from the Euromast). The Prins Hendrik Maritime Museum has many items associated with canal boats and is especially rich in figureheads and other carved details from smaller inland vessels.
Opening times: 10·00 h – 17·00 h; 11·00 h – 17·00 h, Sundays and public holidays. Closed 1 January and 30 April.
Zuiderzee Museum, Enkhuizen (on the west shore of the Ijsselmeer, 62 km/39 miles north of Amsterdam). A very attractive museum in this ancient herring fishing port, its extensive collection includes many examples of painted and carved working, passenger and fishing boats. The *klikbords* (rudderheads) on view show an amazing range of 'horn of plenty' designs.
Opening times: 10·00 h – 17·00 h; 12·00 h – 17·00 h, Sundays and public holidays.
Shipping Museum, Groningen. A small, but very interesting display, containing many fine models, reconstructed barge repair yards in miniature and other waterways items.
Opening times: details from the Groningen Tourist Bureau (VVV), Grote Markt 1a, Groningen.

A model of a traditional Dutch barge-building yard, Groningen Shipping Museum.

Sweden

Dalsland Canal Museum, Håverud, Dalsland (see page 209). One of the attractions of this outstanding complex, with locks, aqueduct and tripping boat, is the small museum.
Opening times: during the rather short summer season the local tourist office, telephone 0530-305 80, will provide details. Refreshments available nearby.
Strömsholms Canal Museum, Hallstahammar (situated above the Hallstahammar locks, on the Strömsholms Canal, north of Mälaren (Lake). A former canal manager's house has been converted into a really interesting and well displayed museum.
Hjälmare Canal Museum, Hällby Docka (see page 212). A small museum devoted to this short length of waterway.

Switzerland

Rhine Shipping Museum, Kleinhüningen Harbour, Basle. An exceptionally well designed exhibition, dealing with all aspects of Rhine transport over the centuries.

Index

Entries in italics denote illustrations
and include text mentions in
certain cases.

OTHER GUINNESS SUPERLATIVES TITLES

Facts and Feats Series:

Air Facts and Feats, *3rd ed.*
John W.R. Taylor, Michael
J.H. Taylor and David
Mondey

Rail Facts and Feats, *2nd ed.*
John Marshall

Tank Facts and Feats, *2nd ed.*
Kenneth Macksey

Car Facts and Feats, *2nd ed.*
edited by Anthony Harding

Yachting Facts and Feats
Peter Johnson

Business World
Henry Button and Andrew
Lampert

Music Facts and Feats
Robert and Celia Dearling
with Brian Rust

Art Facts and Feats
John FitzMaurice Mills

Soccer Facts and Feats
Jack Rollin

Animal Facts and Feats
Gerald L. Wood FZS

Plant Facts and Feats
William G. Duncalf

**Structures – Bridges,
Towers, Tunnels, Dams ...**
John H. Stephens

Weather Facts and Feats
Ingrid Holford

Astronomy Facts and Feats
Patrick Moore

Guide Series:

**Guide to French Country
Cooking**
Christian Roland Délu

Guide to Freshwater Angling
Brian Harris and Paul Boyer

Guide to Saltwater Angling
Brian Harris

Guide to Field Sports
Wilson Stephens

Guide to Mountain Animals
R.P. Bille

Guide to Underwater Life
C. Petron and J.B. Lozet

Guide to Motorcycling, *2nd ed.*
Christian Lacombe

Guide to Bicycling
J. Durry and J.B. Wadley

Guide to Water Skiing
David Nations OBE and
Kevin Desmond

Guide to Steeplechasing
Richard Pitman and Gerry
Cranham

Other Titles:

**The Guinness Book of
Answers,** *2nd ed.*
edited by Norris D.
McWhirter

**The Guinness Book of
Records**
edited by Norris D.
McWhirter

**English Pottery and
Porcelain**
Geoffrey Wills

Antique Firearms
Frederick Wilkinson

History of Land Warfare
Kenneth Macksey

History of Sea Warfare
Lt-Cmdr Gervis Frere-Cook
and Kenneth Macksey

History of Air Warfare
David Brown, Christopher
Shores and Kenneth Macksey

**The Guinness Guide to
Feminine Achievements**
Joan and Kenneth Macksey

**The Guinness Book of
Names**
Leslie Dunkling

100 Years of Wimbledon
Lance Tingay

Kings, Rulers and Statesmen
Clive Carpenter

The Guinness Book of 1952
Kenneth Macksey

The Guinness Book of 1953
Kenneth Macksey

The Guinness Book of 1954
Kenneth Macksey

**The Guinness Book of
British Hit Singles**
edited by Tim and Jo Rice,
Paul Gambaccini and Mike
Read

**The Guinness Book of World
Autographs**
Ray Rawlins

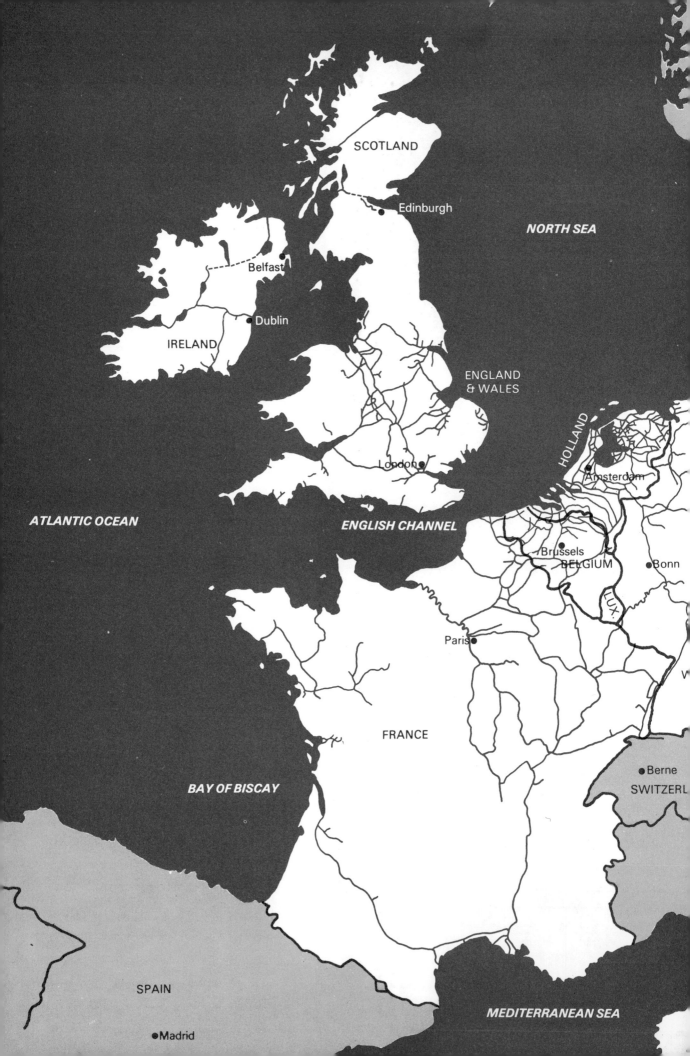